Tiles 143
Wood stripping 145
Woodwork and joinery 145

5. Getting Your Act Together
Entertainers 147
Fancy dress 151
Party catering 153
Party equipment 158
Toastmasters and butlers 162

6. Getting Personal
Glass engraving 163
Named gifts 168
Portraits and houses 175

7. Getting What You Want
Needlework and craft supplies
Basketware and timber 179
Dressmaking 180
Embroidery 181
Jewellery 184
Knitting 185
Spinning and weaving 186

Shops for collectors
Antiquities 187
Arms and military 187
Books and newspapers 188
Buttons 189
Cartoons, maps and photographs 190
Clocks and barometers 190
Commemoratives 191
Craft shops and galleries 192
Dolls 194
Fifties and Deco 195
Limited editions 196
Pewter and silver 196
Records 197
Rugs and textiles 197
Shells 199

Thimbles 199
Wine antiques 200

Specialist shops
Books 200
Food 201
Herbs and plants 204
Household 204
Leisure – indoors 209
Leisure – outdoors 210

8. Getting Service
Children 213
China matching 214
Family trees 214
Fashion and beauty 215
Hire services 218
Household services 221
Pets 224
Vehicles 225
Video 225

9. Getting Cleaned Out
Blinds 226
Drycleaning and dyeing 226
House cleaning 231
Invisible mending 232
Oriental carpets 233
Suede, leather and fur 235

10. Getting Married
Cars and carriages 236
Fashion and beauty 238
Flowers 239
Photography and video 241
Receptions 241

11. Getting Posted
Chocolates 243
Flowers 243
Food 245
Wine and other gifts 247

Penguin Handbooks
Where Can I Get . . . ?

Beryl Downing has been an adviser on where to buy what for much of her journalistic career. Having been a fashion editor, home editor and cookery editor she has been concerned with finding the best value and the most interesting ideas in clothes and cosmetics, furnishing and do-it-yourself, food and catering. Four years ago she joined *The Times* as shopping editor and her Saturday page has become an essential cut-out-and-keep guide to the best in shops and services throughout the country.

Her main principle in giving advice has been that she will never recommend any item that she has not tested personally and as a result she has attracted many loyal readers who trust her judgement and appreciate the efforts she makes to ensure that those who do not live within easy distance of a large, well-stocked shopping centre are as well served and supplied as those who do. Like her popular book of thirty-minute recipes, *Quick Cook*, published by Penguin in 1981, this handbook has been written with a practical appreciation of the pressures of modern living – and the need to find an experienced guide who will save you the time and effort of tracking down exactly the shop or service that you need.

Beryl Downing

Where Can I Get . . . ?

Penguin Books

Penguin Books Ltd, Harmondsworth, Middlesex, England
Penguin Books, 40 West 23rd Street, New York, New York 10010, U.S.A.
Penguin Books Australia Ltd, Ringwood, Victoria, Australia
Penguin Books Canada Ltd, 2801 John Street, Markham, Ontario, Canada L3R 1B4
Penguin Books (N.Z.) Ltd, 182–190 Wairau Road, Auckland 10, New Zealand

First published 1983

Made and printed in Great Britain by
Richard Clay (The Chaucer Press) Ltd, Bungay, Suffolk
Set in 8/10½ pt Univers Light

Text illustrations by Jill Feld

For my mother, the most super supershopper of all

Contents

Introduction 13

Acknowledgements 17

1. Getting Things Made
Beds and bedding 19
Calligraphy and paper 22
Clocks 25
Embroidery and tapestries 27
Fire bellows 28
Furniture 28
Glass and ceramics 37
Interior decor (fabrics and walls) 38
Jewellery and silver 41
Lamps and lampshades 47
Musical instruments 48
Painted decorative effects 50
Picture framing 52
Rugs and carpets 54
Soft furnishings 56
Stained glass 60
Toys 61
Willow baskets 65
Wood-turning 65

2. Getting Dressed
Women's wear 67
Furs 70
Knitwear 71

Lingerie 74
Shoes 75
Accessories 78
Umbrellas 80
Menswear 81

3. Getting Things Mended
Books and paper 83
China and glass 86
Clocks, watches and barometers 90
Disability aids 93
Furniture 93
Furniture – cane and rush 100
Jewellery, silver and objets d'art 104
Leather, skins and fur 107
Metal and machinery 109
Models and toys 111
Photography 112
Pianolas 113
Pictures and sculpture 113
Sports equipment 115
Teeth 115
Textiles 115
Umbrellas 117
Vehicles 118

4. Getting Things Restored
Architectural supplies 119
Awnings 121
Bathrooms 121
Conservatory extensions 122
Fires, stoves and chimneys 123
Fitted furniture and units 126
Gardens and paths 128
Lighting 132
Metalwork and forged iron 133
Plasterwork 138
Rope 139
Stained glass 140
Stone and marble 142
Thatch 142

12. Getting Around
   Group craft workshops and craft courses 249
   Useful addresses 251

   Index 255

Introduction

This is a biased book. There is no point in pretending that it is comprehensive or well balanced or impartial. On the contrary, it is extremely selective, because everyone included has been personally vetted and recommended – by me, by my friends and shopping scouts and by readers of *The Times*, who have so often contributed invaluable suggestions for the shopping page I write for them.

Spending other people's money – even in theory – is enormous fun. You handle beautiful and rare objects that you couldn't possibly afford, you get caught up in the enthusiasm of the expert and begin to find the construction of a corset as fascinating (momentarily) as the binding of a rare manuscript. But making recommendations is a tremendous responsibility. If you make a mistake with your own money, tough luck. If you waste someone else's, you are also misspending their trust.

One of the first lessons I learned years ago when I began shopping around professionally was that you can't always believe what a business says about itself and that what looks good in a picture may be shoddy in reality. So one of the best recommendations any business can have is a satisfied customer who has tried and tested the goods on offer. And not only the goods, but the service that goes with them.

For service, in my view, is what makes buying things a pleasure and what this book is all about – not servility, but expertise. There is a growing appreciation of craftsmanship, a growing need for individuality in a mass-produced world. Large companies simply don't find it economic to perform the small, useful services that used to be taken for granted, but now small businesses are taking root, sometimes because their owners have decided to opt out, basing their lives on a different set of values, sometimes, unfortunately, because they have been made redundant – in some cases not so unfortunately, because being disqualified from the rat race has meant the discovery of new skills which have brought much more satisfaction.

What these new small businesses are reviving is not only services useful in themselves, but also the spirit of assistance which in the sixties and seventies seemed to be dying out. This is a guide to some of the most useful, most unusual and most interesting to me (and therefore I hope to you), with a sprinkling of the most unlikely, just for fun.

The selection of subjects has been guided by the pleas for help sent to me at *The Times* – 'Where can I get my pearls restrung, my pans rehandled, my brushes rebristled, an extra large shirt, a vintage Rolls for my wedding, an after-dinner speaker?'

I am not concerned with the everyday goods that can be found in any High Street, nor with famous stores, unless they happen to offer an interesting service that I or my helpers have found particularly useful. Wherever possible we have sought the expert – some long-established family firms, some new, but all willing and eager to please – with an emphasis on value for money, whatever the price range. We have tried to find people who are not only efficient but helpful and pleasant – and if you follow up any recommendations and are disappointed with the treatment you receive, please let me know, so that further investigations can be made before that company is included in another edition.

I apologize to those who live in Scotland, Wales and Northern Ireland. With just a couple of exceptions, I did not feel that I had enough personal experience of shopping in those parts of the United Kingdom to include the specialists they undoubtedly have – but I hope I shall be able to gather enough recommendations for next time.

Some practical notes: Prices fluctuate according to the costs of materials, but I wanted, where possible, to include actual figures rather than high/medium/low symbols, because I feel it is helpful to prospective customers to know the sort of charges that will be made. Some people are nervous about approaching a craftsman if they think the price will be beyond them. Not everyone was willing to quote figures months ahead, so it does not follow that where prices are omitted they are necessarily higher than those quoted. But those mentioned should be a yardstick. They normally include VAT at 15 per cent – I like to see exactly what I'm paying, and I believe all traders should quote inclusive prices to private customers.

I have not included postal charges for mail orders for two reasons – one, because they will undoubtedly increase during the year of publication, and two, because no one should ever send money or goods to any company without checking first that it still exists. However reputable and successful, the owners of small companies do retire or move when their leases run out.

Telephone exchanges are given rather than STD codes because some exchanges still have different local dialling codes from those applicable when you are telephoning from London or major cities. Opening hours are mentioned only if they differ radically from the normal five-day, 9 a.m. to 5 p.m., or 10 a.m. to 6 p.m., week. Always check before making a special journey.

Some craftsmen have a variety of skills and many shops provide a range of services, so they don't always fit neatly into one category. If you are looking for a special service, regardless of area, the Index lists every subject in alphabetical order.

I hope you may find many of these entries useful and interesting and stimulating. I have a great personal respect for the individual craftsman and small shopkeeper who survive in spite of big business competition, and I hope the variety of specialities mentioned may encourage others to try their hand and discover some untapped skill.

I hope, too, that my selection will not only be of practical use to those who live in the areas mentioned, but will also be a guide to tourists who may be in search of the excellent craftsmanship this country has to offer. We have the best designers in the world and we should say so – often.

Prices were correct at the time of printing, but are only intended as an indication and means of comparison. Do not send cheques to any company without checking first by telephone on postal charges and availability.

Acknowledgements

My thanks to all those who have contributed individual recommendations, and in particular to Bobbie Bouch, Emma Buckmaster, Eve Drake, Julia Ellam, Judi Goodwin, Peta Hoult, Alison Walker and Hilary Wharton for their invaluable research, encouragement and enthusiasm. Thanks, too, to Jane Parry-Williams and especially to Nina Ford for helping me at the last minute to keep my deadline – and my sanity.

Further suggestions would be most welcome. Please send them to Beryl Downing, *Where Can I Get . . . ?*, Penguin Books, 536 King's Road, London SW10 0UH.

1 Getting Things Made

Beds and bedding

CUMBRIA

Cumbria Industries for the Disabled, Petteril Bank Rd, Harraby, Carlisle (Carlisle 25241/2). A wide selection of beds and mattresses, all of which can be made to order in any size, at prices from £87 to £176.75. The organization, which has grown from the original Workshops for the Blind, now provides a variety of work for the severely handicapped people of Cumbria. Run as a competitive business by the Social Services, the workshops also make three-piece suites, caravan mattresses, hassocks and kneelers, and they will make geriatric chairs, covered in fire-retardant vinyl or tweed if required.

Chris Trippear, Shap Wells Cottage, Shap, nr Penrith (Shap 264). Reproduction seventeenth-century four-poster beds. Chris Trippear, who started his career as a boatbuilder, makes convincing copies by taking mouldings from original antiques and reproducing them in glassfibre stained to a dark oak colour and backed with wood to give the right sound quality. He specializes in traditional carvings from various areas of Britain and also makes panelling, chests, court cupboards and cabinets. A four-poster with platform costs around £1,500.

DEVON

Michael Cox, Lower Washbourne Barton, Ashprington, Totnes (Harbertonford 488). Four-poster beds and surrounds handmade to order. The complete beds are available in a selection of styles, mainly from the seventeenth and eighteenth centuries, in pine or mahogany from about £510. The surrounds (posts and cornices), in two styles, are free-standing and will fit round any size bed, adding charm to the most ordinary divan. These are from £325 in pine, £425 in mahogany. Drapes, valances and canopies for both beds and surrounds can be made up in customers' own fabrics.

CO. DURHAM

Theresa Spinks Designs, Watergate Lodge, Watergate Rd, Castleside, nr Consett (Consett 507136 and 501851). Theresa Spinks has been designing and making four-poster beds, canopies and draped beds for the last two years – since she made and dressed two four-posters for her two daughters and all her friends wanted one too. She is now accepting orders from customers in Selfridges and Harrods and has made all the beds for a small private hotel in a period house in West Auckland, Co. Durham. She will travel to any part of the country to discuss ideas for a complete bedroom scheme. Prices start at around £700 and making up takes six weeks.

ESSEX

Edward Teale Ltd, Langley Rd, Clavering, nr Saffron Walden (Clavering 307). Continental quilts converted from eiderdowns and sleeping bags, or made new to order from £24.90 single. Extra channels can be added to quilts that are too small, from £11.20 per channel in feather and down. Other services available include the making of covers, pillowcases, sheets, curtains, bedspreads and cushions and the making and recovering of eiderdowns. A postal service is available anywhere in the United Kingdom.

GLOUCESTERSHIRE

Janet Turner Fine Linens, 7 Eldorado Rd, Cheltenham (Cheltenham 37463). Irish linen sheets and tablecloths, hand-hemstitched or with crochet inserts and edgings. Janet Turner has workers throughout the country making crochet and bobbin lace to traditional patterns, and she mounts and hand-finishes the items herself – very time-consuming and therefore expensive, but very popular, as lace is enjoying a revival. Several embassies have ordered large dining cloths, monogrammed sheets, duvet covers and napkins, all worked by hand. Single sheets with hemstitched edge are £94.80 per pair, with crochet insertions £105.50. A full price list is available.

LONDON

And So To Bed, 638 King's Rd, SW6 (01-731 3593); and at 7 New King's Rd, SW6. Victorian brass beds, antique and reproduction, and four-posters, with antique bedlinen to match, or made to order. Reproduction beds are from £270; antiques start about £300. A brochure is available. The New King's Road shop specializes in bedlinens, including sheets in cotton, poly/cotton and silk, comforters, duvets and antique quilts. They will also make quilts in customers' own fabrics.

The Bedchamber, 8 Symons St, SW3 (01-730 5102). Antique and modern four-poster beds in oak, mahogany or pine, handpainted to match furnishings if required. The reproduction ones are hand-crafted in Northumberland and sent to London in strips. Hugh Blackett then delivers them and puts them up himself – anywhere in the country. Prices are from £1,500 with curtains and drapes. A complete design service is also offered by Liz Williams, who has one of the best collections of chintzes based on original eighteenth-century designs and including an exclusive range of six designs in four colourways, chosen by her from archives and produced in colours mixed to her specifications.

Descamps, 197 Sloane St, SW1 (01-235 6957). Sheets made in any size or shape in Descamps' own fabrics, plus a wide range of co-ordinating sheets, towels, tablecloths and duvet covers. Single sheets from £17 to £30, plus about one third for special orders. A catalogue is available.

Heal's, 196 Tottenham Court Rd, W1 (01-636 1666). Handmade beds and bedding to order. Heal's will make beds in any size; a single spring-interior mattress is from £442, mattress and sprung base from £950, base with traditional horsehair mattress from £1,000. They say that people who can afford to lie in such luxury tell them it's like driving a Rolls Royce after a Mini. Heal's also have handmade pillows from £28, single down duvets from £160, chintz quilts from £228, silk from £336, real eider-down from £672.

Pat Jones, 36 Brookwood Rd, Southfields, SW18 (01-870 1587). Old eiderdowns, cushions or sleeping bags converted into continental quilts. Any sizes are possible, from £25 single, £36 double. Pat Jones will also repair or remake duvets, and although she prefers to discuss orders with customers personally, she will accept mail orders. She can collect within twenty miles.

The London Bedding Centre, 26–27 Sloane St, SW1 (01-235 7544). Beds in any size and shape to customers' own specifications, with bedheads to commission too. They have made beds up to 7 ft square and 9 ft wide, and prices are from £600 to £3,000. A brochure is available.

One Off, 33 Shorts Gardens, WC2 (01-379 7796); and at 24 Chalk Farm Rd, NW1 (01-482 1989). Any shape, size or colour of tubular bed – no timber work. Prices for the frame only are from £150 to £400. One Off will also plan your bedroom, install the bed and design any piece of furniture to your specifications. Leaflets are available.

Stokecroft Arts, 88–94 Caledonian Rd, N19 (01-278 6874). A large range of beds and mattresses which can be made to any size. There are bunk beds, sofa beds and stacking beds too, all with slatted bases and made in solid timbers –

mostly pine, but there is also a range of exotic hardwoods, including afrormosia, iroko and mahogany. The workshop's philosophy is that the end product is better when a craftsman is allowed to make a complete piece, rather than working on sections in a mass-production factory. Yet, because of the use of labour-saving equipment, the prices remain reasonable for the quality – from £106 for a 3-ft single bed. A brochure and price list are available.

MANCHESTER

Burgess Bedding Ltd, Hope Mills, 113 Pollard St, Ancoats, Manchester (061-273 5528). Divans and mattresses made to measure in any size. The most popular requests are for extra-long single beds (6 ft 9 in. by 3 ft) and extra-wide double beds (up to 6 ft 6 in. and even wider). Various types of divans and mattresses are available; a 4-ft 6-in. divan would cost around £250. Write for a leaflet and stockists.

Pinecroft Beds, 10 Lees Hall Crescent, Fallowfield, Manchester (061-224 4275). Peter Kelly makes four-poster pine bedsteads to a cottage-style design. Single, double or made-to-measure sizes are available, and all are easy to assemble. Mattresses and drapes can be supplied. Peter Kelly also makes slatted pine beds in standard and made-to-measure sizes. A double four-poster costs £340, including delivery. A mail-order service is available.

SUSSEX

Stanwater Designs, Stedhame, Midhurst, W Sussex (Midhurst 2578). Beds and bedroom furniture to your own specifications. Designer Janette Garstin will discuss your ideas and furnishings and provide suitable sketches of any type of bed, from a cradle to a four-poster. They can be made in oak, mahogany or old pine or in pine hand-decorated with flowers. Prices start at £672 for a plain half-tester bed. Other handpainted items can also be supplied, plus bed-hangings and covers. Viewing is by appointment only.

Calligraphy and paper

CAMBRIDGESHIRE

Paper Dragons, Unit 19, Roman Bank, Leverington, nr Wisbech (Wisbech 582935). Handmade papers tailored in shape, colour and substance to individual needs. Chris Gander was a mechanical engineer when he took up paper-making as a hobby, so he quickly grasped the technicalities of the subject and now spends a good deal of time teaching the craft to schoolchildren, taking his portable papermill with him. He likes to discuss his customers' exact requirements – whether the paper is for etchings, engravings, fine art – and he will make anything to order, at very reasonable charges. He also has a printing press and is prepared to print certificates, presentation scrolls on handmade paper or other one-offs or short runs that large commercial printers would not undertake.

CHESHIRE

Manley Wright, 41 Chapel Lane, Wilmslow (Wilmslow 532180). Illuminated manuscripts for presentation. Ken Jones has developed his hobby of calligraphy into a full-time occupation now that he has 'retired' and will hand-inscribe poems and texts as wedding and anniversary presents from about £20, depending on the amount of illumination. These can be parchment scrolls or can be framed as pictures by his son Martin, who is a woodcarver. Church inscriptions are also undertaken, and a recent commission was for a two-hundredth-anniversary document for a twin town in Germany, illuminated with symbols of Cheshire.

DORSET

Richard Grasby, Bedchester House, Bedchester, Shaftesbury (Fontmell Magna 811732). A journeyman lettercutter who designs and cuts work in stone. These include memorials, commemorative plaques and foundation stones as well as house names, office signs and the carving of symbols, crests and coats of arms. Richard Grasby works in a variety of stones, including granite, marble, limestone and slate, and he travels extensively. His work is of a very high quality.

Joan Haig, Home Farm, Fifehead Magdalen, Gillingham (Marnhull 820268). Illuminated addresses, heraldic work, family trees, gilding, watercolours and portraits. An illuminated address might cost from £60 to £150. Joan Haig's talents also include spinning and weaving.

LONDON

Alan & Kenneth Breese, 387 King St, Hammersmith, W6 (01-748 8896). Designers and craftsmen in lettering – foundation and head stones, commemorative plaques, signs and heraldry. Their work for public buildings has included museums, universities and St Paul's Cathedral, and they also work to private clients' commissions. Alan Breese specializes in letter carving (house plaques, for instance), Kenneth in calligraphy and painted lettering, including poems as Valentines.

OXFORDSHIRE

Alison Urwick, Crossways, Bloxham, nr Banbury. After an art-school training Alison Urwick worked for two years at the College of Arms, and she specializes in all types of illustrative lettering. Presentation scrolls for retirement and special occasions, simple family trees (not the genealogical research) on handmade paper from about £100 to large ones going back several centuries and with coats of arms at £600 to £800. She also particularly enjoys a commission to illustrate a poem or piece of prose.

SOMERSET

Wookey Hole Caves Ltd, Wookey Hole, Wells (Wells 72243). Paper made by hand in a revived Victorian mill. Wookey Hole is renowned for its caves, but another claim to fame is that paper has been made there for nearly four hundred years. During the seventeenth and eighteenth centuries Wookey Hole was one of many Somerset mills using the pure water from local rivers to produce fine paper, and in 1863 it won an order to make American Confederate banknotes. A new paper shop has opened selling handmade writing paper, watercolour paper, artists' drawing blocks and a variety of posters and cards. Prices are from 35p.

WILTSHIRE

Compton Marbiing, Lower Lawn House, Tisbury, Salisbury (Salisbury 870691). Marbled papers and bindings for albums, portfolios, visitors' and game books and endpapers. Solveig Stone first became interested in marbling when she saw a magnificent collection in the private library at Stanford University, California. No one could teach her the techniques in America so she had to wait until she came back to Britain. Marbling originated in Persia and did not arrive in England until the early seventeenth century, when the Dutch exported toys wrapped in marbled paper, which was so admired that it was smoothed out and kept. The original technique used coloured dyes, but Solveig Stone and her partner Caroline Mann use oil paints on size. Each sheet is made individually by hand and so differs slightly from the next. There are two sizes: 20 × 25 in. at about £1.04; 25 × 30 in. at £1.38. Apart from being used as endpapers for valuable books, they make pretty linings for boxes and bookcases; and interior decorators even paper whole walls with them. A catalogue is available for a stamped addressed envelope, or send £1 for a book of samples.

Mitchell & Malik Ltd, Duchy Manor Mill, Hazzards Hill, Mere (Mere 860965). Hand-marbled papers for the restoration of rare books and also available in a range of stationery. Michael Mitchell re-established this centuries-old craft of paper marbling after five years of research, and his endpapers, hand-marbled in fifteen different stages to produce unique patterns, are used by major conservation libraries world-wide. The stationery range includes address books, albums, blotters, desk accessories, photograph frames, lampshades and collectors' boxes, at prices from £2 to £60. Send £1.15 and a stamped addressed envelope for sample pack and price list. Visitors are welcome at the workshop in an eighteenth-century converted flour-mill in Mere, just off the A303.

W. J. Partridge, Church Farm Workshops, Sutton Mandeville, nr Salisbury (Fovant 213). Private-press limited-edition printing by a retired master printer. Walter Partridge produces hand-press editions for collectors on an 1828 Columbia press under the imprint of Perdrix Press. He binds limp editions himself and has hardbacks and specials bound locally in full calf. Prices are from £3 to £50.

Clocks

CORNWALL

Bill Thompson Lapidary, Carn Glaze Farm, St Just, Penzance (Penzance 788602). Semi-precious gemstones cut, polished and made into decorative clocks, windows, firescreens and lamps. Bill Thompson built his own machinery to grind and polish the stones to translucent slices which show up the beautiful markings. He uses agate, amethyst and rose quartz and will undertake any commissions, including presentation trophies. Clocks are from £50, firescreens £150, lamps £125, windows from 40p per square inch.

LINCOLNSHIRE

Gay Grima, Mount Pleasant, Hainton (Burgh-on-Bain 225). Clockfaces handpainted to order. Gay Grima's clocks have quartz movements and wooden faces about 12 in. square. The numerals can be either Roman or Georgian-style, and the decoration can be simple folk art or more sophisticated designs. She will also paint nursery rhymes or children's scenes, and will make larger play clocks. Prices are from £15, plus postage and packing.

LONDON

Gordon Burnett, The Granary, 61 St Mary Church St, SE16 (01-231 0222). Clocks and watches made to order in a variety of modern designs and materials — silver, wood, aluminium, brass, stone, marble and granite. Having trained in Aberdeen and at the Royal College of Art, Gordon Burnett was awarded a Crafts Council grant in 1982 and set up in this Rotherhithe group of workshops. His designs have a classic simplicity, from a $2\frac{1}{2}$-in.-diameter travel clock in blue steel to the 2-ft-diameter clock he made for the Royal Courts of Justice new hall at Lincoln's Inn. He mainly uses quartz movements. Prices range from £45 for a simple wall clock.

Clive Burr, c/o The Goldsmiths Hall, Foster Lane, E C1 (01-606 8971). A silversmith whose particular speciality is carriage clocks, both conventional designs and original modern ones to commission, Clive Burr often combines exotic woods with silver, aluminium or brass, and uses engraving, engine-turning and enamelling techniques. Prices are from £400.

SUSSEX

Hallmark Industrial Engravers, 4 Tralfagar St, Brighton, E Sussex (Brighton 603498). Engraving on metal and plastic. John Gratwick trained as a banknote engraver and now specializes in period-style clockfaces and barometers. Some of his work has gone to Garrards in London, but he is also willing to undertake any engraving, however small, by hand or machine, or by combination of computer and hand (the computer spaces out the lettering). Signet rings can be engraved with an initial from £1; pewter presentation tankards cost from £3 to £4 by machine, £7 to £8 by hand.

YORKSHIRE

Trevor Booth, Lane Head Cottage, North Lane, Cawthorne, Barnsley, S Yorks (Barnsley 764579). Clocks made to match any period setting or piece of furniture. Trevor Booth has been a cabinet-maker for twenty years, and for the past twelve has concentrated entirely on clocks – bracket, wall and long-case. He

regards clocks as pieces of furniture, rather than ornaments. 'Once you start studying clock design, you realize it's not like making a coffin with a dial on top, as so many people seem to think,' he says. 'If it's too wide or too top-heavy it just isn't "right".' His clocks are certainly 'right' – beautifully crafted in mahogany, rosewood, oak, walnut or yew, or any timber requested, mostly with German movements but some with English ones (these to special commission only, as they are ten times more expensive). Prices are from £400 for wall clocks, £400 to £1,500 for bracket clocks, and between £1,000 and £3,000 for long-case.

Embroidery and tapestries

LONDON

Joyce Conwy Evans, 4 Cedar Studios, 45 Glebe Place, SW3 (01-351 0648).
A designer who has turned her talents to such diverse interiors as the Royal Albert Hall and a Mississippi steamboat, Joyce Conwy Evans also specializes in tapestries and has created magnificent altar frontals for King's College Chapel, Cambridge, and the Chapel of Martyrs and Saints, Canterbury Cathedral. She also enjoys domestic interiors and will design wall-hangings to complement an existing scheme. Her natural instinct is for the dramatic, and she uses colour and texture lavishly.

MANCHESTER

Elda Abramson, Weaving Studio, 30 Claremont Grove, Manchester (061-434 3022). Highly textured woven wall-hangings in hand-dyed yarns, mainly to commission. Elda Abramson usually visits the house or works from photographs and colour swatches. The textures of her work rely on the different reflective qualities of materials like sisal, cotton, synthetic wool and jute. She submits designs and yarn swatches in advance, but a clause in her contract says that clients need not buy the work is they don't like it. That, she says, keeps her on her toes, but no one has ever rejected her work. Prices from £35 to £60 per square foot, depending on size.

Eleri Mills, Textile Workshop 2–4 Oxford Rd, Manchester (061-236 5707). Painted and handstitched panels, wall-hangings and banners to commission. Eleri Mills's work is fresh, spontaneous and very atmospheric. Her freely expressed designs are loosely based on landscape studies and observations of nature. Prices from £200 to £1,000.

SOMERSET

Œnone Cave, Rambler Studio, Holford, nr Bridgwater (Holford 315).
Specialist embroidery with an emphasis on linen cut-work or Ruskin work, as it

is called in the Lake District: John Ruskin brought designs over from Venice to the Lakes, where they were taken up as a local craft and where Œnone Cave learned the skills and helped to revive them. She has written a book on cut-work, does a lot of work for the English Lace School at Tiverton, and will accept commissions for table linen, cushions, needle-cases and ecclesiastical vestments. She also specializes in batik dyeing on silk and in miniature weaving.

SURREY

The Grange Training Centre, Great Bookham, Leatherhead (Bookham 31). All types of needlework from mounting lace edging on tablecloths to embroidering altar cloths. The Centre is run as a charity and employs handicapped girls, whose work is beautiful enough to be commissioned by the Royal Family. They will work on your own designs and can embroider table linen to match your china. They will also finish your tapestries if you find the backgrounds boring. Embroidered luncheon mats are from £13.50 for six, tablecloths from £20. They will also smock your own material for children's dresses.

Fire bellows

NOTE

For other fire furniture made by blacksmiths, see pp. 133–8.

WILTSHIRE

John Jones, 35 Milton Milbourne, Pewsey (Pewsey 2696). Craftsman-made fire bellows in elm and cowhide from £21.50 to £50. John Jones's start as a bellows-maker seven years ago was almost as traditional as the craft itself – he 'happened to mention to a man in a pub' that he had mended his own pair and was immediately given his first commission to make a new pair. He has his own solid brass nozzles turned specially for him, as he couldn't find any he liked, and he uses solid brass nails. He will also undertake repairs – releathering costs between £13 and £25.

Furniture

AVON

Paul Harris, 39 Upper Belgrave Rd, Clifton, Bristol 8 (Bristol 737348). Furniture made to commission. After a career as a Lloyd's broker, Paul Harris 'got fed up with making nothing but money', took a five-year City and Guilds course and 're-tired' to become a cabinet-maker. Among his smaller pieces are carved firescreens –

you make the tapestry, he will frame it for about £65. He also makes attractive Windsor-style chairs which can incorporate an initial in the back splat – high or low versions for children from £100, full-size chairs with or without coats of arms from £125.

CHESHIRE

A. Allen Antique Restorers Ltd, Arden St, New Mills, via Stockport (New Mills 45274). Regency- and Georgian-style furniture made to order in reclaimed antique timber. If you have a set of five antique chairs, Tony Allen can make you a sixth to match. Or he will build a drinks cupboard or TV and video cabinet in virtually any antique style. A plain Regency-style sabre-leg dining chair costs from £250.

Our Kid, 1–3 Bank Square, Wilmslow (Wilmslow 522385). Nursery furniture made to order, with cot and pram quilts, duvets and cushions to match. Heirloom cribs can be draped to order, and there is an original and charming grandmother clock with the long case fitted with shelves to make a narrow cupboard for the nursery – £75.

CUMBRIA

Four Gables Workshop, Four Gables, Brampton (Brampton 2635). High-quality cabinet-making and antique restoration. Roger Nelson and Bill McKie combine traditional methods of construction with the precision provided by modern machinery. Among recent projects have been a series of twelve reproduction Victorian workboxes in walnut, yew, coca-bola or ash, with inlaid tops and carved legs, each £675.

Peter Hall Woodcraft, Danes Rd, Staveley, nr Kendal (Staveley 821633). A small team of skilled cabinet-makers producing good-quality traditional and contemporary domestic furniture. The work includes dining-room furniture, corner cupboards, bedheads, bookcases and display cabinets. Everything is designed to commission by Peter Hall and made in solid English oak. Coffee tables are about £115, dining tables £380, Welsh dressers from £1,000. There is a six months' waiting list.

Ian Laval, Meadowbank Farm, Curthwaite, Wigton (Dalston 710409). A furniture-maker in the traditional style, working in oak, yew and other native British timbers. Ian Laval is involved with every stage of his craft, felling and sawing and seeing the process of furniture-making through to its final polishing. He makes to commission, but there is always a representative selection of timber and furniture to be seen at his farm showroom. Prices are in the region of £2,061 for a 6-ft-long traditional pedestal desk in oak, £850 for a full-size, standing oak corner cabinet with pear inlay.

DORSET

Cecil Colyer, Orchandene, Candys Lane, Shillingstone, Blandford Forum (Child Okeford 860252). Imaginative and beautifully finished furniture to commission. Having taught woodwork for twenty-one years at Bryanston School, Cecil Colyer knows all about the pleasure of the texture of polished wood. He wants people to enjoy the feel of his furniture – not for him the 'Do not touch' notices. He makes elegantly simple tables and chairs and will create special pieces to meet the most unusual demands – a newspaper-holder for someone with the use of only one arm, for instance, and a rocking chair for short-legged people.

John Makepeace Furniture Workshops, Parnham House, Beaminster (Beaminster 962204). Impossible not to mention the leading name in modern British furniture craftsmanship, although John Makepeace's own one-off designs are now in the collectors' and museums' price category. There are, however, signed editions by Makepeace made in the Parnham workshops. These are from £15 for bowls, £100 for stools and dressing mirrors, £260 for folding stools in cherrywood and coach-hide. The house, workshop and gardens are open on Wednesdays, Sundays and bank holidays from April to October between 10 a.m. and 5 p.m.; visits at other times can be arranged by telephone or letter.

ESSEX

David and Jean Whitaker, Frogge Cottage, Frogge St, Ickleton, Saffron Walden (Saffron Walden 30304). Tables, chairs, sideboards, dressers made to individual sizes and in the timber of your choice – English oak, elm and ash and other timbers from the Far East, Africa and America. Designs are based on the best of traditional English country styles adapted for present-day use. Chairs from £80, stools from £16, tables from £290. An unusual speciality is a cottage bed with pegged-together frame – substantial in use, but designed to be moved in four sections up narrow stairs and landings: from £375 in elm to £600 in oak. Work is also done for builders and architects, and a wide range of turned wood is available, including stair spindles, newel posts and finials. The workshop hours are 8.30 a.m. to 6 p.m., Monday to Saturday. A leaflet is available.

John Yeates, Good Wood, 5 Chase Rd, Southchurch, Southend-on-Sea (Southend 614102). A furniture-maker and woodcarver with a particular interest in heraldic design, John Yeates has carved coats of arms on wall plaques and in table tops, and his commissions have ranged from dining tables and double beds to pub signs and lace bobbins. A recent trophy was commissioned by the Burma Star Association in memory of Lord Louis Mountbatten. Heraldic chairs with high backs in the form of a griffon or other beast are from £100 in lime or sycamore and elm; coats of arms from £40.

GLOUCESTERSHIRE

Richard Fyson, Manor Farm, Kencot, Lechlade (Filkins 223). A cabinet-maker for thirty-four years, Richard Fyson designs and makes to commission. His work has included chairs, tables and bureaux (he is particularly fond of walnut) and a lot of church furniture, including pews, pulpits, altar tables and lecterns. He works mainly in British hardwoods, and his claim to make anything he is asked for was proved recently when he extended his skills to include sculpture on being commissioned to make a pair of heraldic lions – and a cow.

Charles Verey, Yew Tree Cottage, Ampney Crucis, Cirencester (Poulton 495 or Bibury 561). A specialist in garden furniture design. Charles Verey's collection designed for Green Bros includes handsome teak seats with Chinese-style latticed backs and a bench made to an original Lutyens design, identical to a miniature in Queen Mary's dolls' house at Windsor Castle. These are available at prices from £95 to £600 through Green Brothers (Hailsham 845414). Charles Verey also designs to commission and particularly likes to work in timbers which can be left without treating and which weather to a silvery grey.

HEREFORD AND WORCESTER

Innova, 18 St Owen's St, Hereford (Hereford 51170). Philip Hearsey is a furniture designer who will undertake anything to order apart from chairs. Commissions have included cabinets, tables, storage units and shelving, mostly in ash, oak and cherry. The lines of his furniture are simple and beautifully tailored rather than outrageously modern, and his prices are realistic.

KENT

Tenterden Rushcraft, rear of 90 High St, Tenterden (Tenterden 3326). Specialists in cane furniture made to order. William Birch comes from a family of furniture-makers who established a factory in High Wycombe in 1850 and became well-known for their chairs. He has been weaving cane since he was nine years old, learning his skill from a local craftsman on the way home from school. Now he makes a range of cane furniture and panels – bedheads in sheet cane are from £33.35 (2 ft 6 in.) to £67.85 (5 ft 6 in.). Special commissions have included elaborate work for a palace in Saudi Arabia.

LANCASHIRE

John Whitehead, 84 Denshaw Rd, Delph, Oldham (Saddleworth 4578). A furniture-maker/designer working mainly in English hardwoods. John Whitehead produces chairs, tables and cabinets – anything except fitted furniture – using oak, ash, chestnut and fruit woods in a clean, uncluttered and modern style. A wall cabinet, for example, would be from £320. He also undertakes architectural and church work using carving, lettering, painting and gilding.

LONDON

Cabochon Furniture Ltd, 7 Tyers Gate, S E1 (01-403 5404). Modern laminated furniture at a reasonable cost. Jim Nicholls and Derek Abbitt concentrate on simple lines with a matt white finish, but customers may choose colours, sizes and finishes to their own specification at extra cost. Tables, shelves and desks are available. Much of the range has been selected by the Design Council. Prices from £30 for a small occasional table.

Casa Fina, 9 The Market, Covent Garden, W C2 (01-836 0289), and branches. As well as a large range of imported ceramics, lights and rugs, there is a range of off-the-peg cane furniture which can be made in a range of six colours. The range includes chests, bedside tables, sofas, screens, coffee tables, bedheads and mirrors from about £87 for a bedside table. It is also available at Casa Fina branches in Bath, Farnham, Harrogate, Leamington Spa, Truro and Tunbridge Wells.

Ciel, 281 Lillie Rd, S W6 (01-385 5167). Tables made to order in any size, shape or colour. Ciel are also specialists in painted effects, marbling, feathering, spattering or lacquering in colours to match furnishings. Prices will depend on size and complexity, but a coffee table 18 × 18 × 30 in. long would cost around £276; sofa tables are from £255.

Dragons, 23 Walton St, S W3 (01-589 3795). Children's nursery furniture designed and nurseries furnished to order. Rosie Fisher (dubbed 'dragon' by her younger sister when they were children – hence the name) started in antiques, moved over to children's furniture, and only two years after opening Dragons was asked to design some of the furniture for Prince William's nursery. She now employs twenty-one artists, each with a speciality, and can offer decorated furniture in any style – copying motifs from fabrics, handpainting Disney creations, Pooh and friends, or her own exclusive characters, a family of delightfully dressed rabbits and moles designed by Penny Streeter. Dragged finishes are available, as are complete murals. In fact 'Anything can be done on anything – and it's all British,' says the chief dragon herself.

Heal's, 196 Tottenham Court Rd, W1 (01-636 1666). Small furniture designed by craftsmen and made to order. Prices will depend on the wood required and the intricacy of the design, but as an example a small nest of tables would start at £100. Heal's also offer a complete interior-design service, charging £150, which is refundable if furniture more than £2,500 is ordered from them.

Hippo Hall, 65 Pimlico Rd, S W1 (01-730 7710). Nursery furniture and furnishings with a charmingly humorous touch, handpainted to commission. Annie Sloane's animal alphabet – delightful animal characters bent into the shape of letters – can be handpainted as a child's name and framed for about £48 for a five-letter name, more for a longer one, or there is a less expensive printed version from about £13.75. They can be sent by mail (plus postage) without glass. Lots of other nursery ideas, exclusive fabrics, wallpapers and co-ordinating nursery bedlinen in stock.

London Architectural Salvage and Supply Company, Mark St, off Paul St, E C2 (01-739 0448). Pine seats made from pews. This company specializes in clearing demolition sites and churches and will make straight seats from 4 ft to 8 ft long, from £75 to £160; corner seats from £190 to £350. They do them in yellow pine, pitch pine, oak and chestnut.

Moobles Design, 10 Median Rd, E5 (01-985 6469). Custom-built, handmade pine furniture, using well-seasoned demolition timber. Rob Prangnell finds much of his pine in old churches and theatres and from it makes desks, dressers, tables, chests, benches. He also makes beds, which are delivered in sections and assembled in fifteen minutes – no problems in getting them up narrow staircases. His designs have a rounded, cottagey look, and he is prepared to tackle anything to commission. Prices are about £185 for a table 6 ft × 2 ft 6 in.; £210 for one 48 in. in diameter.

Norfolk Furniture Company Ltd, 632 King's Rd, S W6 (01-736 4840). Makers of sofas and sofa beds in nine standard styles, and also to specific requirements. Sofas are supplied in calico or can be covered in your own fabric or one from their stock. Prices from £373.50 for a two-seater sofa bed.

Pearl Dot, 2 Roman Way, N7 (01-609 3169). Custom-made furniture by a group of three designer/makers, Robert Williams, Steve Hounslow and Peter Hoare, with the help of four other craftsmen. Apart from one-offs, the emphasis is on batch production and designs which lend themselves to reinterpretation, thus cutting the costs. Their plank-backed chair is well-known – the standard version is £161 – and they make interesting desks, tables and drinks cabinets from £140 to £2,000. Every piece is inlaid with a pearl dot – leftovers from the group's landlord, who was one of the last mother-of-pearl workers in the country. He made large quantities of compass dials for the services, and when the furniture-makers moved in, they bought all the small pearl circles punched out of the centres of the dials, which they now use as their trade-mark.

Chris Sullivan, Kingsgate Workshops, Kingsgate Rd, N W6 (01-328 7496); showroom: 108 Mill Lane, N W6. Many sizes of tables handmade from old, reclaimed pine; Victorian-style pedestal and tilt-top gateleg and coffee tables and a range of bedroom and kitchen furniture. Prices from £99 for a round dining table 2 ft in diameter. The workshop is open during the week, 8 a.m. to 6 p.m. The showroom is open only on Saturdays.

William Tillman, 30 St James's St, SW1 (01-839 2500). Very high-quality reproduction furniture that is now turning up at auction and making a profit for its owners. William Tillman's craftsmen specialize in making exact copies of Georgian furniture with finishes that will withstand modern living. Tables are their speciality; a Sheraton-style mahogany pedestal table is about £1,300.

OXFORDSHIRE

Crowdys Wood Products Ltd, The Old Bakery, Clanfield, Oxford (Clanfield 216). Spinning wheels are among the items offered by this small furniture workshop established in 1964 – there are four types from £135 to £275. They also make furniture to commission, mainly tables and dining and kitchen chairs, which are their speciality and can be made in many types of British and imported hardwoods.

Lucinda Leech, Jericho Furniture Workshop, King St, Oxford (Oxford 56376). All sorts of one-off commissions for domestic, office and church use, with a particular emphasis on tables, chairs and handsome, handmade desks and filing cabinets to blend with domestic interiors. Lucinda Leech was one of the first women to be accepted as a student of furniture making and design at Rycotewood College, and she enjoys making functional pieces with simple, bold lines. She works with a variety of British hardwoods and experiments with unusual ones. In some of her work she blends several timbers in one design – a dining table in cherry and sycamore, for instance, would be about £750.

SUFFOLK

Mendlesham Furniture Workshop, Elms Farm, Mendlesham, Stowmarket (Mendlesham 7107). Roy Clement Smith makes a new generation of the Mendlesham chair, first produced in that village between 1790 and 1830. They are the Windsor chairs of East Anglia, with arms, and made in traditional elm and cherrywood inlaid with boxwood. Each is individually made to order, numbered and can be inscribed. Prices around £250 each. Antique furniture restoration, some upholstery and French polishing also undertaken.

George Sneed, Bacon's Barn, St Michael, South Elmham, Bungay (St -Cross 282). Rush-seated dining chairs based on traditional English designs. George Sneed has been reseating antique chairs for many years and has produced these chairs in answer to the demand from his customers. They are made in ash, which can be left natural or stained black. Dining chairs cost £57, carvers £67, and they can be delivered anywhere on the UK mainland for an additional £5 per chair.

SURREY

David Gillespie Associates Ltd, Dippenhall Crossroads, Farnham (Farnham 723531). Carved screens in Californian redwood, supplied untreated for the client to stain, varnish or wax. The company supplies large screens for large commercial premises and palaces, and is prepared to make to any size. The standard size is $2\frac{1}{2} \times 1$ metre. The fretwork can be in the shape of stars, squares, typical Islamic designs. A brochure is available. Prices are from about £56 to £104 per square metre for a screen carved on both sides, and from £44 to £74 per square metre if only one side is decorated.

Lincoln Road Workshops, Lincoln Rd, Dorking (Dorking 880927). A co-operative furniture designers' workshop where four ex-Parnham graduates share overheads but design and make furniture independently. Philip St Pier, a founder member, has a special talent for intricate cabinet-making, using the contrasting effects of English and exotic hardwoods and working with the timbers in a sensitive way which fully realizes their potential. He also likes to make large conference tables and dining chairs; prices from £180 for a chair, £800 for a table. Rupert Senior makes one-off designs and limited-edition batches and is particularly interested in creating new types of furniture to suit modern demands. Charles Wheeler-Carmichael bases his modern designs on traditional forms, creating classic rather than way-out shapes in English hardwoods and pre-stained sycamore veneers; and David Linley has made a speciality of many-panelled screens decorated in coloured veneers like large-scale marquetry. Prices are from £450 for a four-part screen. He also makes folding desks in brightly dyed plywoods for the young and trendy furniture fancier. All four work closely with the client at the design stage.

Ursula St Barbe Spurr, Haslemere (Haslemere 52428). Papier-mâché trays and stands made to order; also small trays on folding legs – to use as firescreens. Prices from £40.

SUSSEX

Long Barn Furniture Workshop, Muddles Green, Chiddingly, Lewes, E Sussex (Chiddingly 764). Contemporary furniture made to commission by three individual designer/craftsmen sharing a renovated barn. John Wyndham's particular interests are in chair design and the technique of steam bending. He uses British hardwoods – oak, ash, sycamore, beech and cherry – and likes to include metals, plastics and fabrics in his designs. Rod Wales designs tables, chairs and cabinets in various hardwoods and, as well as undertaking individual commissions, is interested in developing limited editions of some designs. Andy Kindler's interests in boat-building and instrument-making led him to cabinet-making and furniture design, and he particularly enjoys designing tables, beds, and seating. He works with English and exotic woods, sometimes incorporating chipboard and other man-made materials to give contrast in colour and texture. All three design and work to a client's budget; a chair might be £100 to £250, desks and dining tables from £800, beds from £350, and cabinets from £450.

Shal Design, 134 Brighton Rd, Horsham, W Sussex (Horsham 69844). Glass-topped coffee tables, handpainted on the reverse by Grace Hosking in colours to blend with your furnishings. There are ten designs, including the Backgammon Table, based on the rescue of Helen by Agamemnon; the Chess Table, decorated with the thirty-two characters in the costumes of the court of the fifteenth-century German emperor Maximilian I; and the Chinoiserie Chess Table, with its leaves, ferns and shells characteristic of the rococo period, when chinoiserie was at its peak. The panels are all signed and numbered – no two are ever the same – and are set in 17-in.-high solid mahogany bases, brass-edged or in Chinese-Chippendale style, made by a local craftsman. Four sizes of glass – 24 in. or 30 in. square; 38 × 18 in.; or 40 × 24 in. Prices from £320.

WARWICKSHIRE

Arden House, Exhall Lodge Farm, Wixford Rd, Bidford-on-Avon, Alcester (Bidford-on-Avon 773575). Reproduction furniture in oak, yew or mahogany. Architect John Green and builder Clive Marcham join forces in their spare time to reproduce sixteenth- and seventeenth-century furniture with a well-worn look. They use timbers between ten and fifty years old with a 12-per-cent moisture content, which means the finished product is less likely to be affected by central heating. An oak refectory table which, if antique, would cost around £2,500, is about £995.

Neville Neal, School House, Stockton, nr Rugby (Southam 3702). Hand-turned spindle and ladder-back chairs to the traditional design by Ernest Gimson, disciple of William Morris. The making of these chairs has continued in an unbroken line since the turn of the century when Gimson set up a craft community in the Cotswolds. He had taken lessons from Philip Clissett, a Herefordshire chairmaker, in 1890 and after setting up his workshop near Cirencester he then taught Edward Gardiner, who moved to Warwickshire and handed on the craft to Neville Neal. The designs are made in dining chairs, carvers and rocking chairs, all with rush seats, and are produced to order in ash from £54 to £120.

WILTSHIRE

Michael Nettlefold, 90 Church St, Great Bedwyn, Marlborough (Marlborough 870791 and Pewsey 3447). Handmade garden furniture in solid pine or hardwood with wood preservative or a high-gloss white finish which withstands being left outdoors in the summer. There is a range of standard pieces –

tables, chairs, sun loungers, garden seats and planter tubs – designed by Michael Nettlefold and made by local craftsman Richard Waters. Tables from £46; sun loungers £125, towelling cushions extra. Also anything made to commission. A brochure is available.

Nicholas Partridge, formerly at Church Farm Workshops, Sutton Mandeville, nr Salisbury; now at Brecon House, 160 North St, Milborne Port, Somerset (Milborne Port 251102). Finely crafted furniture to commission, including tables, chairs and desks. Nicholas Partridge trained at Parnham House and likes to visit the rooms for which his furniture is intended, so that he can design for the space intended and create a blend of tone and line with other pieces in the room. Recent commissions have included a set of thirty-two chairs for the choir of St Mary's Church, Chard, and an American walnut desk exhibited at Parnham House. Dining chairs would cost around £200 each, desks around £1,000, stools £38.

Glass and ceramics

NOTE

I have deliberately not included studio pottery, because it is a very oversubscribed craft. You can find hand-thrown pottery throughout the country and the famous names, such as Lucie Rie, the Leach family, Robin Welch and Emmanuel Cooper, at specialist craft galleries. Some potters who offer personalized items are included in Chapter 6.

CAMBRIDGESHIRE

Brian Blanthorn, Thorpe Hall, Thorpe Rd, Peterborough (Peterborough 263389). Brian Blanthorn is one of the most remarkable new talents in glass-making. He is fascinated by stratified geological formations and has developed a technique of laminating strips of glass, firing them several times and grinding and polishing the result into magnificent bowls and dishes that look as if they have been scooped out of transparent rock. He will make to commission; expect to pay from £50 to £1,000, as the process is extremely time-consuming.

LONDON

Anthony Stern Glass Ltd, Unit 205, Avon House, Havelock Terrace, SW8 (01-622 9463). One of the outstanding talents in modern studio glass, Anthony Stern was already a successful film director when at thirty-two he saw glass being blown and on the spot decided that this was what he wanted to do for the rest of his life. He did an introductory course at the Glasshouse in Covent Garden and then went on to the Royal College of Art, where he became an MA. Many of his bowls and vases incorporate spiral motifs in flowing, swirling colours. His one-off 'Seascape Bowls' are in the Victoria and Albert Museum permanent collection. His work is available in several galleries from about £30 for a small bowl, and he also sells from the showroom attached to his workshop.

SUSSEX

Stephen Jones, 23 Sudeley St, Kemptown, Brighton, E Sussex (Brighton 673924). Iridescent ceramics achieved by a nineteenth-century technique called micro-crystalline glazing, which Stephen Jones revived and improved upon. The original effect happened by accident – an overfiring which produced crystals – and was so difficult to control that ceramicists in Stoke and Copenhagen found it uneconomic and ceased production. Stephen Jones found an old American recipe, experimented until he perfected the technique and now produces delightful and unusual plates, bowls and boxes in semi-porcelain with the tops glazed like frozen pools, in blues, greens and golds. Prices are from £20.

Interior decor (fabrics and walls)

CHESHIRE

Muraspec Textured Wallcoverings, Causeway House, Bath St, Altrincham (061-928 6527/4168), and branches. Specialized textured wallcoverings in wool, raw silk, moiré silk, synthetic suede, wall felts and forty shades of hessian. One-metre-size samples are available free of charge, and customers are given technical advice on hanging. Many of the wallcoverings are made in Muraspec's own factory, and they also stock high-quality wallpaper ranges from Britain, America and Europe, including Van Luit, Osborne & Little and Coles. There are branches in London, Glasgow, Birmingham, Leeds and Bristol.

LONDON

The Chelsea Fabric Shop, 6 Cale St, SW3 (01-584 8495), and 24 Chertsey St, Guildford, Surrey (Guildford 503058). Specialists in co-ordinated furnishings. The Chelsea Fabric Shop has, apart from ranges by well-known names, its own selection of thirteen designs in a variety of colours which have matching tiles, voiles, quilted fabrics and pleated shades. It offers a full interior-design service and can do handpainted shades and lamp bases to match furnishings, although this is likely to cost at least £60.

Colefax & Fowler, 39 Brook St, W1 (01-493 2231), and Colefax & Fowler Chintz Shop, 149 Ebury St, SW1 (01-730 2173). Exclusive furnishing fabrics, including a special range of chintzes taken from old eighteenth- and nineteenth-century documents in the company's archives. These are from about £11 to £19 per linear metre and can be printed in special colours to order. They have their own range of carpets and can design one-offs to order. There are also two weights of cream pure silk shantung which are inexpensive enough to use lavishly in furnishing; the lightweight is £3.57 per metre, 84 cm wide, the medium-weight is £6.10, 91 cm wide.

Coles, 18 Mortimer St, W1 (01-580 1066; sales: 01-580 2288/9). A range of beautiful, classic wallpapers, with some designs dating back to the early nineteenth century when Coles began. Paper can be specially printed to commission (minimum order ten rolls). They also do fabrics and wallcoverings – linen, silk, wool, moiré and mock suede.

Colour Counsellors Ltd, 187 New King's Rd, SW6 (01-736 8326), and branches. A range of 1,500 colour co-ordinated furnishings brought to your own home so that you can choose an entire scheme in the room you intend to decorate. Virginia Stourton began the company in 1970 when she arranged her samples of wallpapers, fabrics and carpets into eight black boxes, each relating to a main colour so that they could be taken out and mixed or matched. The ranges are by famous manufacturers, but the service costs no more than if you bought through a store, and includes the expert advice of the counsellor. There are fifty Colour Counsellors throughout the country; write to the New King's Road address for your nearest contact.

Distinctive Trimmings, 11 Marylebone Lane, W1 (01-486 6456), and 17 Kensington Church St, W8 (01-937 6174). Fringes, borders, bobbles and braids for trimming curtains and soft furnishings. A very extensive stock is available, and if you can't find exactly the shade you want they will make to order. They also offer a mail-order service, matching trimmings to swatches of fabrics. Please enclose a stamped, addressed envelope.

Leslux, 148 High Rd, East Finchley, N2 (01-883 9552/2419). The place to go if you know what tiles or wallpaper you want but are having trouble tracking them down. If you tell Leslux the make and design name or number, they will try to find it for you and, in most cases, get it at a discount. They also have a range of standard designs on show, and they sell paint.

John Lewis Ltd, Oxford St, W1 (01-629 7711), and branches of the Partnership. Bags of polybeads to make your own floor cushions. They come in bags of one cubic foot at about £2.45 and are to order through the cushion buyer. Blocks of foam for cushion-making are also available in various thicknesses and sizes to order.

Liberty, Regent St, W1 (01-734 1234). Quilting of lengths of fabric for you to make up yourself. Outline and motif quilting and also classic quilting is available on most of the fabrics in the furnishing fabric department. Minimum order one metre, maximum five metres in one continuous length. From £11.50 per metre, which includes wadding and cotton backing but not the cost of the fabric.

Marta Moia, 20 Tregunter Rd, S W10 (01-373 0543). Handpainted fabrics for curtains and loose covers. Marta Moia is an artist who also trained as a textile designer, and she combines the two skills to provide a very individual and unusual service. The fabrics are pre-shrunk and the dyes fast, so although you are sitting on a work of art, it won't fade any more quickly than a commercial fabric. Prices from £19 a metre, plus the making-up charges.

Moorhouse Associates, 240 Camden High St, N W1 (01-267 9714). Textile designers with a range which can be printed in colours to individual requirements. The fabrics are all cotton, the designs mainly geometric, and there is a good range always in stock. They deal with private customers, trade and architects. Prices from £4.50 per yard.

John Oliver, 33 Pembridge Rd, W11 (01-727 3735). Exclusive, hand-printed wallpapers and matching fabrics, shown in a friendly shop of twenty years' standing, with none of the intimidating airs and graces of Grand Design. John Oliver is also known for his own colour range of paints in deep, strong colours. His standard range of wallpaper is £15.50 per roll and can be produced in special colours for a 35-per-cent surcharge (six rolls minimum). Customers' own designs can be printed at £150 for the artwork and screen, plus £15.50 per roll in one colour, £350 plus £29.50 per roll in three colours.

Osborne & Little, 304 King's Rd, S W3 (01-352 1456). Trend-setters in fabric design with a very large range and a remarkable versatility – they don't readily fit into any convenient design slot and rather pride themselves on not being stereotyped. They offer a quilting service and curtain-making service on their own fabrics only.

Prints, 8 Portobello Green, 281 Portobello Rd, W10 (01-968 5626). Fabrics printed to commission in strikingly modern abstract designs on cotton or silk for furnishing and for dress design. Sue Timney and her partner Grahame Fowler are trying to produce something a little more individual than the conventional, mass-produced print and have had a great success with Japanese fashion designers. The minimum cost for producing a screen is £90, plus however much fabric you want, but there is also a good range of off-the-peg designs which can be produced in a variety of colours and fabrics.

Quilting Ltd, 33 Mountgrove Rd, N5 (01-226 6039). Mainly quilting for the trade, but private customers' fabric can be quilted too. Only single widths of fabric up to 54 in. wide can be accepted (no joined pieces: you must do that yourself after-wards), and there is no making-up service. It is possible to quilt any woven or printed furnishing fabric (but not jersey), and costs are £1.50 per metre (minimum order £12). Two designs are available: a 1¼-in. diagonal box or the 'onion' design. Customers are encouraged to call in with their fabric rather than order by mail.

Watts & Co. Ltd, 7 Tufton St, Westminster, SW1 (01-222 7169). Genuine Victorian wallpapers printed with the original pearwood blocks used by the company more than one hundred years ago. Colours are to individual requirements, and the minimum order is ten rolls. There is also a range of pure silk damasks in original Victorian colours. Other services include designing and making to commission in gold and silver, and the company also specializes in church embroideries. Expensive and very high quality.

MANCHESTER

William H. Bennett & Sons Ltd, 79 Piccadilly, Manchester (061-236 3551). From this company's forty types of silk, two are particularly suitable for furnishing – rough silk Noil in six colours at £2.95 per metre and Chien Shan Pongee, bleached and dyed shades at £2.85. Minimum order three metres. There is a large range of colours in other weights of silks.

Jewellery and silver

AVON

Gold & Silver Studio, 11a Queen St, Bath (Bath 62300). Designers, makers and repairers of jewellery in gold, platinum, silver, titanium and precious stones. Three craftsmen working on the premises will prepare designs to clients' requirements. They specialize in matching wedding and engagement rings and the re-modelling of outdated pieces. Prices from £3 to £1,000. Also repairs of silverware.

BUCKINGHAMSHIRE

Celia Howard, Design Studio, 18 Rotten Row, Great Brickhill, Milton Keynes (Great Brickhill 278). A talented jewellery designer who is highly re-commended by many of her faithful clients. She designs and makes simple modern pieces, working in gold, silver and enamel, from £9 for a pair of earrings, £25 for a necklace. She also resets stones, makes pieces to match existing jewellery (handy if, like one client, you lose a single earring and don't want to admit your careless-ness to the giver) and undertakes repairs – 'especially,' she says, 'when a shop is too expensive or won't take a job on.' Clients are seen by appointment only.

DEVON

The Gem Shop, The Old Market, Dartmouth (Dartmouth 3620). Jewellery with the accent on unusual stones. Major-General and Mrs Lyall Grant both have diplomas in gemology, and they travel to many countries, including Thailand, India, Mexico and Brazil, in search of interesting pieces. Among other gems they have coral, turquoise, ivory netsukes, Pakistan rubies and emeralds and Brazilian aquamarines and tourmalines. The range, from £1 to £500, also includes mineral specimens and second-hand jewellery.

DORSET

Cecil Colyer, Orchandene, Candys Lane, Shillingstone, Blandford Forum (Child Okeford 860252). Silver tableware to commission. Cecil Colyer's designs have strong, simple modern lines, and, as his first love was woodwork and furniture design, silver is often combined with wood – silver goblets with rosewood stems, for example. He also makes for special occasions and anniversaries.

Goldfinger Jewellery, 2 Gundry Lane, Bridport (Bridport 56340). Modern or traditional jewellery made to commission in gold, silver and precious stones. John and Jocelyn Pardoe both trained as jewellers and worked in the trade before opening their own workshops, where they will adapt and reset customers' own jewellery as well as designing new.

David Law, Charnwood, Milldown Rd, Blandford Forum (Blandford 52813). A silversmith specializing in coffee and tea sets, candlesticks, presentation goblets, napkin rings and church silver. He has a highly individual modern style with simple, robust lines and prefers to create his own designs rather than work to other people's ideas. Napkin rings and christening spoons are around £30; a full set of coffee pot, milk pot, cream, sugar and tongs or spoon in a presentation case would be about £3,500.

ESSEX

Peter Shorer, 40 Devonshire Rd, Ilford (01-590 8364). Reproductions of antiquities in gold, silver or plated alloys. Peter Shorer comes from a family of jewellers and has combined his skills with his interest in conservation of antiquities. He developed a special method of making moulds of precious antiquities in silicon rubber which reproduces every dent but does not harm the original. He makes reproductions and moulds of artefacts for research and exhibition and also makes a range of jewellery for museums – the Darnley ring given to Mary Queen of Scots, for example, and an Anglo-Viking ring found in Fishergate, York. Prices from about £3 in alloy to £90 in gold.

GLOUCESTERSHIRE

Robert Welch, The Mill, Chipping Campden (Evesham 840522). An internationally known silversmith and designer of tableware. When in 1955 Robert Welch first leased this eighteenth-century silk-mill he didn't know that it had once belonged to Charles Robert Ashbee, who left the East End of London in 1901 with 150 workers to establish his Guild of Handicraft in the more congenial surroundings of Chipping Campden. Ashbee was a social reformer who wanted to escape from industry. Robert Welch, on the other hand, while sharing the commitment to craftsmanship (and the desire for a congenial workplace), has established a healthy relationship with industry, and he designs for Old Hall and Prestige among others. But it is for his beautiful one-off pieces that he is renowned; his commissions have included goblets to commemorate the 900th anniversary of the Tower of London and gifts from the government to foreign heads of state. His modern coffee pots and candelabra with classically simple lines will cost in the region of £1,000 and are certainly among the antiques of the future.

LINCOLNSHIRE

Derek Birch, 34½ Hungate, Lincoln (Lincoln 30120). A specialist in church silver. Derek Birch's commissions have included a chalice for Canterbury Cathedral, a pair of ciboria for Lincoln Cathedral and a replica of Richard II's sword. He also undertakes private commissions and will design domestic silver and jewellery in silver, gold and gemstones. His smallest pieces have included silver thimbles engraved with representations of a family name, Peacock or Bell, for instance (from £10).

LONDON

Jocelyn Burton, 50c Red Lion St, W C1 (01-405 3042). A versatile silversmith and jeweller whose work has included a series of coins for the World Wildlife Fund and a platinum goblet presented by Rustenburg Platinum Mines to the Worshipful Company of Goldsmiths to commemorate the introduction of a platinum hallmark. Her designs are often inspired by natural and plant forms; seahorses, snails or grasshoppers, for instance, may form part of the stems of goblets or tops of bowls and salt cellars. Her work is distinctive and very tactile.

Howard Fenn, The Granary, Hope Sufferance Wharf, St Mary Church St, S E16 (01-237 3778). A silversmith who particularly enjoys combining silver and slate, achieving an attractive blend of light, shade and texture. Howard Fenn will design anything to commission and has made a magnificent bronze chess set in which the head of each piece is in the form of its initial letter (K for king, R for rook etc.), set horizontally like linotype. This cost £360. He also designs handsome modern clocks set on slate bases inlaid with fine lines of silver (£195) and slate boxes inlaid with silver (about £60).

Sarah Jones, 14 Basinghall St, E C2 (01-600 5908). Silver and jewellery to commission. Sarah Jones is known for her charming bowls of miniature silver and enamelled flowers, one of which was presented to the Queen. She also makes attractive and amusing jewellery which is available at the shop from about £15, and handsome beaten tableware. She has great imagination and versatility and is willing to undertake 'anything anybody asks me to make'. She is a Freeman of the Worshipful Company of Goldsmiths.

Stephen Maer, 18 Yerbury Rd, N19 (01-272 9074). Modern non-figurative jewellery designed to commission in gold and silver with precious and semi-precious stones. Stephen Maer has a small range of stock items for instant gifts, including earrings from about £10, pendants, cuff links and rings from £15 to £500. He is a past chairman of the Designer Jewellers Group and Fellow of the Society of Designer Craftsmen.

Alison Richards, 94 Constantine Rd, N W3 (01-267 4881). Jewellery designed to commission or remodelled from your own pieces. Alison Richards, a De Beers prizewinner, particularly enjoys working with 18-ct gold and cabochon stones, as she finds the look softer than the brittleness of faceted ones. Her strong classical style is seen in her setting of rare Roman intaglio stones in seal rings. Prices are from £40 for a pair of small earrings.

Ruth Robinson, 55 Chiltern Court, Baker St, W1 (01-935 5994). Interesting modern necklaces and chokers made of a mesh of silver wire interspersed with beads or semi-precious stones. Ruth Robinson is an inventive designer who experimented for a year before producing a wire as fine as hair and yet strong enough to be worked like miniature rolls of wire netting. In some cases the silver wire is blended with anodized aluminium, brass and copper wire, giving a graduated shaded effect. She also has revived the Etruscan technique of granulation – heat-fusing miniature silver or gold balls to a surface without solder – and this she uses for brooches, clasps and earrings. Prices are from £24 for a small silver-wire choker to £300 for large chokers with pearls and lapis lazuli.

MANCHESTER

Andrew Coomber, 39 Granville Rd, Fallowfield, Manchester (061-224 7969). A talented Scottish silversmith who fled south of the border to escape the 'thistle' jewellery syndrome of the tourist market at home. Now he designs beautiful and unusual pieces to commission in silver, incorporating enamelwork, precious and semi-precious stones. He encourages his clients to discuss their ideas at length, then produces sketches for approval. He also makes commemorative pieces, trophies and all kinds of presentation pieces for anniversaries, including handmade hardwood boxes incorporating silverwork. A simple pair of silver earrings costs £20, a gold and silver engagement ring £250, a specially designed diamond necklace anything up to £15,000. He usually also has a small range of ready-made jewellery available.

SOMERSET

Peter Critchley, Dormans, Combe St Nicholas, Chard (Chard 3695). Delicate studies of British birds painted on ivorine and set in silver or gold as pendants. If you have an antique pendant, the picture can be painted to fit. Peter Critchley is a regular exhibitor at the Royal Society of Miniature Painters and will undertake special commissions of favourite subjects. Costs will depend on the mounting; a silver locket might be about £63.25, one in gold about £150. His work can be seen at Mappin & Webb in London.

Judith Uiterwijk, Well Cottage, Latcham, Wedmore (Wedmore 712773). Jewellery and silver boxes a speciality. Judith Uiterwijk uses walrus ivory for necklaces and for the lids of some of her boxes (£38 to £72) and Peruvian picture opals for brooches, rings and earrings from £40. The large picture opals, whose formation actually looks like a painted picture of mountains or seascapes, are set in the lids of silver boxes at about £224. Commissions for jewellery or silverware can be arranged.

SUFFOLK

John Grenville, 14 Guildhall St, Bury St Edmunds (Bury St Edmunds 4884). A designer and maker of modern silver, church work and jewellery and restorer of antique church silver. John Grenville has a small range of stock pieces for anniversary gifts, hand-forged christening spoons and napkin rings from £50, hand-raised christening beakers from £195, and also a range of jewellery in gold, silver, copper, bronze and enamels. He has been established for thirty-five years, having originally studied drawing and painting; his work has been included in many exhibitions and is in the collections of the Worshipful Company of Goldsmiths and the Victoria and Albert Museum.

SUSSEX

Simon Beer, 164 High St, Lewes, E Sussex (Lewes 4207). A specialist in ecclesiastical and domestic silverware, including cutlery, Simon Beer trained at the Sir John Cass College and has won several awards for his work. Commissions have included a set of communion plate for Southwark Cathedral and a crucifix for

Leeds Castle. His work is striking and innovative, with a strong geometric influence.

Rodney Pettitt, Ashdown, Brigting Rd, Robertsbridge, E Sussex (Robertsbridge 880657). Reproduction of traditional designs in domestic silver. Rodney Pettitt doesn't claim to be a designer, but he is an accomplished silversmith and can copy anything to order. If you have an item missing from your silver tea set, for instance, he will make it to match the originals. Prices depend on weight, but a small plain sugar bowl would be about £175, a coffee pot from £600.

Ray Smart, 56 Harebeating Drive, Hailsham, E Sussex (Hailsham 842620). Trained as a commercial jeweller, Ray Smart became frustrated by having to make 'the usual sort of thing you see in a High Street jeweller's' and set up on his own seven years ago, making curved, gentle jewellery with an Art Nouveau influence and using silver, gold and stones from semi-precious to diamonds. He has a wide range, from simple silver rings from about £7 to important pieces at £300 or £400.

WILTSHIRE

Jakki Becker, 17 Water Lane, Salisbury (Salisbury 5762). Enamel miniatures mounted in silver or gold as earrings and pendants. The naturalistic designs of birds, flowers and bees are painted free-hand, and each is fired several times before being set in the mount. Inscriptions, or initials and dates for christenings, can be arranged. Prices from about £15.

YORKSHIRE

Debby Moxon and Ian Simm, The Duncan Craft Workshops, Ilkley Rd, Otley, W Yorks (Otley 467778, evenings). Young, original jewellery by two young, original designers. Debby Moxon is concentrating on a range of titanium and silver jewellery in geometric forms, using grid patterns to give a multi-coloured harlequin effect (prices from £9.75 for small studs to £43.50 for a necklace). Ian Simm likes to blend different materials in the same object – mainly silver tube and coloured wire, creating brooches with strips of colour like a military ribbon and slender silver and wire pins and bangles. Prices from £7. Both designers will undertake commissions and repair work. Visitors are welcome at the workshop.

Leonard Singleton, 108a Totley Brook Rd, Sheffield, S Yorks (Sheffield 365978). A specialist in mother-of-pearl. Leonard Singleton is the third generation of a family who originally made buttons and handles for the cutlery trade in pearl, horn and tortoiseshell. For the past twelve years he has concentrated on modern jewellery, mainly abstract designs, but not too way-out – he describes it as classical.

He works mainly to commission in natural black Tahiti pearl and white mother-of-pearl, sometimes combining this with cultured pearls. There is also a standard range of designs, from £1.95 for a pair of simple ear-studs and from £19.50 to £150 for pieces set in gold.

Lamps and lampshades

CHESHIRE

The Handicraft Shop, 5 Oxford Rd, Altrincham (061-928 3834). Lampshades made or re-covered to order in customers' own materials. The cost is from £12, which includes lining. The shop has a team of outworkers who can undertake most handicraft services, including quilting fabric for bedspreads and embroidering to commission – they have even embroidered backs and seats of a complete three-piece suite.

DORSET

Bridget Fairlie, Brian Cottage, Holwell, Sherborne (Bishop's Caundle 285). Handmade lampshades to order. Bridget Fairlie will make any shape, any size, to match customers' furnishings or to tone. Her range of silks includes exclusive Thai silks at £10 per metre, and other materials are available. Her charges are extremely inexpensive for such high-quality handwork, so there is a waiting list.

LONDON

Clare House, 35 Elizabeth St, SW1 (01-730 8480). Handmade lampshades made to order. There is a large selection of bases in the shop, but wooden bases can also be made to order and other bases can be converted. They also have a large selection of chintz, muslin, silk and other fabrics suitable for lampshades and carry samples of card and fabric laminates.

General Trading Company, 144 Sloane St, SW1 (01-730 0411). Your own ginger jars or vases converted into lamps by mounting them on wood bases and adding brass lamp fittings and silk flex. From £25.

Alison Saunders, 13 Caroline Place, W2 (01-727 1630). Silk lampshades made specially to order in any shape and size, in several qualities and in a wide variety of colours. The standard of work is high – Mrs Saunders has been making lampshades for top retailers and interior decorators for twelve years – and she will visit private clients within a forty-mile radius. Sizes start at 10 in.; the price for a 14-in.-diameter shade is about £27.

Yardstick Designs, 51 Kinnerton St, SW1 (01-235 9091). All types of lamp bases and shades. Ellie Bradfield had such difficulty in finding exactly the right lamps to put the finishing touch to her own interior schemes that she decided to specialize and now has a wide range of antique and modern bases. She will convert your own vases and will re-cover lampshades or supply new shades in plain or handpainted card or in silk. Prices are from £15 for a simple conversion; re-covering £3.25 (stretched), £3.50 (pleated), per inch of base diameter. Also handpainted card, £1.75 per inch of base diameter.

MIDDLESEX

Roger of London, 344 Richmond Rd, East Twickenham (01-891 2122). Lampshades made to order, and vases and statues converted into lamps. There is a large selection of silk, dupion, and synthetics suitable for lampshades, and they will also make up customers' own fabric. This shop will also wash, clean and repair lampshades and chandeliers. Closed Wednesdays.

Musical instruments

CAMBRIDGESHIRE

Robert Welford, 1 Victoria Rd, Cambridge (Cambridge 353423). Classical guitars made to commission. Robert Welford started his craft as a hobby and now makes for leading guitarists. He uses Indian rosewood for the ribs, Swiss pine for the front, Brazilian mahogany for the necks and ebony for the fingerboards, but as the shape has to conform to certain dimensions it is in the rosettes round the sound-hole that he feels a maker can best express his artistic talent – there are as many as twenty thousand tiny pieces, each smaller than a pin-head, inlaid to form an intricate mosaic to decorate the guitar. Prices are around £1,000.

CORNWALL

Ben Green, Maze-Hill, Queens Acre, Boyton, Launceston (Launceston 3510). Reproductions of medieval instruments. Ben Green became interested in ancient music through studying Celtic history and culture, and his first instrument was a psaltery, often mentioned in the Old Testament Book of Psalms. Since then he has researched and made lyres, zithers, tambourines, hammered dulcimers and bowed psalteries, hoping that other people will share his enjoyment in these early instruments. He makes them in Brazilian hardwood and ebony and they cost from £90. They can also be handpainted.

CUMBRIA

Martin Morris, Townfoot, Hunsonby, Penrith (Langwathby 224). New stringed instruments of the violin family, both modern and baroque, made to order. A biochemist with a love of the cello and a talent for carpentry, Martin Morris uses beautifully figured English sycamore for the sides and backs of his instruments and imports spruce from Germany for the fronts. He hopes eventually to trace a suitable spruce tree in this country in order to produce wholly British instruments. His clients include members of the Northern Sinfonia, BBC Philharmonic, Scottish National and London Philharmonic orchestras. Violins are about £1,400, violas £1,600, cellos £2,500 and double-bass £2,300. Please telephone for an appointment.

DORSET

Dominic Cardozo, Manor Farm House, West Orchard, Shaftesbury (Sturminster Newton 72685). Violins made from fine Continental maple and pine – for centuries the timber for violins has come from the mountains of Central Europe and has to be matured for ten years before it can be used. Mr Cardozo's violins are in the traditional Stradivarius style, and he also makes violas in the usual $16\frac{1}{4}$-in. size and in his own adaptation, $15\frac{1}{2}$-in. Prices from £500.

John Dike, Nottingham House, Ring St, Stalbridge, Sturminster Newton (Stalbridge 62285). Maker of violins, violas and cellos. John Dike makes the violins and cellos to designs based on old Italian instruments, using maple, spruce and pine. Prices are from about £500. Repairs and restoration work also undertaken.

HAMPSHIRE

Paul Bickle, The Violin Workshop, 4 Lenten St, Alton (workshop: Alton 84007; home: Bishop's Waltham 5292). Exact copies of antique violins and violas. Paul Bickle specializes in designs by Gagliano and by Guarneri del Jesu, who made very few instruments – a genuine one would be around £300,000, as only about 150 of them still exist. The copies are made traditionally, with maple back and sides and mountain spruce tops, and the cost depends on the degree of antiquing, which can take twice as long as the actual making. Prices are from £500 to £1,500. Cellos are also made to commission, and repair work is undertaken for all three instruments.

MANCHESTER

David E. Vernon, 898 Chester Rd, Stretford, Manchester (061-865 7438). A maker and repairer of string instruments, including violins, violas, cellos and classical guitar. David Vernon also restores mandolines and violas, supplies accessories such as cases, bridges, bows, strings, adjusters and tailpieces, and arranges insurance and valuations. A violin costs about £1,150, and a lot of patience is required, as there is at present a two-year waiting list. The shop is closed on Mondays.

STAFFORDSHIRE

Brynn Hiscox, 81 New Rd, Armitage, Rugeley (Armitage 491331). All types of steel-string acoustic, classical and electrical instruments custom-built to order. Specialities are two instruments developed by Brynn Hiscox – a scaled-down classical guitar for children as young as five years and an all-wood round-back acoustic guitar which combines the sound-projecting properties of the parabolic curve with the natural resonating qualities of fine timbers. Prices from £350 (children's), £550 (roundback).

TYNE AND WEAR

Barry Oliver, Washington Arts Centre, Washington (Newcastle upon Tyne 467599). Violins made to order. Barry Oliver was the first craftsman to move into the workshops in Washington Arts Centre when it opened in 1976, and he brought with him a stock of seasoned wood bought when he was in Italy at the violin-making school in Cremona. Each instrument, based on the Stradivarius design, takes about 300 hours to make and costs around £2,000.

Painted decorative effects

HAMPSHIRE

Wilson & Henson, 12 East St, Alresford (Alresford 3932). Marbling, stippling, sponging and other specialist paint finishes applied to furniture and walls. Althea Wilson will also paint lamp bases and shades to suit existing decorations and will copy antique china designs on to tiles, or create original designs. Anthony Henson makes the furniture to be painted – cabinets, record-player units to measure, plant boxes, for example – or customers' own furniture may be painted. Althea lives above the shop and will show clients examples of her work in her own home. Prices are from £7 per tile, £100 for a pair of lamp bases and shades.

LONDON

Higgs & Maunsell, The Workshop, 46–52 Church Rd, Barnes, SW13 (01-741 2944). Handpainted decorative knobs. Geoffrey Higgs and Charles

Maunsell have a range of beech knobs for doors and furniture in many shapes and sizes, and will paint them to order with motifs taken from furnishing fabrics or with any design you choose. Prices are from £1.50 each and they can be supplied by mail.

MANCHESTER

Sue Talbot, 48 St Georges Rd, Fallowfield, Manchester 14 (061-445 6524, daytime; 061-248 7297, after 7 p.m.). Old furniture transformed by hand-decorating in the Central European tradition. Chests and chairs, mirrors, picture frames, wardrobes and tables that have seen better days are restored and repainted with a highly polished black lacquer-look finish reminiscent of Victorian papier-mâché. Designs are inspired by birds, plants and flowers. Sue Talbot will decorate your own furniture, find a particular antique piece for you, or even get something made. She also works with coloured stains. Prices from £12 to about £100.

NORFOLK

Mary MacCarthy, The Old Stores, 7 Seven Bridge St, Stiffkey, Wells-next-the-Sea (Binham 468). Finely shaded, handpainted designs on walls or doors. Mary MacCarthy will do all types of pictorial decoration, from flowers and folk designs to formal and elaborate eighteenth-century work. She has also painted an entire room to look like marquetry and a shop-front to look as if it were made of Delft tiles. Send a photograph of your room with your ideas, and Mary will send her suggestions and an estimate. Costs are from £100 per day, plus expenses. A frieze in an average-sized room would take approximately three weeks. She will also decorate furniture; prices vary according to the amount of work involved.

SOMERSET

Oliver Canti, Lilac Cottage, Stathe Rd, Burrowbridge, Bridgwater (Burrowbridge 707). An antique restorer who also enjoys decorating furniture – stencilling, gilding, handpainting motifs, marbling, sponging, ragging. These special finishes particularly suit old pine that can't be stripped. Oliver Canti is a fine arts graduate and will undertake any commission, including murals.

SURREY

L. W. Maybank & Sons Ltd, 9 Greenways, Walton-on-the-Hill, Tadworth (Tadworth 3701); also at 39 Summit Drive, Woodford Green, Essex (01-550 6834). Decorative finishes, including graining, stippling, dragging and marbling. The company specializes in Louis XIV-style decoration, and much of the work is done for interior designers, but commissions from private clients are also undertaken.

Picture framing

CHESHIRE

Amadeus Gallery, 94 Park Lane, Poynton (Poynton 974541), and the Framing Studio, 82 Welling Rd South, Stockport (061-477 6714). Two galleries offering framing services and run by two ex-engineers with a love of pictures. Brian Young of the Amadeus Gallery and Dave Johnson of the Framing Studio started the business in Poynton while they still had jobs 'just in case' disaster struck. For two years they worked a full shift and then went straight to the gallery for an extra half-day's work. Now they concentrate entirely on pictures and have opened the second studio in Stockport. They specialize in modern etchings and watercolours from £35 to £100, with a few Victorian watercolours from £80. They have a choice of more than 100 mouldings for framing, mostly used with card mounts in any colour, and prices are from £12.08 to £16.10 for a picture 15 × 12 in.

Manley Wright, 41 Chapel Lane, Wilmslow (Wilmslow 532180). Specialists in woodcarving and picture framing. Martin Jones has a large selection of woodcarvings from £6 to £200 and will carve house names to commission. He stocks 150 picture mouldings and thirty-five mounts and will either provide a framing service or sell the materials for customers to do their own framing. His colleague, Paul Walsh, is an expert at marquetry and will design wall clocks with marquetry faces to order.

GLOUCESTERSHIRE

Geoffrey Vivien, The Grange, Woolstone, nr Cheltenham (Bishop's Cleeve 2122). A picture-framer who sees his craft as, ideally, a creative partnership with artists, print-makers, interior decorators and picture-lovers. He works mostly for private customers, has also undertaken large commercial assignments and likes to extend framing in all directions – fan-boxes, medal-cases, bookends, mirrors (a special feature are children's mirrors incorporating favourites such as Beatrix Potter characters). The Cotswold workshop and gallery is open during the week and at weekends.

HERTFORDSHIRE

Centre of Restoration and Art, 20 Folly Lane, St Albans (St Albans 51555). Picture-framing materials and a framing service. A choice of 100 mouldings in stock which can be sold in any lengths, with a wide range of mounts and accessories. Pictures brought in for framing cost from £5 for a 10 × 8 in.

LONDON

Blackman Harvey Ltd, 29 Earlham St, Covent Garden, WC2 (01-836 1904), and 11 Masons Avenue, Coleman St, EC2 (01-726 2502). Expert picture framers and art gallery. A selection of more than 300 wood and aluminium mouldings is available, with fifty colours of card mounts, including acid-free board (known as museum board because it prevents valuable pictures from discolouring), and a selection of linen, velvet, cork and suede. A standard aluminium frame 10 × 8 in. costs from £7.50; a special size in wood would be from £11; or you can buy the mouldings or sandwich frame and accessories to do your own framing. The company also restores oil paintings and watercolours, repairs frames and regilds, and has a stock of original prints, lithographs, watercolours and engravings. There is a large research library, and pictures can be supplied on almost any theme for hotels, restaurants and private collectors.

Fix a Frame, 280 Old Brompton Rd, SW5 (01-370 4189). Learn how to frame your own pictures. Anthony Royds brought the idea back from America, where DIY framing shops are a booming business, and he offers more than 100 wood frames and twenty in aluminium, with forty colours of mounts, plus acid-free board, and linen and textured mounts. Customers take in a picture and are given advice on the right mounts and frames for it; the frame is cut to size, and instruction is given on the assembly. It all takes about an hour and everyone comes out with a sense of achievement – and an inexpensively framed picture. Prices are from £4.10 for a 10 × 8 in. wood frame, including backing, glass, picture wire and fittings. Note the opening hours: Tuesday to Friday 11.30 a.m. to 8 p.m.; Saturday 10 a.m. to 6.30 p.m.

Emma Lindsay, Studio 9, 465 Battersea Park Rd, SW11 (01-228 3155). Mounting and framing of watercolours and prints. Emma Lindsay specializes in pictures which need a more abstract treatment than a heavy gilt frame. She will tint frames and mounts specially to tone with the painting, or can provide stained, lacquered or stippled frames from about £8 for a 10 × 8 in. picture.

Sebastian d'Orsai (A.B.) Ltd, 8 Kensington Mall, W8 (01-229 3888). Specialist in frames and reproduction mirror surrounds which can be handpainted to any colour scheme and with designs to match fabrics. Prices from £50 to £150.

WILTSHIRE

Edward and Julia Rooth, 18 Market St, Bradford-on-Avon (Bradford-on-Avon 4191). Picture cleaning and framing. Decorated mounts, with washes, lines or gilded bevels, and staining, veneering, colouring and polishing of frames are all done on the premises. The Rooths are members of the Institute of Paper Conservators; they stock a large range of acid-free boards and can arrange for the restoration of both watercolours and oil paintings. They advise on framing, and collect and deliver within fifty miles.

Rugs and carpets

CHESHIRE

Caroline Slinger, Old Canal Warehouse, Whipcord Lane, Chester (Chester 378766). Hand-tufted rugs and carpets made specially to individual requirements. Caroline Slinger trained as a painter, and her preference is for modern and pictorial designs – English gardens with paths and flowers or a desert island with sea and waves and palm trees, commissioned by John Makepeace. She also creates textured designs in one colour, achieving a sculptural effect with different heights of pile. She works only in wool and can have any colour specially dyed. Any size is possible up to about 18 ft, and the cost is from £20 per square foot.

CUMBRIA

Susan Foster, 9 Windermere Rd, Kendal (Kendal 26494). Rugs woven from rags and wool in flat or shaggy textures, in stock and to commission. Many of Susan Foster's designs are based on traditional Persian and Navaho rugs, and she also makes cushions and wall-hangings, belts, bags and some clothes. Prices for rugs are from £100 to £200. The workshop, five minutes' walk from the town centre, is open Wednesday, Friday and Saturday from 10 a.m. to 5 p.m.

Wetheriggs Country Pottery, Clifton Dykes, Penrith (Penrith 62946). Hand-loomed rugs made from the wool of local Jacob, Herwick and other rare breeds. Wall-hangings and cushions can be commissioned to match the colours you choose in your rug. The weaving shed is part of a nineteenth-century industrial monument which also houses the pottery.

Steve and Belinda Wilson, Eden Valley Woollen Mill, Ainstable, nr Armathwaite (Croglin 406). Rugs and floor cushions woven to order. Steve Wilson trained as a computer programmer (he hopes eventually to programme his loom to individual colour schemes) and makes his rugs with a wool weft on a cotton warp for extra durability. A 3 × 5 ft rug is about £50, a large floor cushion £30.

DEVON

Sue Mace, Glan-yr-Afon, Staverton, nr Totnes (Staverton 456). Bold, handwoven rugs, wall-hangings and cushions to commission. Sue Mace won a Commonwealth scholarship in 1976 to study in India, where she learned weaving, dyeing, block-printing and design. She uses natural Berber wools and dyes them with woodshavings, indigo and madder root, achieving a subtle range of natural colours. Her designs are strong and her textures particularly soft to the touch. A hanging about 4 × 3 ft would be around £160. Visitors are welcome to visit her workshop at Riverford Farm, Charlie's Cross, Totnes, by appointment.

DORSET

Tom and Elizabeth Wotherspoon, York House, Puddletown, nr Dorchester (Puddletown 308). All-wool, hand-tufted rugs and wall-hangings made to commission. Apart from designing rugs to match the style and colours of clients' furnishings, the Wotherspoons make children's rugs in various shapes, including hippos and elephants. Prices are from about £10 per square foot, depending on the depth of pile.

GLOUCESTERSHIRE

Colin Squire, Sheldon Cottage, The Bottoms, Epney, Saul (Gloucester 740639). Rugs, wall-hangings, cushions and bags to commission. The rugs, in modern designs, are flat-woven in a variety of constructions and in natural fibres. Any colours are possible; prices are from £80 for rugs, from £12 for cushions and bags. Colin Squire also designs furnishing and dress fabrics to order.

LONDON

Patrick Vaughan, 45 Garfield Rd, SW19 (01-542 9401). Trained as a textile designer, Patrick Vaughan now specializes in rug-making. He has several standard designs, to order in colours to tone with clients' furnishings; he also designs to commission. Subjects can be modern or traditional – he has copied pictures, tufted an entire map of the world and produced a rug in the shape of an artist's palette. Several clients have described his rugs as too good to walk on and have hung them like tapestries. Prices from £10 a square foot.

YORKSHIRE

John French, Woodhall Lane, Pudsey, W Yorks (Pudsey 552844). Hand-made wool rugs to order. John French specializes in bold colours and abstract designs and creates each rug individually. The effects are strikingly modern and luxurious. Prices depend on the height of pile and the complexity of the design; colours are specially dyed. A simple design in one or two colours would be from £80 to £150 per square metre. Wall-hangings can be commissioned to match. There are also two ready-to-tread ranges.

Soft furnishings

CHESHIRE

Cottage Cutains, Hayfield, via Stockport (New Mills 45396). Festoon blinds in ivory-coloured cotton lace made to measure. The fabric is woven in a flower pattern based on a Victorian lace design; each blind is supplied with fixtures and fittings and is raised and lowered by a cord-and-pulley system that can be fixed at any position at the window. They can also be supplied in kit form by mail order, from £29.62 for a window 3 ft deep by 4 ft wide. Sheila Collier will also make soft furnish-ings, curtains, blinds, cushions and loose covers to order in clients' own fabrics.

Jane & I, 26 London Rd, Alderley Edge (Alderley Edge 583007). Made-to-order furnishings in a selection of famous-name fabrics, plus a full interior-design service if required. Matching bedlinen and valances, curtains, loose covers and tablecloths are available. Nurseries are a speciality – appliquéd cot quilts to individual requirements and with a child's name are from £30.

Jenny Kersh Designs, Brinksway Trading Estate, Brinksway, Stock-port (061-477 1625). Cushions in every conceivable colour, shape and size made to match every room and every scheme. Jenny Kersh makes nursery cushions, quilt cushions and wall-hangings to go with your wallpaper or bedcovers, with match-ing filled pillows and, for older children, cushions with their names or favourite pets. She usually uses clients' own fabrics and often incorporates antique lace as a trimming. A doorhanging with a child's name costs from £8.50, a small heart cushion in satin and lace £8.50, larger cushions, appliquéd and embroidered, from £15 to £30. A throwover bedcover, with a frilled valance (double), is about £250. There is also a large stock of ready-made cushions.

DORSET

The Julian Workshop, 1 Cheap St, Sherborne (Sherborne 815473). Three-dimensional appliqué on soft furnishings to commission. Jane Burden has a highly individual style of appliqué – flowers, for instance, are cut out petal by petal and built up into the actual flower form. She uses washable cottons or silks and satins to tone with customers' furnishings and will undertake cushions (from £25 to £40), duvet covers, cot covers, Roman blinds, curtains and chair covers.

KENT

Sally Gordon Boyd, Homeweaves, 53 New St, Sandwich (Sandwich 617272). Handwoven wool rugs from £22, cushions from £12.50, scarves and bags from £8.25, all in natural colours – shades of off-whites, fawns, browns and greys. Special lengths can be woven to order. There is also, in the same colours, a range of hand-knitted sweaters for men and women in standard sizes, from £17 to £35 – inexpensive for handwork. A brochure of designs is available, and the workshop is open to visitors on Tuesdays, Thursdays, Fridays and Saturdays, 10 a.m. to 6 p.m., throughout the year and on Sundays, noon to 6 p.m. May to September.

LANCASHIRE

Yvonne Davies Design, 58 Deeplish Rd, Rochdale (Rochdale 352808). All types of handmade blinds, including Austrian, Roman and roller blinds made in your own fabric from £1.75 per square foot. Festoon blinds are from £3.25 per square foot, and pleated paper blinds can be handpainted with any design from single motifs to complete landscapes. Yvonne Davies also designs and makes soft furnishings to commission. She will undertake bedspreads with quilted panels or outline quilting, all kinds of curtains and blinds, including nursery curtains for cribs, cot quilt tops, fitted sheets and bumpers. A double bedspread with frilled sides and base including pillow flap costs from £40. An outline-quilted single bedspread is from £65.

James Robertshaw & Sons Ltd, Albion Works, Larkill, Farnworth, Bolton (Bolton 74764). Laminated blinds made from your own fabric and supplied with spring roller and fittings. Send your fabric rolled to avoid creases, and make sure it is 2 in. wider and 12 in. longer than the finished length you require. Various styles are available, with or without fringe. The cost, exclusive of fabric, is from £20.76 for a blind 3 ft wide × 3 ft drop. The largest possible is 96 in. wide × 60 in. drop. The company also makes cane and wooden blinds, available in five colours.

Silkworm, 19 Firswood Rd, Lathom, nr Skelmersdale (Skelmersdale 31538). Pure silk cushions in a variety of colours from subtle blues and greys to vivid jades. Irene Hardwick's trade-mark is a raised appliqué flower motif which she uses singly and in clusters to decorate her very pretty plain and quilted cushions. Prices are from £15 to £20. She will undertake bedspreads if you are willing to wait – in expensive silk satin they are about £200 – and she also does a range of accessories.

LINCOLNSHIRE

Alison Bell, Gravel Pit Cottages, High Toynton, Horncastle (Horncastle 6591). Roller blinds in cotton sateen, hand-printed in a variety of designs to match your furnishings. You buy your own roller blind kit, send the exact measurements of your window or door, and the fabric, printed, sewn and stiffened, is returned for you to fit on to the blind kit. A catalogue is available; send a first-class stamp.

LONDON

Blind Alley, 27 Chalk Farm Rd, NW1 (01-485 8030). The originators of pictorial and decorated blinds. When Janet Moodie started in 1972, she was one of the first to conceive the idea of painting blinds to create a fantasy or illusion. She now has an extensive range of hand-printed and free-hand airbrushed designs and will undertake any special commissions. Standard ranges can be made up in any colours. Those who cannot get to Camden Lock may send swatches of fabric and measurements, and Blind Alley will submit suitable sketches and price quotes. A brochure is available for 50p.

Camden Cushion Company, 36a Commercial Place, Camden Lock Market, Chalk Farm Rd, NW1 (01-482 2270). Patchwork cushions in leather or satin. Floor cushions, 3-ft square, in colours of leather to tone with your decor; appliqué satin cushions, 18-in. square, in ten designs and seventeen colours, from £7.99 each.

Susan Charles, 3a Bathurst St, W2 (01-262 8094). Hobby horses, unicorns and zebras made to match a child's bedroom. The heads, made in calico and hand-painted with waterproof inks, have delightful expressions, the reins are in hand-plaited silk cord, and the poles are decorated with satin ribbons. Prices from £29.95, plus postage.

Conran Shop, 77 Fulham Rd, SW3 (01-589 7401). Many major stores will make up materials bought from them, but the Conran Shop is unusual in offering to make up your own materials. Blinds from £54, lampshades from £15, upholstery for a small two-seater £395 and seven metres of fabric. Curtains and cushions too.

Liberty, Regent St, W1 (01-734 1234). Tented ceilings and walls covered to match by the pin and batten method. From £500, excluding fabric. Also stippling and marbling of walls, dados, columns and pillars, from £100 each.

Miracles, 436 King's Rd, SW10 (01-352 0828). Blinds, any colour or design, to your specifications. They have a basic set of designs and can airbrush almost any pattern, picture or colour. A blind for a medium-size window would cost between £90 and £150, and they can do blinds for most sizes of window.

Rainbow Quilts, Unit 12, 21 Wren St, WC1 (01-278 4974). Beautiful bed-covers in a range of 100 shades of plain chintz, quilted in satin-stitch to create a luxurious three-dimensional look. These are to commission; send a sample of curtain or upholstery fabric and Andrea Coggins will create the design specially for you. There is also a standard range of ten designs – one traditional, one Art Nouveau style, the others mainly abstract and geometric. Many of Andrea's designs stem from her fascination with kaleidoscopes and wave forms, and the results are swirling, free-flowing shapes. All are available in any colour or mixture of colours. These are from £126 to £270 (single), £175 to £375 (queen size), £213 to £456 (king size). There are cushions to match, from £13 to £20. Examples of the work can be seen on colour slides at the Crafts Council and the Design Council in London. A brochure is available.

Sleep Tight, 7 Southwood Lawn Rd, N6 (01-348 4328). Handmade and handpainted cot quilts, made to order. Each quilt comes with cot 'bumpers' to place round the inside of the top of the cot to protect the baby's head from hitting against the bars. These are appliquéd with motifs echoing the main theme – Little Boy Blue on the quilt, with the sheep in the meadow and the cow in the corn on the bumper; Mary Mary flanked by her flowers; or whatever theme appeals to you. Susan Maxwell and Diana Magner guarantee that no quilt will be exactly like another and their work is beautiful enough to use as a wall-hanging when the cot is outgrown. The paints used are machine-washable, and prices range from about £50 for a carry-cot quilt to £200 for a single-bed size.

MANCHESTER

Caroline Jubb, Unit 10, Manchester Craft Village, Oak St, Manchester 4 (061-832 4274). Traditional patchwork to commission, incorporating embroidery and using silk and satin to give a luxurious finish. Cushions, kimonos, bedspreads and triangular cushions can be designed to match fabric and wallpaper and can incorporate an embroidered message or a name. Cushions are from £10 to £20, single quilts £140, kimonos from £80. The workshop is in a former fruit-and-vegetable market, now converted into an interesting craft centre.

OXFORDSHIRE

Libby Calvert, Marsh Cottage, Aston, Oxford (Bampton Castle 850658). Patchwork bedspreads made to individual colour schemes and measurements.

Libby Calvert was first inspired by a Victorian quilt owned by her great-aunt, and has developed the art of patchwork with a particular emphasis on colour. Send her a piece of your curtain fabric and carpet, and she will choose the prettiest cottons to tone – sometimes using a large bird or flower motif from your fabric as a central picture. Everything is made to commission; standard-size double quilts 8 ft square are from £250, singles from £210. Cot spreads and cushions are also available.

TYNE AND WEAR

Suzanne Conyngham Greene, 31 The Grove, Gosforth, Newcastle upon Tyne (Newcastle upon Tyne 854512). Suzanne says she organizes for people – advising, providing samples of fabrics, curtains, blinds, wallpapers and carpets, producing catalogues for furniture and lighting, making up curtains and soft furnishings and supervising workmen in your home. She charges the small businesses' rate of £7 an hour plus travelling expenses (though the first consultation is free) and approximately £10 a width for making, delivering and hanging lined curtains with simple headings. She will also remake old curtains (price according to work involved). She has a large selection of fabrics and papers, including Osborne & Little, Bakers, Pallu & Lake, Tissunique, Parkertex, Colefax & Fowler and the Laura Ashley Decorator's Collection.

Bev Dixon, 6 Lindisfarne Rd, Newcastle upon Tyne (Newcastle upon Tyne 810666). Patchwork, appliqué and quilting to order. Bev Dixon will come to your house or go to the shops with you to choose a colour scheme, and then will make a quilt with co-ordinating curtains, cushions, blinds, tablecloths or any other accessories. The quilts range from around £30 up to several hundred; cushions are from £7 to £25.

Stained glass

AVON

Unicorn Glass Workshop, Tooses Farm, Stoke St Michael, Bath (Oakhill 840654). Modern stained-glass window and door panels to commission. Frances Johnston is a fine arts graduate with a life-long interest in birds, so colourful plumage figures prominently in her designs. For a fee of about £15 she will prepare a full-scale design to fit in with your specifications, and she welcomes visitors by appointment to her workshop, established in a fifteenth-century farmhouse. She also has a range of hand-blown glass set into leaded shapes to hang in your windows – birds, fish, flowers, available in a range of colours to suit individual colour schemes – and nursery decorations painted with names or messages. A coloured brochure is available.

CUMBRIA

Gwenda Payne, 96 Lowther St, Penrith (Penrith 65347). Stained glass made to order. Gwenda Payne will make Tiffany-style lamps (from £20 to £80), terraria, mobiles, windows and door panels. She also prints on glass and will undertake repairs at £5 per hour, plus materials.

GLOUCESTERSHIRE

Kate Baden Fuller, 45 Park Rd, Blockley, Moreton-in-Marsh (Evesham 700208). Unique appliqué mirror mosaics. Kate Baden Fuller cuts pieces of plain and coloured glass, some finished in antique silvering, and creates mosaics applied to screens, tables and headboards. Small mirrors are available from £40, but most pieces are from £150 to £1,200 for a screen. Also stained glass and some repairs.

LONDON

Waymouth Jones, 40 Allfarthing Lane, SW18 (01-874 4361). Stained-glass windows and screens to commission. Claire Waymouth and Graham Jones will undertake any type of designs – Claire specializing in painting in the traditional style, Graham in the modern manner. Prices range from £30 to £60 per square foot.

Toys

BEDFORDSHIRE

John Marriott, 86 Village Rd, Bromham, Bedford (Oakley 3173). Hand-built rocking horses worth handing down to your grandchildren. John Marriott came back from civil engineering in Saudi Arabia looking for something more satisfying to do that was sufficiently specialized not to compete with the big factory producers. His horses are made in selected hardwood, finely carved, and have a painted or varnished finish. There are three sizes, a choice of rockers or stands and various colours of manes, tails and saddles. The largest takes about 100 hours to make, and if you want any size for Christmas you must order by June. Prices from £45 for a baby horse 18 in. high to £450 for a large one on a stand. He will also undertake repairs to antique horses.

CORNWALL

David Plagerson, 5 Cliff View Terrace, Gunnislake (Gunnislake 833035). An enterprising and talented woodcarver who found himself unemployed and followed a well-known survival pattern by setting about building an ark. His hand-carved and painted arks, with Mr and Mrs Noah and up to thirty-six pairs of animals, are now collectors' pieces and cost from £295 to £490, according to the numbers of animals. He also does a circus ring with animals and performers (£330), a nativity set (£75), and a collection of animals in unpainted woods with attractive grains (£3 each) – very pleasing to the touch and the eye.

CUMBRIA

Ian Butler & Ruth Lawley, Croglin Toys, 1 Mulcaster Place, Croglin, Carlisle (Croglin 405). Orders accepted for virtually any wooden toy. Ian Butler trained as a joiner and, because of his keen interest in children, used to run holiday play schemes in Yorkshire. His specialities are a climbing frame (£120), slide (£30), Wendy house (£80) and Cumbrian farmyard (£14.50), and he will also make easels, baby walkers and tricycles, all of which show his special attention to durability, finishing and safety.

LANCASHIRE

Croft Design, 1 Lincoln St, Cornholme, Todmorden (Todmorden 2795). Highly ornamental and unusual jigsaws for adults, individually designed and made in stained plywood by Paul Croft. His surrealistic designs are very colourful and complex, but he also does simpler illustrations including butterflies and firesides. Prices are from £10 to £30.

Robin and Nell Dale, Bank House Farm, Holme Mills, Holme, via Carnforth (Burton in Kendal 781646). Hand-turned wooden stump dolls made from beechwood and handpainted. Individual dolls are made to commission – choose from story-book characters, fashion dolls in modern or period costume, soldiers in uniform. Robin and Nell Dale also make chess sets based on *Alice Through the Looking Glass* or King Arthur. Prices are from £20 to £2,500.

Frank Egerton, 94 Appley Lane North, Appley Bridge, nr Wigan (Appley Bridge 3861). Toys for adults – they're much too sophisticated for children; in fact Frank Egerton calls them 'three-dimensional illustrations'. He trained as a potter, taught in a college of art for ten years and turned to woodcarving because it was something he could do in his spare moments. He only makes one-offs, so each piece is unique, and each carved and painted toy has a quirky originality which will appeal to anyone who can afford to indulge an offbeat sense of humour. Prices from £12 to £500.

John Woods, 180 Chorley Rd, Westhoughton, Bolton (Westhoughton 816246). Traditional carved rocking horses, with leather saddles and horsehair manes and tails, made by John Woods and handpainted in dapple grey by his wife,

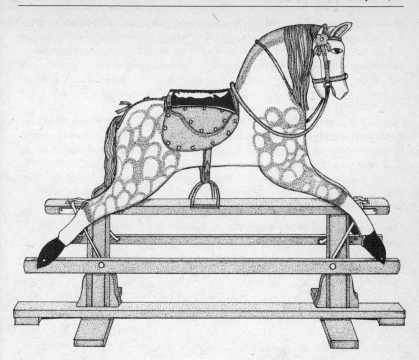

Dorothy. There are five sizes, from 24 in. high (£50) to 57 in. high (£500). Two to three months' delivery, longer towards Christmas.

LONDON

Susan Dumper, 176 Greenvale Rd, Eltham, S E9 (01-850 9303). Period dolls, beautifully made in porcelain with articulated limbs, or with cloth bodies and porcelain heads, arms and legs. Susan Dumper has been making dolls since she was a child – her first was modelled out of fireplace putty – and she is particularly interested in small dolls, mostly about 6 in. but some as small as 1 in., all perfectly modelled. A selection of her dolls is available at Nelsons Wharf, 43 Greenwich Church Street, S E10, but she will also undertake interesting individual commissions if customers are willing to wait. She likes unusual requests – for instance, supplying a body for an odd head when no one knows just what the original complete doll looked like – but again, only small dolls. Her standard range of period-style dolls is from £8 to £10 for 3-in. dolls, £12 to £30 for 6-in. dolls, all in costume. Specials are, of course, considerably more.

Keith Padmore, 19 Ray Walk, Andover Rd, Hornsey, N7 (01-272 4641). Hand-carved and painted model toy shops in the Victorian manner. Keith Padmore is a window cleaner with an artistic flair who wanted to own a model shop since he saw one in the Toy Museum when he was a child. He made a butcher's shop, with all the painted joints of meat, for his two small daughters, but it was snapped up by an antique dealer and he has been busy making a variety of shops ever since – the little girls are still waiting. There are milliner's and grocer's, baker's and toy shops, all mounted behind glass for display, or with a hinged front for those who want to play. Sizes are from 13 × 14 in. to 24 × 14 in., and prices are from £200. He also makes Victorian-style shop signs – giant painted eyes for the optician, for instance – from £50.

MIDDLESEX

Margaret Glover, 42 Hartham Rd, Isleworth (01-568 4662). Reproduction wax dolls made to commission. Margaret Glover used to make soft toys for her daughter before she became interested in wax and had to develop her own techniques, as very little has been written on the subject. Her dolls are made in the same way as the waxworks at Madame Tussaud's, with the hair and even the eyebrows and lashes implanted. They are based on famous children in paintings – Bubbles, for example, or Claudine from Renoir's *Les Parapluies* – or you can have, among others, Christopher Robin. Prices are from £85 to £500 – this for a 12-in. Queen Victoria in full coronation robes.

YORKSHIRE

Peglegs, 36 Greentop, Pudsey, W Yorks (Leeds 550478). Handmade rocking horses made in Quebec yellow pine, painted dapple grey and fitted with real horsehair manes and tails. Stephen Hope was a craft teacher and made his own plans from dismantling and restoring antique rocking horses. His methods are entirely traditional; his only concession to modern technology is that he strengthens the legs. A local specialist makes real leather saddles to his specification, and they can be removed – just like those of the original rocking horses, which were meant as trainers for prospective riders. One size only, on bowed rockers, £495, including delivery anywhere on the mainland, or by quotation elsewhere.

Peter Stocken, Puzzleplex Ltd, Stubbs Walden, Doncaster, S Yorks (Doncaster 700997). Hand-carved three-dimensional puzzles in beautifully grained woods, with an initial or motif of your choice in the centre. Each piece is intricately made to interlock in every direction – some are so complicated they can take three days to put together. In various shapes: four-leafed clover, heart, dragon, various animals and geometrics in rosewood, yew, walnut, beech, ebony and several other exotic coloured woods. From £30, or from £300 with a 30-oz. silver initial incorporated into the carving.

Willow baskets

CAMBRIDGESHIRE

Jane Greening, Periwinkle Crafts, Periwinkle House, Old Rectory Drive, Dry Drayton, Cambridge (Crafts Hill 80637). All types of baskets made from Somerset willow. Prices are from £9 for a small log basket, £15 for a picnic hamper, £18.50 for a laundry basket; shopping baskets are from £6.75 to £9.50. They are available in white, buff, brown or any combination, and can be delivered anywhere in the country. Jane Greening will also repair English willow baskets – a baby's crib, for instance – but not imported shopping baskets. Telephone for an appointment to view the baskets at Periwinkle House.

CUMBRIA

Hedgerow Baskets, Daffiestown Rigg, Longtown (Longtown 791187). Baskets made to order from English willow, mostly grown in Somerset. Steve and Sue Fuller hope eventually to be self-sufficient when their own osier beds mature. Their range includes log baskets at £15.50 and babies' cribs at £30, and they will undertake commissions or repairs. A price list is available for a stamped addressed envelope.

OXFORDSHIRE

English Nursery Heirlooms, Britwell House, Britwell Salome, Oxford (Watlington 3255). Traditional Moses baskets handmade in willow and trimmed to order. The most popular draperies are in ivory silk or poly/cotton, trimmed with antique-style lace; the prices, complete with safety mattress, are from £86. Willow stand to match, with seed-pearl-trimmed lace on each leg, at £35. There is also a range of small accessories.

Wood-turning

STAFFORDSHIRE

George Hodson, Castle View, Coppenhall (Stafford 58831). High-quality wood-turning. George Hodson makes a large number of lace bobbins and bobbin winders and a selection of attractive decorative items, from goblets and hour-glasses to trinket boxes in the shape of full-size apples and pears. He also makes table and standard lampstands and bric-à-brac shelves, and can copy drawer knobs, finials and other turnery to order. All his work is hand-polished – no stain or varnish unless expressly requested – and his work is extremely reasonably priced – the apples, for instance, are £3.50, pears £3.75, hour-glasses £16.

WILTSHIRE

Rod Naylor, Turnpike House, 208 Devizes Rd, Hilperton, nr Trowbridge (Trowbridge 4497). Wood-carving and sculpture in a variety of styles. Rod Naylor will make to order small pieces such as chess sets, trophies and mirror frames and also large murals and fireplaces. He works only to commission and uses the best exotic timbers. He also restores high-quality antique furniture for museums, the National Trust and private clients, undertaking cabinet work, carving and turning of missing parts.

Prices were correct at the time of printing, but are only intended as an indication and means of comparison. Do not send cheques to any company without checking first by telephone on postal charges and availability.

---

2 | Getting Dressed

Women's wear

GLOUCESTERSHIRE

Rosemary Gill, Old White Hart, Downend, Horsley, nr Nailsworth (Nailsworth 3554). Quilted jackets and waistcoats in a highly individual style. Rosemary Gill went to art school but had no formal training in quilting, which she started six years ago, and so had no pre-conceived ideas. She machine-quilts strips of fabric and then decorates them with braid and ribbons, beads and appliqué. She uses mainly Liberty prints and can incorporate customers' own silks, cottons and velvets to match a blouse or skirt. Prices are from £30 to £55, and she also makes children's sizes.

LANCASHIRE

Silkworm, 19 Firswood Rd, Lathom, nr Skelmersdale (Skelmersdale 31538). Pure silk shawls, scarves, quilted waistcoats and quilted evening clutch-bags. Irene Hardwick uses Chinese and Macclesfield silks, which she decorates with a single raised appliqué flower and leaf motif. Long narrow scarves with flower fasteners are from £4.95, triangular crêpe de Chine shawls £24, clutch-bags £7.50 to £15.50. A wide variety of colours is available; send a sample of fabric if you want to match something special.

LINCOLNSHIRE

Roz Leon, The White House, Lowgate, Lutton, Spalding (Holbeach 363703). Having studied fashion design, Roz Leon started to handpaint on silk and cotton 'because I was too impatient to screen-print – I wanted to see immediate results.' She specializes in classic silk shirts (£19.95), sweatshirts (£8.95) and T-shirts (£11.99) – some painted free-hand, others stencilled – but she is prepared to do almost anything on anything in any colour.

LONDON

Buy & Large Ltd, 4 Holbein Place, Sloane Square, SW1 (01-730 6534).
Stylish clothes in sizes 16 to 24, with a particularly good selection in the 20-to-24 range. The shop was once run by a couple of titled ladies, who conducted the business like a coffee morning; Mrs Christina Lane, who has owned it for the past twelve years, not only maintains the sociable atmosphere but takes endless trouble to provide her customers with a good choice of well-known brand names, ordering specials when possible. She has dresses, jackets and coats, and prices are upper-middle – £38 to £150 for a dress, for instance.

Monica Flynn, 137 Sloane St, SW1 (01-730 6945). Designer clothes in sizes 16 to 24–26. Monica Flynn has been right through the fashion trade, from picking up the pins (which they don't do any more) to designing and buying. She decided to specialize in larger sizes because she is a 24 herself, and when she opened fourteen years ago she found she couldn't even buy the simplest cream silk shirt in anything larger than a 14. She now scours Europe for the very best shapes to flatter the larger woman, sometimes even teaching the manufacturers how to make up styles she likes to her own large patterns. Not for her customers the outsize Crimplene tent. These are very beautiful clothes in lovely fabrics, so they are expensive – a few skirts at £75 to £90, dresses from £100, pure silk blouses £150 (no coats) – but there is a degree of exclusivity because she only keeps one of each size in any style: you won't find racks of the same model.

The Frock Exchange, 450 Fulham Rd, SW6 (01-381 2937). Second-hand clothes bought and sold. When she opened twelve years ago, Gabrielle Crawford was one of the first to deal in clothes bought from and by people with busy social lives who don't like to be seen in the same thing twice. She accepts clothes on a sale-or-return basis and insists on first-class condition – often there are top designer labels, including Yves St Laurent, Bill Gibb, Ozzie Clarke. At Christmas this is the place to find an evening gown for £30 to £60 which would have cost hundreds when new.

Long Tall Sally, 21 Chiltern St, W1 (01-487 3370); also at 3 New Market Rd, Grand Parade, Bath, Avon (Bath 66682); 13 Chapel Place, Tunbridge Wells, Kent (Tunbridge Wells 34131); Royal Exchange Shopping Centre, Manchester (061-832 3331). Clothes specially designed for women over 5 ft 8 in. Run by Judy Rich, who, at 6 ft, knows the problems, these shops stock well-made and elegant clothes in sizes 12 to 18, with some size 20, all cut on longer-than-average lines so that sleeves and waists are properly proportioned. There is a budget range (shirts and skirts from £14.95, dresses £24 to £34) and a designer range. Swimwear, tights and slips are also available. Mail order through the Chiltern Street address.

Kate Rumens, 6 Pembridge Mews, W11. Embroidered and appliquéd silk dresses and separates. Kate Rumens specializes in high-quality silks and wools and enjoys making elaborately decorated clothes. She also has a range of simple, elegant shapes that can be made to order up to any size and sent anywhere. Prices are from £75 for a heavy raw-silk kimono, and a brochure is available.

Sassa, 10a Gees Court, W1 (01-408 1596). Stylish clothes in large sizes (16 to 30), some available also by mail order. Dresses, coats, suits, blouses and evening wear from about £35. A brochure is available.

Helen Trist, 5 Dovedale Studios, 465 Battersea Park Rd, SW11 (01-223 9643). Handpainted silk clothes and lingerie by mail order. The name is a composite of Helen O'Keefe, the artist, and Anne Stafford (whose mother's name was Trist), the designer. They produce simple silk T-shirts from £29 and evening skirts in silk taffeta at £145, plus separates, dresses, nightdresses and negligées in habutai, crêpe de Chine, spun silk and silk satins. A catalogue of their designs is available, and if you want something individual, send a sample of fabric to be matched and the colours will be mixed specially for you.

MANCHESTER

Nicolette and Linda Hutson, 7 Holly Bank, 9 Oxford Place, Manchester (061-248 6863). Tapestry woven waistcoats and jackets made to order. Nicolette and Linda Hutson came over from America in 1974 and have been producing garments and wall-hangings with a most original combination of textures, incorporating metal threads, satin and taffetas, velvets and chenilles. One of their specialities is the Scandinavian rya technique, which produces an effect like feathered ruffles. Prices are from £200 for a jacket, £150 for a waistcoat.

SUSSEX

Julian Akers Douglas, Barham Farmhouse, East Hoathly, Lewes, E Sussex (Halland 397). Traditional smocks in natural calico, with cream or stone smocking, in off-the-peg sizes, from children's ages 2 to 6 from £28, to adults, small, medium and large at £65 midcalf or knee length (postage extra). Special sizes can be made to order – the largest was made for a man with a 49-in. chest. Julian Akers Douglas also produces exact replicas of the traditional Sussex round smock made in linen or natural silk with elaborate smocking and embroidery – one of the few remaining originals is at the Victoria and Albert Museum. She also makes trousers, scarves and skirts to match.

TYNE AND WEAR

Hazlewood Antiques, Hazlewood Avenue, Newcastle upon Tyne (Newcastle upon Tyne 816809). Ruth Statham and Claudia Seaton were the first specialists in twentieth-century collectables in the North-East when they started four years ago. They have an extensive collection of clothes, quilts and linen from 1850 to 1950, Art Deco and Art Nouveau furniture and decorative pieces. The stock ranges from 1950s summer dresses for under £10 and silk and chiffon evening dresses for between £20 and £45 to beaded Edwardian dresses at around £100, and there are beaded bags for £5, baskets of lace collars and cuffs, drawers of buttons, shelves of sheets and linen cloths and piles of Northumbrian and Durham quilts. Open Monday–Saturday, 11 a.m. to 5 p.m.

Furs

LONDON

Murray Bennett, 11 South Molton St, W1 (01-629 2757). Fur renovation and remodelling, from rabbit to mink. Unfashionable furs can be updated (stoles converted to waistcoats, for instance), and current styles can simply be cleaned. They also buy and sell second-hand furs and will make up new ones to order.

Maxwell Croft, 105 New Bond St, W1 (01-629 6226), and 46 Milsom St, Bath (Bath 64989). A name synonymous with top styling and top quality in furs. Maxwell Croft was one of the first to style rabbit like mink and mink like trenchcoats, and you can be sure of seeing glamorous furs and glamorous people in the elegant, third-floor showroom in Bond Street. Anything can be made to order – at a price, of course – but you could find a bargain in the annual sale held both in London and Bath.

Herman Fur Hire, 61–5 Conduit St, W1 (01-734 3805/4). Fur coats, jackets and stoles to hire for one glamorous evening. Most types of fur are available; fees are from £20 for a stole, and a fairly substantial deposit is required for valuable fur coats. Furs may not be taken out of the country. This company also provides many of the furs seen on stage, film and television.

YORKSHIRE

Nova Scotia Furs, Unit 15, The Piece Hall, Halifax, W Yorks. Mink and fox coats and jackets to order. A trained furrier offering a made-to-measure service which usually works out less expensive than an off-the-peg coat. No fuss or fancy furnishings in his basic workshop, but don't let that put you off. He also repairs and remodels existing coats and always has a rail of second-hand furs for sale, as well as some new ones. Mink coats are from about £2,000.

Knitwear

AVON

Breckdale Hand Knit, The Coach House, 73a Prior Park Rd, Bath (Bath 334839). Traditional hand-knitted Aran sweaters in stock and to order in any non-standard sizes, including children's. There is a range of styles for men and women: sweaters with crew, polo or V-neck, zip jackets, button-through jackets, V-neck cardigans, lumber cardigans, button-through jackets with polo collar, waistcoats and hats, scarves and mittens. A brochure with photographs of the range is available. Prices for standard sizes from 34 in. to 44 in. are from £26, plus postage; unusual sizes extra.

Mary Dawson, Hillstead, Weston Park East, Bath (Bath 319422). Children's and adults' sweaters, with a range of repeat motifs. There are nine designs – trains, sheep, ducks, pigs, elephants, teddies, strawberries, flowers and Fair Isle, knitted in Shetland wool on a home machine. Any colour combinations are possible, and if you have something special you want to match you can send a piece of fabric and have your sweater knitted in colours to tone. Children's sizes cost from £9.95, adults' from £29.50, both with postage extra. A leaflet of the designs is available.

CAMBRIDGESHIRE

Cambridgeshire Knitters, 27 Madingley Rd, Cambridge (Cambridge 357752). Anne Farmer specializes in hand-knitting in all yarns – wool, silk, cotton and mixtures – and will attempt any commission. If you fancy a poodle with 3D ears flapping from your bosom or Plato's head with 3D hair you only have to ask. She and her team of knitters will adapt patterns, copy old favourite sweaters, or create garments from pictures or drawings for which there are no patterns. Prices are from £38, plus the cost of wool.

Patricia Corbett Shawls, 3 Clare Rd, Cambridge (Cambridge 357735). Traditional christening shawls in finest white Shetland lace wool, with a choice of narrow or broad border. Circular, 4 ft 6 in. or 5 ft diameter, £25 and £30; 4 ft 6 in. or 5 ft square, £40 and £45. Patricia Corbett will also make the shawls in a choice of seven colours for adults – she will send wool samples on request. Mail order only.

CHANNEL ISLANDS

Le Tricoteur, Pitronnerie Rd, St Peter's Port, Guernsey (Guernsey 26214). Traditional guernseys made in worsted yarn, navy and eleven other colours. Sizes range from child's 22-in. to man's 54-in. Basic prices are from £7.50 for the smallest child's size to £16.95 (36-in.), £17.50 (38-in.) and £18.45 (40-in.). These are the prices applicable in Guernsey; VAT is added for mail orders to the mainland, and postage is extra.

CORNWALL

Elspeth Allsop, Wainwrights, Doddy Cross, Menheniot, Liskeard (Widegates 473). Sweaters knitted to any size. Mrs Allsop machine-knits at home and finishes all garments by hand. She designs for men and women and does particularly pretty knitted lace for jumpers and stoles. She prefers to work on a local basis – no mail order – but her prices are particularly reasonable: from £16 for a sweater or waistcoat, and from £36 for a dress or suit.

HERTFORDSHIRE

Dorothy Greenwood, 22 Station Rd, Berkhamsted (Berkhamsted 73875). Original Fair Isle and picture knitting in wool or cotton. Dorothy Greenwood started her career by studying chemistry, physics and maths, and it was by chance that she became a professional knitwear designer; having decided to make a sweater, she couldn't find a pattern she liked, so she created her first pop art design by copying an H P sauce bottle. She progressed to Lowry-like figures and was asked to show her work in a craft exhibition. Now she sells to top stores here and in America. She has a range of fifty designs, which can be made in colours of the customer's choice, all made on a home machine and hand-finished. Prices are from £25 for adults' sizes, £17 for children's.

LONDON

Chas Bird, 36 Hosack Rd, SW17 (01-673 8488, evenings). Fair Isle and picture sweaters knitted to order in Shetland wools. Chas Bird uses an electronic machine and can reproduce almost any design you choose in any colour and any size. If you want Fair Isles, he will send sketches of the pattern with a wool chart and you can choose the colours or simply the background colour and give him an idea of the shades you want to predominate. Prices are from £32, including postage.

Inca, 45 Elizabeth St, SW1 (01-730 7941). Peruvian handmade knitwear, accessories and craftwork. There are four ranges made from vegetable-dyed hand-spun wool, alpaca (in natural shades of brown, cream, grey and black), multi-coloured wool and cotton. A good range of sweaters and some rugs, mats, runners and cushion covers is available by post, and other crafts, including carved gourds, pottery and baskets, are available at the shop. Prices from £3 for a pull-on hat and £20 for a patterned sweater.

MANCHESTER

Knitwitz, Unit 9, Manchester Craft Village, Oak St, Manchester 4 (061-835 1017). Jackie Needham makes original fashion knits to special commissions, working mainly in wool, mohair and silk yarns. She incorporates a lot of sequins and fancy beading in her work and knits by both hand and machine. She can usually offer a range of garments off the peg, including hats, scarves and leg-warmers. A mohair slipover to order is around £20, a three-quarter-length jumper around £60.

NORTHUMBERLAND

Almost Unwearoutable Socks, Nicholl Knitwear, Piper Close, Corbridge (043 471 2283). Socks and stockings knitted by four local husband-and-wife teams on traditional sock machines made around the turn of the century. They are usually knitted in a 4-ply mixture of 60-per-cent pure shrink-resistant wool and 40-per-cent nylon, and they do live up to their name. One wearer wrote to say that he had just walked the length of the Roman Wall and although his shoes had worn out, his socks had not. Almost any colour is available in 3 ply, 4 ply (single) or 8 ply (double), all with reinforcement in toes and heels. The average length for socks is 12 in. and for stockings 23 in. including turnover top; other lengths to order. Sizes from shoe 4 to 14. New additions to the range are fingerless gloves with extra-long wrist-bands (from £3.50, button-front cardigans (£25), striped classic sweaters (£23.57), plain (£20). Prices for the socks range from £4.84 to £13.06. There are also knitted gaiters, children's sweaters and matching shooting stockings.

OXFORDSHIRE

Maggie White, The Chapel, Swinbrook, nr Burford (Asthall Leigh 489).
Brilliantly coloured machine- and hand-knits to order. Maggie White started hand-knitting for friends; she intended to go to art school and was knitting to support herself while she prepared a portfolio. But her designs were so successful that art school had to wait. She uses Shetland wools in stunning colours and mostly in bold geometric designs – splendid for ski-wear. Prices from about £50.

TYNE AND WEAR

Penny Plain, 7 St Mary's Place, Newcastle upon Tyne (Newcastle upon Tyne 321124). Wool and cotton sweaters knitted and hand-finished in Yorkshire and Scotland. There are traditional Fair Isles and modern picture and motif designs for men and women at prices between £19.50 and £50. A mail-order catalogue is available. Lots of other original and unusual clothes, shoes, jewellery, pottery and gifts.

Lingerie

CHESHIRE

She, 49 Park Lane, Poynton (Poynton 877636). Specialist lingerie, corsetry and swimwear in a wide range of sizes. Barbara Sciel aims to provide a friendly and personal service and can fit sizes 32C to 46DD. She also provides maternity swimwear from £15 and mastectomy swimwear from £35.

CORNWALL

Pretty Things, Carpenna, Budock Water, nr Falmouth (Falmouth 72721). Pure silk or cotton lingerie made in any size. The range includes petticoats and half-slips, camisoles, briefs, French knickers, nightdresses, negligées and pyjamas, all in natural, pink, blue or black crêpe de Chine, lace-trimmed. The majority of orders are for silk – prices from £11 (briefs) to £106.50 (negligée) – but Audrey Blackford and Janet Martin will make up their designs in pure cotton if required.

LANCASHIRE

Margaret Horner, 11 States Rd, St Anne's on Sea (St Anne's 724830).
Pure silk lingerie made to order. Margaret Horner started making lingerie for her daughter, but she believes in making beautiful lingerie for larger figures too, and her standard range of camisoles, French knickers, slips, nightdresses and negligées

is available in sizes 10 to 18. She stocks five pastel shades in crêpe de Chine and satin, and can obtain black, navy, red, silver and mulberry on request. Prices are from £12.75 for briefs to £135.95 for a lace-trimmed negligée. She will also copy customers' favourite lingerie to commission (no bras). All her business is mail order – she can't cope with callers to the house.

LONDON

Olive Bennetto, 64 Woodhayes Rd, Neasden, NW10 (01-459 1994). Bras, swimwear and lingerie made to order. Olive Bennetto deals mainly by post, but will also see clients by appointment. She will copy any bra no longer obtainable or will restyle to her own patterns and in natural fabrics for those who are allergic to synthetics. The first bra will be between £25 and £40, depending on style; repeat orders are one-third less. Lingerie includes French and cami-knickers, slips and half-slips, suspender belts, nightdresses and negligées, in silk and other fabrics. A nightdress will cost from £42.

Contour, 2 Hans Rd, SW3 (01-589 9293), and 1021 Upper Level, Whitgift Centre, Croydon, Surrey (01-681 1153). Specialists in corsetry, swimwear and mastectomy fittings. June Kenton trains all her own staff and has a workroom at the Knightsbridge address where alterations can be made to ensure an exact fit. She has young, attractive styles in all sizes, including DDs and maternity bras, and stocks a wide range of leading brands from Europe and America from about £6. Her swimwear comes in the same fittings as corsetry – long- and short-bodied and in many styles. She is also a specialist in mastectomy bras and prostheses, and she makes the allowable VAT deduction on such items (including mastectomy swimwear) on the spot.

Rigby & Peller, 12 South Molton St (upstairs), W1 (01-629 6708). Clients who still want made-to-measure corsetry, including laced corselettes or over-wired bras, can have them made here (individually made bras are from about £50). It is an old-established company, now owned by Contour; and also offering a top-quality range of ready-to-wear corsetry and swimwear.

Shoes

Peter Lord and other Clarks shoe stockists. For people with one foot larger than the other, Clarks will make up pairs in odd sizes – one shoe half a size or a size larger than the other, for instance. The service is available at most Clarks stockists in most of the popular women's styles and also in all men's casual styles and some children's fittings. Orders take four to six weeks and cost about one and a half times more than the same shoes in standard, matching sizes.

CHESHIRE

Gordon Clarke, 178 Market St, Hyde (061-368 1674). Made-to-measure shoes for awkward feet. Surgical shoes are a speciality, and everything is hand-made in leather. All styles are available, including lace-ups, boots and casual shoes. Prices are from £131, including measuring, fittings and making a special last for each customer. The service takes two to three months.

Stockport Odd Feet Association; secretary: Gillian Evans, 17 Deva Close, Poynton (061-483 7026; a.m. only). A nationwide voluntary organization that helps people who have odd-size feet to shop for shoes. Special deals with retailers and manufacturers give members discounts if they buy two pairs of shoes to get one pair that fits. The organization will also try to match you with a mate who has the same size odd feet as you but in reverse, so that you can share two pairs – if you can agree on the style. Membership is £1.50. Please send stamped addressed envelope with inquiries.

CUMBRIA

J. Strong & Son, Glencote, Caldbeck, Wigton (Caldbeck 424). Wooden clogs with leather uppers in five colours and seven styles, or made to order for awkward sizes. J. Strong established his clog shop in Caldbeck in 1945, when shoes were a 'coupons-only' luxury. Today he and his son make a range of clogs in men's, women's and children's sizes and in several colours. They can be fitted with extra rubber soles for protection, or traditional steel caulkers for morris and clog dancers. Prices are from £13.20, plus postage, for ladies' styles.

LONDON

Crispins, 28–30 Chiltern St, W1 (01-486 8924), and in the Royal Exchange Shopping Centre, Manchester (061-833 0022). Named after St Crispin, the patron saint of shoemakers, this is certainly a sanctuary for people with over-sized feet, as the owner, Dawne Gutteridge, wears size 9 shoes and knows all about the misery and the scorn meted out to women looking for larger-than-average but smart shoes. 'In Italy they thought I had the figure wrong when I asked for size 42. They fell about laughing and offered to sell me the boxes to wear!' Many women are made to feel like freaks when they look for large sizes, so Dawne has specialized in 8s to 11s, with four fittings; AAA to C. Very stylish, and mostly between £20 and £60 – less for sandals. There is another Crispins shop at 5 Chiltern Street (01-935 7984), which specializes in narrow fittings in standard sizes up to 7½.

Deliss, 41 Beauchamp Place, SW3 (01-584 3321). Shoes made to measure in any colour, fabric or leather, including silks, satins, brocades, straw, suede, calf, snake, ostrich or whatever. Perfect for a wedding party (givers or goers) if your budget will stand at least £176 a pair. They also make shoes and boots for men from £225.

Egeli Shoemakers, 2 Windmill St, Tottenham Court Rd, W1 (01-636 5861). Ladies' and gentlemen's made-to-measure shoes. Prices are from £195, depending on the complexity of the fitting; an information sheet is available. They will also make up shoes in any design and material, including evening or wedding dress fabrics. Orders can be taken at the customer's home or office, as well as at the shop, and a postal service is available.

Gamba, 46 Dean St, W1 (01-437 0704), and 55 Beauchamp Place, SW3 (01-584 4774); also at 78 Church St, Weybridge, Surrey (Weybridge 45031). Shoes for theatre, ballet, television and special occasions. Children's leather ballet shoes are from £5.50, adults' shoes made up in fabric to match a wedding dress or ball gown from £25 to £30. This service takes about five weeks.

John Lobb, St James's St, SW1 (01-930 3664). One of the most famous and most expensive names in made-to-measure footwear, established in 1850 and still in the same family. Handmade calf shoes are about £504.85, or you can have your feet encased in ostrich leather at about £1,020. The first pair you have made will take from four to six months; subsequent pairs will take two to three months. For clients out of town there is a catalogue and a self-measurement chart. Every year they go to Scotland twice, the USA twice and to Europe once to visit their clients.

Annette Rose, 39 Vivian Way, N2 (01-607 5464). Court shoes dyed and handpainted to match an outfit. Annette Rose is a Swiss designer who keeps a stock of plain court shoes in unprepared leather which she paints with leather dyes, copying a motif from a fabric, or creating whatever design the customer wants. She also keeps samples of the colour mixes used, so that she can offer an after-sales service by touching up scuffed areas. Shoes in a plain colour are about £70, with a contrast toe-cap about £90 and in special designs from £100. The service takes about three weeks.

Savva, 37 Chiltern St, W1 (01-935 2329). Specialists in ladies' leather shoes for theatre and television and for private customers. Tony Savva followed, so to speak, in his father's footsteps and has so many famous people on his books he doesn't know where to begin name-dropping. His productions have included *Murder on the Orient Express* and *Death on the Nile* and when we talked he had just finished Bo Derrick's shoes for *Bolero*. He doesn't make special lasts for every customer and so will not undertake problem feet, but he keeps an extensive range of lasts which can be adapted to individual customers' needs. Hence the price is much less than the usual made-to-measure – about £50 a pair.

Small and Tall Shoe Shop, 71 York St, W1 (01-723 5321). Shoes by mail order is an unusual service, but Small and Tall will go on changing pairs that don't fit until you are completely happy. A service charge is made on goods returned – £1 on shoes, £1.50 on boots, 85p on sandals – and a brochure is available for both the small (13 to 2½, fittings B to E) and the tall (8½ to 11, fittings AA to E). Not all styles are available in all fittings, but special colours can sometimes be ordered at an extra cost of £3 a pair. Prices from £19.95 to £37.95. Closed on Mondays.

James Taylor & Son, 4 Paddington St, W1 (01-935 4149). Bespoke and orthopaedic shoes. James Taylor walked to London from Garboldisham in Norfolk and set up his company in 1857. In 1952 it was taken over from his two grandsons by a German shoemaker whose son, Peter Schweiger, is now managing director. The company handles orthopaedic work for several London hospitals and makes bespoke shoes for many customers here and overseas. Prices are from £281.75 and orders take up to ten weeks; but the products can last for fifteen to twenty years.

Trickers, 67 Jermyn St, W1 (01-930 6395). Gentlemen's city and country shoes made to order. As well as the traditional city shoes Trickers make riding boots and shooting boots to measure, plus their standard country ranges. The uppers are handmade, with the soles machine-stitched and finished. Prices are from £170 for the first pair and £155 for subsequent pairs. They will also make tapestry up into slippers (£50) and velvet slippers embroidered with initials or crests. A catalogue is available.

NORTHAMPTONSHIRE

Magnus, 2 High St, Harpole, Northampton (Northampton 831271); also at 63 South End Rd, London NW3 (01-435 1792). This company claims to have the largest range in the world of men's footwear, sizes 12 to 15 in a variety of widths. They also do a ladies' range, sizes 8 to 11 and in widths AA to EE, although not in every style. A catalogue for each range is available. Average prices.

Accessories

DERBYSHIRE

Cargo, The Old Workshop, North St, Cromford, Matlock (Wirksworth 4574). Peter and Clare Ludbey have their workshop in what was once a weaver's cottage, not far from the place where Richard Arkwright started his first cotton mills. They make a variety of accessories – belts, purses, briefcases, handbags – mainly in cowhide from about £8. There is also a range of flat sandals made to measure from £9.95, and they will make instrument and tool cases to order. They don't use clothing leather, but will undertake heavier repairs to straps, saddles and similar leather goods.

DORSET

Joan Haig, Home Farm, Fifehead Magdalen, Gillingham (Marnhull 820268). Scarves, stoles, knee rugs and floor rugs made to order. Joan Haig weaves her own handspun yarns – wool in natural fleece colours and dyed silks. Scarves are from £30, stoles £70, floor rugs £130 (5 × 3 ft).

GLOUCESTERSHIRE

MacGregor & Michael, 37 Silver St, Tetbury (Tetbury 52179). Hand-stitched leather goods made with traditional techniques, using oak-bark tanned hide and other natural leathers. The range includes travel bags, briefcases and attaché cases from £120 to £300 and shoulder bags from £50 to £150, as well as a range of accessories, including belts. Some items are available from stock but most work is made to commission. Telephone before visiting.

LONDON

Asprey & Co. Ltd, 165 New Bond St, W1 (01-493 6767). The gentlemen's fitted cases for which Aspreys have been famous since 1847 are still made in their own workrooms above the shop. If you want one in baby crocodile with 9-ct gold fittings it will set you back nearly £14,000. It includes a tube of toothpaste, but at that price if you don't like the flavour they will probably change it. They also make wallets, dressing cases, playing cards, embossed with whatever you want in gold.

OXFORDSHIRE

S. & J. Cooper, 24 Market Place, Faringdon (Faringdon 20517). Tradi-tional saddlers who make bespoke saddles to fit the horse and the rider. Each one takes at least thirty hours to make and only the best materials are used. The cost is between £200 and £400. Stanley Cooper also undertakes special commissions for instrument cases and other unframed bags – when he has time.

SURREY

Terrapin Design, 4 Castle St, Guildford (Guildford 62711). Leather hand-bags to commission. There are various types, some with handles as well as shoulder straps, classic framed bags, briefcase bags or whatever you fancy in any leather and any colour. Prices are mostly between £20 and £60. Mike Hill and his wife (who collects terrapins, hence the name) started at local agricultural shows ten years ago, opened their shop three years ago and have continued to grow during the recession, so Mike reckons 'We must be doing something right.' Joy makes waistcoats in all sizes too – men's, women's, children's – in sheepskin (£79.95) or leather (£36.50), and suede T-shirts (£24.95). There is also a stock of ready-made leather goods.

TYNE AND WEAR

Le Prevo Leathers, Blackfriars Craft Centre, Stowell St, Newcastle upon Tyne (Newcastle upon Tyne 617648). Handmade leather handbags and accessories. Stuart Hails was one of the first to revive the tradition of craftsmen working at Blackfriars Priory when he opened his workshop there seven years ago. Now the building has been restored and three other workshops have opened. Many leather workers still concentrate on stiff, hand-tooled leather bags, but Stuart moves with the fashion and is producing soft sausage handbags (£12.50), supple suede bow ties (£3.50), wide laced corset belts (£7.50). He also makes leather Gladstone bags copied from an old design, with steel frames, brass fittings and real locks and keys. They are between £50 and £100, depending on size.

Umbrellas

LONDON

Abdank Ltd, 5 Chiswick Common Rd, W4 (01-995 9718). Special-occasion umbrellas made to order. Jan Gurawski will design umbrellas to complement individual outfits – one of his prettiest was a Victorian style made from the same material as a bride's dress and with a carved ivory handle. Prices will be about £50.

T. Fox & Co. Ltd, 118 London Wall, E C2 (01-606 4720). This third-generation family firm was established 140 years ago and was the first to use nylon for umbrella covers. There is a large range of standard umbrellas in nylon or cotton from £10.95 to £100, and special umbrellas can be made to order from £25; or, if you have an antique handle, they will make a complete umbrella to fit.

James Smith & Sons Ltd, 53 New Oxford St, WC1 (01-836 4731). Umbrella specialists, established in 1830 and still in the same family. There is a large stock of all types of umbrella, and special ones can be made to order if a particular length or style is required. Walking-stick umbrellas, for instance, are from £29.50.

Menswear

CHESHIRE

T. Todd Ltd, 15 Charles St, Hoole, nr Chester (Chester 22127). Clothes and shoes for large men. This is a family business, established in 1897 and thought to be the second oldest shop in the Chester area – about two miles from the city centre. They stock jackets up to 54 in., jeans and trousers up to 56 in., casual wear up to 56 in., shirts up to 20 in., knitwear, belts and shoes in sizes 11 to 14. They also have a range of ladies' coats, raincoats and dresses up to size 26. As much as possible is British-made, and prices are average – trousers from £16 to £36.50, men's knitwear £10.95 to £40, dresses £18.50 to £45.

LONDON

Harvie & Hudson, 77 Jermyn St, SW1 (01-930 3949). Shirts made to measure in exclusive fabrics to Harvie & Hudson's own designs. Prices are from £55 in cotton; there is also a large range of off-the-peg shirts from £32.

Hilditch & Key Ltd, 37 and 73 Jermyn St, W1 (01-734 4707 and 01-930 5336). Bespoke shirtmakers founded in 1899 by two enterprising young men who travelled to the universities to 'fit the sons of gentlemen'. The company is now an international name, with branches in America, Switzerland, South Africa and Australia, and shows two collections a year of its special fabrics. Men's made-to-measure shirts are from £45, and there is also a ready-made range for men and women from £29.95. These can be made up in fabrics of the customer's choice for a little extra (from £36). Other accessories include socks, ties, robes and knitwear, pyjamas and nightshirts, designed to co-ordinate with the H & K fabrics.

Mayfair, 60 Neal St, Covent Garden WC2 (01-240 2785). A huge selection of shirts in a tiny shop – and all available by mail. There are hundreds of fitted, semi-fitted and standard shirts with 'normal' sleeve lengths, and about forty styles in special sleeve lengths from 32 in. to 37 in. and in collar sizes 14 in. to 19½ in. These are made specially for the owner, Jacqueline Cooper, in many fabrics and colours, and she stocks all the good off-the-peg shirt names too.

James Meade Shirts Ltd, Freepost, London SW9 8BR (01-274 7700). Wide range of sizes in men's shirts, by mail order. There are twenty-nine sizes, collars 14 in. to 18 in., including half-sizes, and up to five sleeve lengths per collar size. Sixteen colours in plains, stripes and sporty checks – £25 each, including postage.

Prints, 8 Portobello Green, 281 Portobello Rd, W10 (01-968 5626). For the modern Beau Brummell – a small range of cotton shirts in classic shapes but very bold prints created by Sue Timney and Grahame Fowler, who specialize in fabric design. The shirts, in standard sizes only, are £25 to £30 each.

Sulka, 19 Old Bond St, W1 (01-493 4468). Men's dressing robes handmade to order in seven days. Available in cotton, silk and cashmere from £85 to £1,200. Bespoke shirts too, and a range of pyjamas in stock sizes which can have longer-than-usual arms and legs to order – cotton from £42, silk from £65. A small range of ready-to-wear cashmere and silk blazers and silk raincoats.

Turnbull & Asser Ltd, 71 Jermyn St, SW1 (01-930 0502), and 43 Dover St, W1 (01-499 1357). One of the most famous names in men's made-to-measure shirts. The company was founded in 1885 (Mr Turnbull dropped out in the 1920s, but the Asser family still keeps the connection), and the present managing director says the biggest change is not in the shirts but in the customers. He remembers the time when Sir Malcolm Sargent retreated in horror at finding two ladies in the shop; now some of its most faithful customers are female – and buying for themselves, not their husbands. Bespoke shirts – more than forty dozen shirts hand-cut on the premises each week – are from £40, and there is a large range of off-the-peg shirts, pyjamas, suits and ties. Downstairs is one of Winston Churchill's voluminous velvet siren suits. During the war there was always a Churchill siren suit in the shop for repair – not because of enemy action, but because he kept burning holes in them with his cigars.

YORKSHIRE

Seymour Shirts, 136 Sunbridge Rd, Bradford, W Yorks (Bradford 726520). Made-to-measure shirts in a wide range of fabrics, including Sea Island cotton, cotton/wool mixtures, poly/cotton, brushed cotton and nylon. Prices are from £18.50 to £42 and sizes are from children's to 24-in. collar. Styles include collar-attached, loose collars or plain neckband, and extra collars and cuffs can be supplied for replacement when the originals are worn. The company also makes pyjamas and nightshirts to measure and specializes in clerical shirts. A postal service is available from the address given; personal service through the menswear department of Rackhams, Bradford.

Prices were correct at the time of printing, but are only intended as an indication and means of comparison. Do not send cheques to any company without checking first by telephone on postal charges and availability.

3 Getting Things Mended

Books and paper

BERKSHIRE

The Eddington Bindery Ltd, Hungerford (Hungerford 82275). Restoration and conservation of all books from the fifteenth century, including paper washing and foxing. Work is also done for museums and libraries and there is a special service for sporting clients – handmade morocco-bound game books (from £180) and scrap books bound in personal racing silks from £90. Collections can be made in London.

CHESHIRE

Garrick Book Shop, 8–10 Wellington Rd South, Stockport (061-480 4346). A workshop attached to the shop will bind a typed manuscript or thesis and rebind new books with specialist leather bindings. Repair and restoration of modern and antiquarian books can also be arranged.

CUMBRIA

Miranda Holmes-Smith, Lawson Cottage, Renwick, nr Penrith (Lazonby 402). Conservation of early books. Miranda Holmes-Smith learned her skills from a specialist who rebound the Book of Kells in Dublin, and she also worked on rare books damaged in the Florence floods. She will rebind and is also a paper conservationist, capable of dealing with old vellum manuscripts. The emphasis is on conservation rather than restoration, and there is a minimum charge of £50.

DEVON

Sydney Delow, Kerswell, Liverton, Newton Abbot (Bickington 611). Book restoration, leather or cloth – restitching, relining, replacing or renewing covers, gold blocking. Prices are from £20 for minor repairs. Sydney Delow does restoration work for museums and also binds magazines and graduates' theses.

DORSET

Frank Brown, 24 Camden Way, Castle Park, Dorchester (Dorchester 66039). All types of book repair, from paperbacks to full leather bindings. Frank Brown, who set up his own workshop ten years ago after serving his apprenticeship, will undertake binding, washing and defoxing, edge gilding and gold tooling of new and antiquarian books. An octavo book one inch thick might cost from about £10 for a cloth binding to £20 if sewing was needed. The same size in leather would be £20 to £50. He also undertakes commissions for family bibles and albums and was once even asked to design a book with a false board, obviously intended for smuggling. (The commission was never completed.)

LONDON

Caroline Bendix, 14 Blake Gardens, SW6 (01-736 8692). Restoration of books and paper, gold tooling, new bindings, presentation copies. Individually commissioned visitors' books can be made from £40. Visits are possible in and around London.

BookEnds Bindery, 1b Orleston Rd, N7 (01-607 0511). A workshop in which every craft member has a special skill in the restoration of rare books. They repair both the pages and the bindings, and where any repair would detract from the value of a rare book, they make special containers so that no movement can contribute to the wear and tear. Collectors, dealers and galleries from many parts of the world send their treasured volumes to Tim Siney and his team for their expert attention. Cloth bindings are from £20, leather from £40.

Camberwell School of Arts and Crafts, Peckham Rd, SE5 (01-703 0987). All forms of paper conservation. The college runs several courses, works with museums and can arrange for private work to be done. It will restore family documents, parish archives, photographs, maps and charts.

Kate Colleran, 17 Frognal, NW3 (01-435 4652). Conservation of works of art on paper – prints, drawings, watercolours and ephemera. Kate Colleran teaches at the Camberwell School of Arts and Crafts and uses only materials that are conservation-approved. She will also undertake postcards and posters, rice-paper pictures and curiosities such as pre-cinema 'magic lanterns'.

Studio Bindery, 4 Park Rd, New Malden, Surrey (01-949 2664). Book restoration and rebinding in fine leathers, or books bound to customers' specifications in a variety of materials. Old-fashioned account book binding is among their specialities. Charges from £10.

Elisabeth Thistlethwayte, 62 Lyndhurst Grove, Camberwell, S E15 (01-703 9076). Conservation of early printed books and manuscripts. Having worked as an apprentice paper conservationist and bookbinder, Elisabeth Thistlethwayte gained further practical experience at the conservation departments of the Bodleian Library, Oxford, and Trinity College Library, Dublin. Much of her present work is for libraries, with particular emphasis on the preservation of original binding structures and materials. Her charges are by the hour – about £6.

MANCHESTER

Melissa Hughes, 163 Horton Rd, Fallowfield, Manchester 14 (061-225 1274, after 6 p.m.). Conservation of prints, drawings and watercolours. Melissa Hughes is a paper restorer at Manchester City Art Gallery and in her spare time will treat mould, staining and discoloration, repair tears, reline badly damaged work and undertake patching and retouching. She handles rare and valuable work, but is also willing to restore old family prints which may have nothing more than a sentimental value.

OXFORDSHIRE

Athene Bindery, Church St, Wootton-by-Woodstock (Woodstock 812737). Binding of books, new manuscripts and magazines in vellum, leather with gold leaf and book-cloth hard-back cases. Christopher Shaw and Sarah Pope do not do major paper restoration which includes cleaning and washing, but they can mend tears and they restore valuable books for dealers and private customers. Cloth restoration is from £9, leather from £12, depending on the condition. They also undertake the binding of photograph albums, visitors' books, wedding and christening albums and presentation volumes.

SUSSEX

Limberlost Crafts, 27 Denne Rd, Horsham, W Sussex (Horsham 52658). Antiquarian books restored and rebound, mainly in leather, but also in cloth. Anthony Windrum, having spent his career in publishing, has been closely involved with books for many years and is a member of the Society of Bookbinders and Book Restorers. He will mend small tears in paper but does not claim to be a paper conservationist. He and his talented family sometimes collaborate on the books he writes on local history; his wife, who is a painter in watercolours and oils, contributes the illustrations and his daughter, an expert in needlepoint, designs an embroidered panel for the cover.

YORKSHIRE

John Henderson, Bookbinders, 70 Micklegate, York, N.Yorks (York 24414). A family firm of traditional hand bookbinders and restorers. They have a wide range of calf, morocco, vellum, pigskin, sheep, parchment, cloth and marbled or plain boards and can carry out paper repairs and washing. They specialize in antiquarian books – a fourteenth-century English Book of Hours was one of the oldest they have handled – but also undertake presentation and other bindings in any style.

China and glass

AVON

Ruth Bridgeman, Abbotsleigh Cottage, Freshford, Bath (Limpley Stoke 2218). All repairs and restoration of china and pottery, including dolls' heads. Mould making, modelling of missing parts and filling chips. Ruth Bridgeman's work is of a high standard, and she restores for dealers as well as private customers.

CORNWALL

Clare Beauchamp, Trevince, Redruth (St Day 820355). Antique porcelain restored. Clare Beauchamp concentrates mainly on English and Chinese porcelain for dealers and private clients, but she is willing to undertake all remodelling and repainting, including some enamelling. She has a waiting list of about eight weeks and asks distant customers not to send pieces by post without telephoning first.

Susan Hutton, Sunnybanks Cottage, St Breward, nr Bodmin (Bodmin 850761). China repairs and restoration. Susan Hutton will undertake small cracks and mends from £2 and remodelling from £15. She trained in London and does work for the National Trust as well as for private clients.

CUMBRIA

Cumbria Crystal, Lightburn Rd, Ulverston (Ulverston 54400). A small glass studio which will accept minor repairs. They mend chips and smooth down rough edges from £3.50 per glass. They will also supply stoppers to fit decanters, and where a broken stopper is stuck in the neck, they will drill it out and fit a new one. Prices from £12.50. A postal service is available.

HAMPSHIRE

Just the Thing, High Street, Hartley Wintney (Hartley Wintney 3393).
Restoration of antique porcelain by Sue Carpenter, who owns this antique shop.
Chips, cracks, remodelling and handpainting undertaken. Minimum charge £5.

Mary Rose Wrangham, 25 St Martins House, Clarence Parade, Southsea (Portsmouth 829863). A china restorer who worked for dealers and private
clients for fourteen years and also gives intensive short courses to one student at
a time. Beginners attend from 10 a.m. to 4 p.m. every weekday for three weeks to
learn the basics of remodelling, painting and joining, and the course costs £300,
including materials. Minimum charges £10 for repairs to cracks or chips, £25 for
remodelling.

KENT

Doris del Renzio, 29 Dover St, Canterbury (Canterbury 69560). Repairs
to all types of ornamental china, glazed or unglazed. Doris del Renzio has a diploma
in art and design, and has also studied pottery – she uses the cold method, which
is unsuitable for tableware or pieces in everyday use, but she models and paints
and will also undertake repairs to dolls and papier-mâché, using other materials
but achieving an excellent effect. Much of her work is done for dealers; her charges
are about £10 per hour.

LONDON

F. W. Aldridge, Elizabethan Works, 2 Ivy Rd, E17 (01-539 3717). Bristol
blue glass linings for silverware. There are usually about 40,000 blue glass blanks
in stock, many made from moulds nearly 200 years old, so you can be sure of
finding an exact match. Linings are available for salt, pepper and mustard pots,
sugar, butter and cheese dishes, vases, rose bowls, biscuit barrels, sweetmeat
dishes, preserve pots and prawn cocktail dishes. Specials are possible but take a
long time. Large stocks are also available of stoppers for perfume bottles, apothecary bottles and decanters. Collection service in London and registered postal
service elsewhere. They will also repair drinking glasses and decanters. Open 8 a.m.
to 5 p.m. Brochure available.

Ceramic Restorations, 14 Theberton St, N1 (01-359 5240). Porcelain, pottery and bone china restored. Richard Collins has been remodelling and repainting china for twelve years and undertakes antique and modern pieces, from Dresden figurines and Minton majolica to Art Deco and modern Royal Worcester. He has a minimum charge of £6 and deals with decorative, not domestic, china. He also grinds chips on drinking glasses and decanters (from £3).

China Repairers, 64 Charles Lane, NW8 (01-722 8407). Repair of decorative porcelain and early pottery and also of Battersea and Bilston enamels, using china restoration techniques. Angela Drayson and Pegeen Mair use an old converted petrol oven for firing, and anything that is too big to go in (over 19 in.) is mended and glazed with a cold method. Costs are from £6 for an ordinary cup handle, and from £25 for the remodelling of a hand. They also grind and rebevel chipped drinking glasses (from £5.50 per glass).

Bonita Emms, 45 Gunterstone Rd, W14 (01-603 7105). Mostly antique porcelain restoration, some glass. Figurines and modelling are a speciality. Many restorers use an epoxy resin mixture to remodel missing parts, but Bonita Emms makes them in porcelain, painting, glazing and firing to match the original exactly. She does a considerable amount of work for dealers. Small chips in the rims of cups or plates are from £7, replacement of missing hands or flowers on figurines from £75, smaller remodelling from £15.

General Trading Company, 144 Sloane St, SW1 (01-730 0411). Chipped drinking glasses and decanters ground down from £2.50.

Glass Linings and Repairs Ltd, Unit 5, Lopen Works, Lopen Rd, off Silver St, N18 (01-803 6727). A large stock of blue and clear glass linings for silverware. Most sizes are available immediately from £3 to £5. Odd sizes can be made to order within three weeks – the company has 1,300 moulds or will make a special mould of your piece of silver. Repairs can also be undertaken within a week to glass, decanters, vases, bowls and objets d'art.

Thomas Goode, 19 South Audley St, W1 (01-499 2823). Invisible mending of china, including repainting and gilding to blend with the pattern. From £5.50 for a chipped cup; plate rivets from £1 each. Chipped glasses polished from £3.50 to £4.

Living Art, 35 Kenway Rd, SW5 (01-370 2766). A specialist craft gallery which also offers a range of repair services. They will remove chips from drinking glasses and put silver collars on decanters; clean, restore and frame pictures; provide new bindings for first editions, scrap books and musical scores or restore old bindings in leather or cloth; antique clocks and musical boxes, gilded and lacquered furniture and china can all be restored and repairs can be made to silver. They also engrave glass, table mats or silver to specification for large organizations and private clients.

Studio 1D, 1 Kensington Church Walk, W8 (01-937 7583). All types of antique and modern porcelain restored, including invisible mending and modelling and visible conservation as for museums. Prices start at £5 for a small chip. The studio also offers two-week beginners' courses at £230. There are four a year.

Studio 9, 465 Battersea Park Rd, SW11 (01-228 3155). Restoration of all kinds of china and enamel. This trio of expert restorers, Belinda Johns, Penny Booker and Annabelle Elletson, do a good deal of Chinese restoration work for the trade and private clients, and they also specialize in modern studio pottery. Minimum charge £8.

MANCHESTER

Kendal Milne, Deansgate, Manchester (061-832 3414). John Dearden in the glass and china department will grind down chips in wine glasses or decanters and rebevel from about £4 per glass.

MIDDLESEX

Kate Lane Roberts, 36 Holmesdale Rd, Teddington (01-977 8655). Mainly restoration of antique porcelain, but Kate Lane Roberts is prepared to tackle any china mending and can also cope with glass and enamel repairs. She remodels and repaints, mends chips (from £8), restores figurines (from £35), and also offers private tuition.

NORFOLK

Piers Hart, New Zealand Cottages, Barnham, Thetford (Elveden 212). Specialists in tantalus repairs. The Piers Hart eight-man team are craftsmen in exotic woods, crystal and precious metals and are able to restore and repair antique tantalus, making new parts when necessary, and arranging to match and replace broken decanters. Basic attention to a tantalus, including repolishing the woodwork and re-silver-plating the fittings, is from £70. A new decanter cut to match the original ones is from £90, and this takes about six weeks.

SURREY

Barbara Norman, 9 Downs Lodge Court, Church St, Epsom (Epsom 26570). China restoration of all periods, including remodelling. Barbara Norman undertakes simple joins, without painting, from £15, joining and matching decoration from £20 and remodelling from £25.

SUSSEX

Doreen Brown, Fairlight, Cockmount Lane, Wadhurst, E Sussex (Wadhurst 3432). Mainly antique porcelain and pottery restored for dealers and private clients. Doreen Brown is also particularly interested in the history of her subject. She is a Friend of the Victoria and Albert Museum and of Dyson Perrins, the museum attached to the Royal Worcester company, and will research unusual and interesting pieces for her clients.

WILTSHIRE

Geoffrey Boyle, Winters Penning, Green Drove, Pewsey (Pewsey 3250). Antique and modern porcelain restored for dealers and private clients. Geoffrey Boyle remodels and paints and particularly enjoys restoring figurines and animals or mending and retouching armorial plates. Colour is important – he doesn't enjoy plain white porcelain.

Jane Winch, Westport House, Malmesbury (Malmesbury 2119). Antique and modern porcelain restored, from an early Georgian footbath or a delicate Chelsea figure to a 'mundane soap dish lid' as long as it is ornamental. Jane Winch works with two partners, Pat Paterson and Hilda Jones, each with special aptitudes for modelling, colouring and putting things together, and they undertake work for dealers and private clients.

YORKSHIRE

Janet Larkin, Unit 19, The Piece Hall, Halifax, W Yorks (Halifax 68043, evenings). Pottery and china repairs, from a broken cup to a damaged piece of antique china, by experts at ceramic art restoration. They will remodel and repaint and will also remend badly repaired pieces that have been crudely stapled. Minimum charge £5. The workshop is in a magnificent eighteenth-century colonnaded building, well worth a visit in itself.

Clocks, watches and barometers

BERKSHIRE

Martin Watch Laboratories, London Rd, Binfield, Bracknell (Bracknell 54935). Restoration and repair of all types of watches and clocks, even church clocks. John Martin has been a clockmaker for forty years and makes special parts that other menders cannot reach. He will travel up to 100 miles from his workshop to advise, and says he can make anything out of metal, given the time and the money!

BUCKINGHAMSHIRE

The Watch Shop, 29 Totteridge Rd, High Wycombe (High Wycombe 27313). Antique, modern and long-case clocks repaired and restored. Robert Evans and his wife will recondition cases, relacquer, resilver dials, make parts. Some old clocks have mechanisms as idiosyncratic as their makers, but so far, says Mr Evans, he hasn't met one that he hasn't been able to repair.

CHESHIRE

Barry Lennard, 93 Brook Lane, Alderley Edge (Wilmslow 532070). Restoration of old clocks and antiques. Barry Lennard is a cabinet-maker whose skills include wood-turning, carving and polishing. He uses antique timbers (mahogany, oak and walnut) to match with period furniture, and he will undertake all types of restoration, from replacing a missing knob on a chest of drawers to restoring a fine piece of Chippendale.

KENT

Nigel Coleman, High St, Brasted, Westerham (Westerham 64042). Restoration of barometers, including cabinet-making, resilvering and fitting of new tubes – an important service, as no antique barometer exists with its original tube working. Early ones were made in walnut in the eighteenth century, most were made between 1800 and 1830, and when impurities get into the mercury, air affects the tubes and they have to be replaced. Complete restoration of a stick barometer costs from £50, according to the type of tube. A banjo barometer would be from £75.

LONDON

Roy Bennett, 5 Leeland Mansions, Leeland Rd, W13 (01-567 7030). Restoration and repair of antique clocks and watches. Roy Bennett is an expert of twenty-five years' standing and has dealt with all types of clocks, including a seventeenth-century crucifix clock for a church and an eighteenth-century repeater watch for which he had to make several parts. He resilvers dials and can arrange to regild the case of carriage clocks. His favourites are long-case clocks, and he will also tackle good modern clocks. His work is not cheap, but it is of very high quality. He gives you a five-year guarantee, and collects and delivers all over the country.

Obsolete and Modern Watch Materials, 36–42 Caledonian Rd, N1 (01-837 3838). 'Difficult and impossible' repairs to watches. When Bob Szewczyk, a self-taught watchmaker, was demobbed in this country from the Polish Resettlement Corps in 1947, the only work open to him was in coalmining, farming or the building trade. He chose building and with a little Polish ingenuity managed to get himself transferred to an East End watchmaker. Because no one else seemed interested in saving obsolete watches, he specialized in buying up parts 'here, there and everywhere', and is now more likely than anyone else to have an elusive part for a very old watch. He will also tackle small clocks.

A. R. Roberts, 61a Goldhawk Rd, W12 (01-743 1411). Spare parts and tools for mending clocks and watches. The shop has specialized in the supply of all sorts of spares for fifty-three years, and if you want to tackle your own repairs this is where you will find the missing link.

SOMERSET

Terence Morriss, 11 Patwell Street, Bruton (Bruton 3448). Restoration of antique clocks of all periods. Terence Morriss specializes in long-case, bracket and carriage clocks (no watches) and also restores period furniture, including marquetry, veneering, brass inlay, French and oil polishing. He can collect and deliver within fifty miles.

SUSSEX

Mainly Clocks, 39 Tarrant St, Arundel, W Sussex (Arundel 882871).
Clocks, watches and musical boxes repaired and restored. Robert Beresford is prepared to turn his hand to almost anything mechanical, even converting Victorian coin-operated toys to take 2p, 5p and 10p pieces. He says he mends anything not completely derelict, 'because I don't like to be defeated'. Among his clients is the Curiosity Museum, Arundel, and he is prepared to travel to private clients within eighty miles.

Disability aids

MANCHESTER

Hiltec Services, Hilton Square, Pendlebury, nr Swinton, Manchester (061-793 9263). A rehabilitation workshop which repairs and adapts aids for the disabled and will also consider the manufacture of one-off items or special equipment where no alternative supply exists. The service is available to individuals and establishments and is sponsored by Salford Health Authority and the Manpower Services Commission. The workshop is manned by people who have suffered some form of mental illness, for whom this rehabilitation work can provide an incentive to seek employment in the community. Hiltec also run a leisure information service with details of 6,000 leisure activities, including hobbies, holidays, voluntary services, adult education, social groups and clubs, in and around Greater Manchester.

Furniture

AVON

Tim Dewey, The Cottage, Kelston, Bath (Bath 26810). High-quality restoration of antique furniture. Tim Dewey works for members of the British Antique Dealers Association and for American dealers shipping choice pieces to the US. He is also prepared to accept the least spectacular pieces of furniture for repair – even a kitchen chair – provided a first-class job is required, and will design and make new wood furniture to commission.

CHESHIRE

A. Allen Antique Restorers Ltd, Arden St, New Mills, via Stockport (New Mills 45274). A small workshop employing a specialist team of craftsmen who restore all types of antique furniture. They will do clock repairs (cases and works), boulle work (tortoiseshell and brass), oriental restoration, ivory, marquetry, inlaying, veneering, fretting, carving, gilding and resilvering, leather inlay work and gold tooling, French polishing, modern finishing and upholstery. Work is undertaken for museums and stately homes, and all repairs are guaranteed.

Greenwood of Oulton Mill, Oulton Mill, Little Budworth, nr Tarporley (Little Budworth 282). Experts at stripping and renovating antique pine furniture, including replacement of legs, knobs and drawer mechanisms. They use a water-based sealer inside cupboards and finish the outside of the piece by hand with beeswax. The showroom is in a 1781 flour-mill, and if you visit on a fine weekend there is a pleasant picnic area nearby.

CUMBRIA

Peter Hall Woodcraft, Danes Rd, Staveley, nr Kendal (Staveley 821633). Jeremy Hall is the son of a skilled furniture-maker and has joined the family business to specialize in antique restoration. He undertakes gilding, carving, lacquering, marquetry, inlay, crossbanding, releathering of table tops and bureaux, brasswork repairs and re-upholstery work, using webbing and horsehair and other traditional materials and techniques.

DEVON

Roderick Butler, Marwood House, Honiton (Honiton 2169). Restoration of antique furniture and valuations. These expert services are offered as a contribution to the amenities of the local community, but the main speciality of the family business, started more than forty years ago, is to deal in antique English furniture from the early seventeenth century to Regency. As Roderick Butler feels that 'There is not much enjoyment in bringing home two dozen bow-fronted chests of drawers,' there is particular emphasis on the unusual, and he concentrates on tracking down pieces signed by the maker or those with particularly interesting or curious features.

Tony Vernon, 15 Follett Rd, Topsham, Exeter (Topsham 4635). All antiques restored, whatever the condition. Tony Vernon is a cabinet-maker and joiner and is prepared to rebuild a piece almost from scratch. Having worked for ecclesiastical restorers and on pieces for the National Trust he will do anything from reveneering to wax or French polishing. He will travel within fifty miles of Exeter; otherwise work comes to him from as far afield as London and Gloucester.

DORSET

Robert Bagnell, Dorset Antique Restorer, Stables Farm, Bradford Peverell, Dorchester (Martinstown 312). General restoration work on antique furniture. Robert Bagnell inherited a talent for carpentry and 'took up a wood plane as soon as I could walk'. He was trained on the British Antique Dealers Association restoration course and specializes in boulle work (tortoiseshell and brass), with some marquetry, japanning and lacquering.

Dominic Juett, Ivy House Antiques, The Cross, Shillingstone, Blandford Forum (Child Okeford 860278). Careful restoration of antique furniture, with particular attention to matching the original with old woods and veneers and polishing and colouring by hand. Dominic Juett had a basic woodworking training and does not undertake specialist repairs to lacquer work, marquetry or brass inlay, but he will restore other woodwork, however bad its condition, as near as possible to its original state.

Tolpuddle Antique Restorers, The Stables, Southover House, Tolpuddle, Dorchester (Puddletown 739). Specialists in unusual restoration that cannot be tackled, they say, 'by the little man round the corner'. Two experienced antique restorers offer particular expertise in early English oak furniture, marquetry, lacquer, japanning and gilding in addition to general restoration. They can also call on other craftsmen to undertake cane and rush seating and upholstery. Members of the British Antique Furniture Restorers Association.

ESSEX

A. Dunn & Son, 8 Wharf Rd, Chelmsford (Chelmsford 354452). Specialists in the restoration of marquetry. Founded by Albert Dunn in 1898, this is still very much a family business run by Bob Dunn, his wife, his son, two daughters and son-in-law. The company did the inlay on the original Orient Express and are now refurbishing the present train with the same coloured veneers. They also restore boulle (tortoiseshell and brass) and work for top London dealers as well as for private clients. They also make top-quality reproductions.

Anne Holden, The Glebe House, Great Waltham (Chelmsford 360503). Repairs to chairs, cabinets, bureaux, chests. Anne Holden trained as a cabinetmaker and will also undertake the restoration of veneers and repolishing. Collection and deliveries can be made in Essex.

Carole Thomerson, Poole Craft Studios, Great Yeldham (Great Yeldham 237754). Re-upholstery of the highest quality for museums, collectors and private clients. Carole Thomerson trained at the College of Furniture and has restored many historic pieces for the Victoria and Albert Museum. She takes immense trouble to find the fabrics appropriate to each piece and will arrange to have fabric specially woven if a piece warrants it – and if the client can afford it. Arrangements can be made to have furniture transported anywhere in the UK. She also designs and makes furniture to commission.

GLOUCESTERSHIRE

Richard Fyson, Manor Farm, Kencot, Lechlade (Filkins 223). Restoration of fine furniture. Richard Fyson has been a cabinet-maker for thirty-four years and his special skills include carving, gilding and lathework. He does not claim to be a specialist in marquetry, but if a piece for restoration needs small marquetry repairs he will undertake it.

HAMPSHIRE

L. F. Harris & Sons, 7a Lower Brookfield Rd, Fratton, Portsmouth (Portsmouth 829870). Furniture restorers who specialize in desk leathering. They work for dealers and for private clients and provide a quick service anywhere. A 4 × 2 ft desk would cost around £35 to releather. They also re-upholster small Victorian and Georgian furniture and have a cabinet-maker who will make to commission.

LONDON

M. D. Fisher, 22 Sunbury Workshops, Swanfield St, E2 (01-739 9850). A family business of expert marquetry cutters, now in its third generation. Maurice Fisher and his son Edward have been specializing all their lives in French and English reproductions. They make inlays of all types, including fans, shells and florals for the reproduction furniture trade, and also restore antique inlay for some of the top dealers. They will undertake private restoration work too and some brass inlay.

H. J. Hatfields, 42a St Michaels St, W2 (01-723 8265). Restoration of fine antique furniture, from medieval to the early nineteenth century. This company was established in 1834 and has a long history of top-quality craftsmanship, with specialist skills which include gilding, bronze and metal work, marquetry, boulle, ormolu, terracotta, ivory, clocks, sculpture and works of art.

Richard Holmes, The Chairman, 1 Baronsmead Rd, Barnes, SW13 (01-748 6816). A specialist in chairs who will also undertake any cabinet-making repairs to antique or modern furniture. Richard Holmes will turn small new parts and has a particularly sensitive feeling for wood and the pieces he works on. He also designs and makes furniture to commission, particularly parquetry work and inlaid tables. He will collect smaller pieces in the London area, and travel further if expenses are paid.

The Upholstery Workshop, 13–15 North End Rd, W14 (01-603 9009). Re-upholstery of modern and antique furniture of all periods. The workshop has a huge range of sample fabrics by all the well-known names, and some not so well-known, and reckon to take about six weeks to complete an order. Members of the Master Upholsterers Association.

Watts & Co. Ltd, 7 Tufton St, Westminster, SW1 (01-222 7169). All fields of high-quality restoration, including furniture, needlework and tapestry, silver, metalwork and wrought iron.

MIDDLESEX

B. Hawkes & Sons Ltd, Springwell House, Hayes End Rd, Hayes (01-573 2318). Makers and restorers of fine billiard tables. Anthony Villis is an expert craftsman and will advise customers in their own homes on the restoration of tables. He makes reproductions of old tables up to 9 ft, using only solid mahogany frames and slate beds (a billiard table needs the weight of slate to keep it solid and still). Prices are from £550 for a 6-ft size. Larger tables are all reconditioned old models.

OXFORDSHIRE

The Desk Shop, 41 St Clements, Oxford (Oxford 245524). Restoration of desks and other antiques and reproductions. These specialists will repair lifted veneer, remake plinths and match missing drawers. They also turn knobs and handles to match existing ones or will make sets specially to suit a piece. Releathering and tooling are also offered; a 4 × 2 ft pedestal desk would cost around £55 to releather. They travel all over the south-eastern part of the country and can arrange collection and delivery anywhere. Desks also made to commission.

SOMERSET

Castle House Antiques, Bennets Field, Wincanton (Wincanton 33884). High-quality antique restoration and cabinet-making. Specialities include boulle, lacquer work and marquetry, and pride is taken in the reasonable charges made for work of outstanding quality. They can usually arrange collection and delivery anywhere in the south.

SURREY

Michael Hedgecoe, Rowan House, 21 Burrow Hill Green, Chobham (Chobham 8206). Specialists in the restoration of valuable antique furniture. The twelve-man team will repair, carve, upholster, regild, polish and wax, and will make exact copies to make up sets of chairs – a top-quality service which originated with Michael Hedgecoe's spare-time talent for mending his friends' furniture. He now restores furniture for stately homes, National Trust property, dealers and private collectors in Europe and America. Collection and delivery is available throughout the country, and Michael Hedgecoe is prepared to travel anywhere in the world to advise on restoration.

Ursula St Barbe Spurr, Haslemere (Haslemere 52428). Conservation of papier-mâché and restoration of furniture, including water gilding, oil gilding and lacquer, tortoiseshell and mother-of-pearl inlay. Ursula St Barbe Spurr, who also undertakes the restoration of china, lace and pictures, was until recently at the St Barbe Restoration and Antiques Centre in Haslemere. She is now happy to advise and discuss commissions if you telephone the number given, and she will travel anywhere to collect and deliver or give estimates. Her work can be seen at the House of Antiques, Petersfield Road, Portsmouth, Hampshire.

SUSSEX

John Hartnett, 20 Church St, Brighton, E Sussex (Brighton 28793). Restoration of antique or modern furniture. John Hartnett is a cabinet-maker whose family business was started by his great-grandfather in Paris in 1880. He deals mainly with private clients and some removal and insurance companies for fire and flood damage; he can undertake carving, lacquer, inlay, gilding, leather insets, upholstery and French polishing. He can also arrange for chair recaning. The minimum charge for the repair of a chair is £12, and cabinet work is charged at £8 an hour, which, as he points out, is less than it costs to have your car serviced.

Meeting House Interiors, 26 Meeting House Lane, Brighton, E Sussex (Brighton 26802). Meeting House Interiors have a team of designers and crafts-men to repair and re-upholster furniture, including leather, and three factories to make traditional and reproduction furniture to their customers' requirements. They are willing to quote for design schemes anywhere in the world, at a fee of £10 per hour plus expenses. At their showroom they have an up-to-date range of exclusive fabrics from all the leading English fabric houses.

TYNE AND WEAR

Leighton and Clark, Fairhome, Benwell Village, Newcastle upon Tyne (Newcastle upon Tyne 744437). Specialists in desk renovation, tooled leather tops, stripping and polishing pine, oak and mahogany desks from home or office. They will also refurbish other antique furniture and visit clients' houses to give estimates. Prices vary according to the amount of time needed, but are roughly £20 for stripping and finishing a pine chest, £70 to £80 for a button-back chair (fabric extra), and £180 for a kneehole desk needing to be stripped, polished, fitted with new handles and a new leather top. Most work is ready within three weeks. Ian Macrae Leighton and Gordon Clark also sell antiques.

WARWICKSHIRE

Nicholas Joyce, Alscot Estate Yard, Alderminster, nr Stratford-upon-Avon (Alderminster 345). Restoration of antique furniture, including rebuild-ing, reveneering and repolishing. Nicholas Joyce took a British Antique Dealers Association restoration course at Chichester and worked with a large antique dealer in Scotland before opening his own workshop in 1976. He particularly enjoys walnut, oak and early mahogany, but will undertake any restoration work – even pieces that appear beyond hope.

Taylor & Brook, 5 Greenhill St, Stratford-upon-Avon (Stratford-upon-Avon 69604). High-quality upholstery of antique and modern furniture. Colin Brook particularly enjoys furniture of the Victorian age, because it was 'the heyday of upholstery', and he uses traditional methods for period pieces. A Victorian chaise longue will cost from £120 to re-cover, excluding materials and depending on condition. He can supply a good range of fabrics and can also arrange for chairs to be recaned.

WILTSHIRE

Godfrey Beese & Partners, Church House, East Grafton, Marlborough (Marlborough 810394). Repairs to all kinds of antique furniture. Godfrey Beese describes himself as 'an antique restorer first, cabinet-maker second' and does a lot of fire-damage and insurance work, including French polishing and replacement of desk leathers. He will collect and deliver within sixty miles and is prepared to travel anywhere 'within reason' if expenses are paid.

Furniture – cane and rush

BUCKINGHAMSHIRE

Wycombe Cane and Rush, Victoria St, High Wycombe (High Wycombe 442429). Recaning of antique and modern chairs and supply of cane panels, headboards and small furniture to commission. The company, established 100 years ago, originally made cane chairs and gradually developed the repair side. When the owners retired, Peter and Julie Gilbert, who worked for them, took over the business, working both for the trade and for private customers. A cane bedroom chair seat is from £17.25. They also do rush seats in Dutch rush – about £28.75 for a dining chair, £40.25 for an armchair – and will undertake repairs to woodwork.

CHESHIRE

Stephen Dexter, 9 Manchester Rd, Wilmslow (Wilmslow 523044). Reseating of antique chairs in cane and rush. Stephen Dexter is a perfectionist and will make sure that the pattern of cane is as the original. The charge for cane is 17p per hole; rush seats are from £16.

The Handicraft Shop, 5 Oxford Rd, Altrincham (061-928 3834). Recaning of antique and modern chairs can be arranged through this specialist shop. Four standard patterns are offered, and a small bedroom chair will cost about £18 to reseat. Rush seats are from £22 in Eastern European rush; Dutch rush, available on request, is more expensive.

Gill McKay, 1 Barlow Rd, Chapel-en-le-Frith, Stockport (Chapel-en-le-Frith 814365). Rush and cane seating in various patterns, and bergere suites recaned. Dining chairs are from £16. Victorian furniture is a speciality.

James Smithies, 9 Manchester Rd, Wilmslow (Wilmslow 523044).
Reseating of old and antique chairs in French split cane and natural rush. Charges
are about £16 to reseat a rush dining chair, 16p per hole for recaning – chairs,
bergere suites and bedheads. They will also undertake picture framing.

CUMBRIA

**Cumbria Industries for the Disabled, Petteril Bank Rd, Harraby, Carlisle
(Carlisle 25241/2).** Cane and bergere furniture repaired from £3 per hour. The
workshop, employing severely handicapped people, also makes a range of beds
and other furniture.

Marianne Henry, Briar Cottage, Melmerby, Penrith (Langwathby 701).
Chairs reseated in English rush from £16 for a small dining chair. No cane –
Marianne Henry passes cane inquiries to Miranda Holmes-Smith, who lives nearby
and who returns the compliment by sending rush inquiries to Briar Cottage.

**Miranda Holmes-Smith, Lawson Cottage, Renwick, nr Penrith
(Lazonby 402).** Recaning of chairs in all patterns from 20p per hole – more for
complicated pieces. Collection can be arranged locally – or further afield if she
'happens to be going in your direction'.

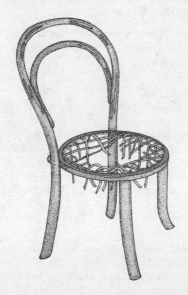

DERBYSHIRE

Joan Gilbert, 50 Ashbourne Rd, Derby (Derby 44363). Antique chairs, bedheads and bergere suites recaned. Chairs re-rushed. All patterns can be done and prices are from about £17 for a small bedroom chair. Seats in English rush from 12p per square inch (measure across the middle of the seat in both directions to assess roughly the total). Fine weave is a speciality. Joan Gilbert works for restorers and stately homes as well as for private clients.

DORSET

Alison Leslie-Jones, The Old Vicarage, Stourton Caundle, Sturminster Newton (Stalbridge 62453). Reseating of chairs in cane and rush. Alison Leslie-Jones taught herself to cane eight years ago when she found the price asked by an antique dealer too high. Friends brought chairs to her 'to practise on' and she gradually learned all types of patterns and, in response to requests, rush seating too. Her standard is now high enough for Sothebys to send her work, and she restores for dealers as well as private clients. Complicated patterns are charged by the hole; ordinary bedroom chairs might cost £7 to reseat, dining chairs £15 to £20.

HEREFORD AND WORCESTER

Isabel Bray, 26 Sandy Bank, Bewdley, Worcs (Bewdley 400103). Chair recaning, both antique and modern. Mainly six-way cane at about 18p per hole. Collection and delivery is free within ten miles.

HERTFORDSHIRE

Centre of Restoration and Art, 20 Folly Lane, St Albans (St Albans 51555). Specialists in recaning in any pattern from all parts of the world, including many that other caners will not tackle. Prices are from £17 for a bedroom chair seat. Alan Messenger is also a carpenter and joiner and will undertake repairs to small pieces of furniture, stripping, staining and wax or French polishing where required.

KENT

Tenterden Rushcraft, rear of 90 High St, Tenterden (Tenterden 3326). Recaning in all patterns and re-rushing. Prices from 20p per hole in cane, and about £30 per seat in rush. Synthetic rush is available for those who want to reseat their own chairs (£5.90 per kilo).

LEICESTERSHIRE

Margaret Littlewood, 18 Main St, Queniborough, Leicester (Leicester 600501). Cane and rush repairs of high quality. Margaret Littlewood learned her skills as a hobby through the Women's Institute and became so expert that requests came thick and fast. She specializes in split caning, particularly of bergere suites, and also reseats chairs in new rush from about £30. A dining chair will cost from £12 to recane.

MERSEYSIDE

Wellington Crafts, 123 St John's Rd, Waterloo, Liverpool (051-920 5511). Recaning with a specialist emphasis on bergere, medallion backs and ray backs. Neville Hymus can offer all caning patterns and will also reseat chairs in rush and cord. A standard bedroom chair will cost around £12.08 in six-way cane, a dining chair from £17.25 in rush. He will also recane modern furniture, where the panels of cane are simply held in by glue, and will do minor repairs to spindles.

OXFORDSHIRE

Kate and Tony Handley, Country Chairmen, Home Farm, Ardington, nr Wantage (East Hendred 362). Restoration of cane and rush seated chairs and frame repairs. Cane patterns are from 25p per hole (more for double and blind caning), and rush seats are available in two grades – thick at £14.25 per square foot and fine at £17.50 per square foot.

SUFFOLK

George Sneed, Bacon's Barn, St Michael, Bungay (St Cross 282). Cane and rush seating repairs backed up by a collection and delivery service anywhere in the country. George Sneed, a furniture-maker for twenty years, has specialized in re-rushing and recaning because of the enormous demand. He uses traditional English and Continental patterns and prices are from about £23.50 for a dining chair 17 × 15½ in. with standard rush seating using sixty strands per foot. Recaning depends on the pattern; an average seat would cost about £25. Delivery charges are according to distance, and a brochure giving details of prices and patterns and delivery zones is available.

SURREY

Pat Dodd, 91 Merton Way, West Molesey (01-979 6635). Recaning in several patterns, including fan-back, medallion and double, and reseating in Dutch rush and seagrass. Patrick Dodd is registered blind and works to RNIB charges, which are extremely reasonable. He also reseats modern chairs with pressed cane (ready-made).

SUSSEX

Alan and Wendy Manser, Barn Cottage, Elsted, Midhurst, W Sussex (Midhurst 6762). Recaning in all types of patterns, including 'the ones a lot of other people can't do'. Prices are from about £14 for a small bedroom chair, more for complicated patterns. Rush seating is also available, from about £25 for a dining chair. The Mansers offer free collection within ten miles and will travel anywhere if required. Their commissions include work for the National Trust.

TYNE AND WEAR

Joy Rich, 49 Larkspur Terrace, Jesmond, Newcastle upon Tyne (Newcastle upon Tyne 811739). Recaning of chairs or bergere suites. Prices are from £15 for a simple bedroom chair; armchairs with sides and back are from £30.

WILTSHIRE

Michael and Robina Pitts, Chairpersons of Marshfield, 119 High St, Marshfield, Chippenham (Marshfield 431). Chair caning and rush seating in a sixteenth-century malting house – Marshfield was a popular stopover on the old Bristol to London coaching route. Fine quality cane seating on chairs and bergere suites from about £15 for a bedroom chair. English rush seats from about £22 for a dining chair. The Pitts have a wide range of other weaving fibres and cords too, and will undertake simple upholstery.

Jewellery, silver and objets d'art

DORSET

Nigel Blades, The Workshop, 21 Princes St, Dorchester (Dorchester 68659). Restoration of small objects, including ivory, mother-of-pearl, papier mâché, tortoiseshell, marble, china and glass. Nigel Blades also repairs clock cases, chess pieces, knife handles, trays and walking sticks. He can arrange for chairs to be recaned, and will try to search out an expert to repair almost anything.

June Philips, 7 Brownsea Rd, Sandbanks, Poole (Canford Cliffs 709800). Beads and pearls restrung. Many jewellers will restring cultured pearls, but few are willing to bother with beads. June Philips threads imitation pearls for £2 per row, cultured pearls for £3 per row. Knotting is extra. She can also supply a good selection of clasps from £1.50 for inexpensive necklaces and from £6 to £40 for more valuable ones. She will also remodel customers' own beads and pearls.

HEREFORD AND WORCESTER

Timothy Blades, 54 High St, Ross-on-Wye (Ross-on-Wye 64560). A designer jeweller currently doing a lot of modern work with titanium, but also expert at repairing antique pieces. He will restring pearls from £3 to £25, according to length and knotting, will reset stones and specializes in repairing the metalwork on violin bows. He likes to tackle unusual things and says he 'gets a kick out of doing things which people say can't be mended'.

KENT

Melvyn Bradley, 27 West Hill, Dartford (Dartford 78650). Modern and antique jewellery repairs and renovation. Melvyn Bradley is a practical jeweller who served his apprenticeship in Hatton Garden. When he first started his workshop he concentrated on repairs for the trade but now deals with private customers too. He doesn't consider himself to be a designer, but will remodel clients' old jewellery and will tackle repairs other jewellers 'have forgotten how to do'.

Breeds, 37 Monson Rd, Tunbridge Wells (Tunbridge Wells 25768), and 27 The Mall, Bromley (01-290 5443). Repair and restoration of cutlery and silverware by one of the few remaining retail cutlers in the country. Breeds was founded in 1829 and apart from selling a wide range of cutlery and scissors will sharpen knives, scissors, pinking shears, saws, hair clippers and chisels, will reblade and rehandle knives and has a master cutler who can restore Victorian and Edwardian hand-forged carving sets and knives. The company also replates cutlery, entrée dishes and tea sets and can supply replacement blue glass liners.

LONDON

F. W. Aldridge, Elizabethan Works, 2 Ivy Rd, E17 (01-539 3717). Repairs to silver-plated tableware. They will also supply and fit handles, insulators and finials for silver tea and coffee pots. Open 8 a.m. to 5 p.m.

Charles Clements, 4 to 5 Burlington Arcade, W1 (01-493 3923). Rebristling of handmade brushes, backed in silver, tortoiseshell and ivory. This

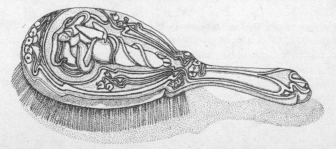

is a laborious service, which is why so few places will undertake it, and you can expect to pay about £3.25 per horizontal row of bristles. The company also has a large selection of knives – they were originally specialist cutlers – and you will find sports knives, hunting knives, scissors, clippers and a variety of manicure and brush sets.

Liberty, Regent St, W1 (01-734 1234). Pearls cleaned and restrung from £10 in the fine jewellery department, which advises attention to pearls every nine to eighteen months, according to wear.

The Pewter Shop, 18 Old Burlington Arcade, W1 (01-493 1730). All types of antique and modern pewter restored by registered pewterers. They will remake lids, handles, feet, using original cast moulds, and will remove silver plate from old pewter, or will polish. Charges are from £10.

Anna Plowden, 39 High St, Kingston-upon-Thames, Surrey (01-549 6471/2). One of the top fine arts restorers in the country, with a royal warrant to prove it. Anna Plowden and Peter Smith, with eighteen skilled craftsmen, will restore anything from life-size marble statues to ancient jewellery, ceramics and bronzes.

Sloane Pearls, 49a Sloane St, SW1 (01-235 9163). Cultured, freshwater and real pearls re-threaded from £5.50 without knots, £6.50 with knots, 16-in. length. Any length possible. You can also take your old-fashioned graduated pearl necklaces to be modernized and restyled – interspersed perhaps with semi-precious beads and crystals and finished with an antique or modern clasp.

Peter Smith Ltd, 39 High St, Kingston-upon-Thames, Surrey (01-549 6471). Top-quality restoration of all three-dimensional fine arts – metal, marble, ceramics, ivory, mounting of objets d'art, everything but furniture. They do work for museums, auction houses and private collectors worldwide, and are experts in techniques that many other restorers no longer practise. 'If nobody else can do it they send it to us.'

SUSSEX

Graham Schofield, Studio 2, Namrik Mews, St Aubyns, Hove, E Sussex (Brighton 722212). Restoration and repair of silver of any period, antique and modern, Graham Schofield was apprenticed through the Goldsmiths Hall in London and worked in the trade for many years before setting up his own workshop in a Victorian coaching yard ten years ago. He is among the few silversmiths to undertake replating – a teapot might cost £20 to £30 to plate, but traditional techniques are used and each item is left in the tank long enough to get a good deposit of silver which will not easily wear off.

WILTSHIRE

Shenstone Restorations, 23 Lansdown Rd, Swindon (Swindon 44980). Restoration of ivory, mother-of-pearl, tortoiseshell, ebony and other woods. Blair and Caroline Shenstone also specialize in inlay and marquetry and will undertake anything from tea caddies and carved chess sets to small furniture. They also repair cane and rush (from £25) and work both for dealers and private clients. They will travel within thirty miles and also make monthly visits to London.

Leather, skins and fur

LONDON

Connolly Brothers (Curriers) Ltd, Wandle Bank, Wimbledon, SW19 (01-542 5251). Specialists in treating leather upholstery – office chairs, car seats, sofas on the *QE2*, the seats in the House of Commons (on the chairs, not the members). They offer a one-day service on motor vehicles, either in their own workshops or at the customer's premises. To clean, feed and refinish the leather interior of a Jaguar would be about £109.25; a three-piece suite costs from £201.25. A renovation kit containing hide food, cleaner, coloured lacquer and cloth swabs is £25. They also produce a special hide food for the care of leather furniture at home: £3.95 for a 6-oz. jar, £4.40 an 11-oz. jar, including postage.

J. Crisp, Leather Gilders and Restorers, 48 Roderick Rd, Hampstead, NW3 (01-340 0668). Leather restorers who have specialized in unusual and valuable pieces since the company was founded by the present owner's great-great-grandfather. Work is done for various museums, and one of the most interesting recent pieces was Admiral Nelson's chair for HMS *Victory*. The black stains on the arm and back differed slightly and with diligent research they discovered that the mark on the back had been made by Nelson's tarred black pigtail and the one on the arm by ink, presumably for his letters to Lady Hamilton. On a less historic level, Crisps supply leather desk tops by mail order. You can choose from a selection of patterns and gilt tooled borders, supply your measurements or a paper template, and the top will be returned with instructions and adhesive. Prices from £10 to £150.

Gerrard Hire, 85 Royal College St, NW1 (01-387 2765). Repairs to animal skin rugs and restoration and recasing of stuffed birds. The original company, founded by Edward Gerrard in 1850, specialized in taxidermy, but now concentrates on hiring stuffed animals for display. The stripping and repair of a skin rug, including restoration of the head, might be about £125. Recasing of a bird – perhaps one bought in a sale in an unattractive case – is from £17.25.

Handbag Services, 16 Beauchamp Place, SW3 (01-589 4975). All types of repairs to handbags, from replacing zips and handles to complete restyling. They specialize in crocodile and can make an elderly hand-me-down look like the latest model from a top designer. They also deal with small luggage repairs and will make petit point into evening bags. They have a mail-order service anywhere.

Jeeves Snob Shop, 7 Pont St, SW1 (01-235 1101), and branches at 11 Heath St, NW3 (01-794 4100), 59 Connaught St, W2 (01-262 0200), and 54 South Audley St, W1 (01-491 8885). High-quality shoe mending – the word snob originated about 1780, according to *Webster's Dictionary*, and is a colloquial expression for a shoemaker, or a cobbler's man. Jeeves repair all shoes and boots including those for golf, riding, safari, climbing, ski-ing, walking and just loafing about. Ladies' leather heels from £3.40, men's leather soles from £5.10, boot zips from £1 per inch, minimum charge £11.40. They also polish and shine boots from £5.50, showerproof shoes from £5.10, and do handbag and luggage repairs.

London Cobblers, 1 Wellington Place, St John's Wood, NW8 (01-722 8424). High-quality shoe repair, from new heels to a complete rebuild. All types of footwear dealt with, including shoes for climbing, riding, golf and ski-ing. Ladies' leather heels are from £3.50, men's half-soles from £10.50, and they can patch uppers, put in new stacked heels, replace boot zips, polish and shine boots and showerproof shoes.

Mayfair Trunks, 3 Shepherd St, Mayfair, W1 (01-499 2620). Suitcases, briefcases and all types of luggage repaired on the premises by a long-serving and skilled staff. The company has been in business for fifty years, is a royal warrant holder and is one of the few in London specializing in luggage. Handbag repairs are accepted too, but these are sent out. Charges from about £4.

SUSSEX

Suede and Leather Care, 30 Preston St, Brighton, E Sussex (Brighton 27488). Specialists in suede and leather restoration who have a department for restoring, refurbishing and replacing leather car upholstery on Rolls Royces, Bentleys and vintage cars.

TYNE AND WEAR

Bart. J. Snowball, 44 Dean St, Newcastle upon Tyne (Newcastle upon Tyne 322894). Specialist saddlers who will also repair leather cases, trunks, handbags, whips, horse blankets and school gymnasium equipment such as vaulting horses and climbing ropes. They have also refurbished the leather seats of an old Bentley, reseated a club fender, and made gun, binocular and camera cases to order. They will also undertake canvas repairs to tents and boat covers.

Metal and machinery

CUMBRIA

Clive Walton Engineering, Rivendell, Cumrew, Heads Nook, Carlisle (Croglin 232). A small company which began in 1976 with two borrowed machines and has now greatly expanded, offering welding, toolmaking, milling and turning, making parts for musical instruments, obsolete domestic machinery, steam engines or lawn mowers. Clive Walton will also do aluminium welding and supplies parts for boats, bikes, trailers and cars.

HERTFORDSHIRE

Iron Things, 2 Hatfield Rd, St Albans (St Albans 68432). All types of metal repairs, including small items. Iron Things will make and repair fire baskets, gates, balustrades, lamps, gate hinges, pan handles and 'all the difficult little things'. They also make metal fire canopies. Prices are based on a charge of £10 per hour.

KENT

Melvin Pinnock, 4 St Martin's Avenue, Canterbury (Canterbury 63279).
Repairs of any metal but pewter. Melvin Pinnock will undertake ironwork restora- ·
tion, replace hinges on harpsichords, copy brass handles and ornaments – no job
is too small, and his prices are very competitive.

LONDON

**Leon Jaeggi & Sons, 232 Tottenham Court Rd, W1 (01-631 1080), and 124
Shaftesbury Avenue, W1 (01-434 4545).** Repair and retinning of copper pans
– widely used by the catering trade and by private customers. Prices from £1 per
diameter inch, depending on the condition. Firm quotations from the head office
and factory (Staines 63663).

**Olympic Sewing Machines, 1c and 1d Shepherds Bush Rd, W6 (01-743
6683).** Repair and sales of all makes of sewing machines in any condition – new,
old, antique and falling apart. The company offers a forty-eight-hour service and
has a large range of spare parts.

Sewcraft, 150 King St, W6 (01-748 0808). Dealers in all makes of sewing
machines who will also undertake repairs. They have a nationwide mail-order
service. A catalogue is available.

Voysey & Knapp, 20 Goodge Place, W1 (01-636 8741). Art metal restoration
and manufacture. This company will repair brass, copper and silver items, make
chandeliers, zinc liners for jardinieres to commission, convert vases to lamps, mend
copper pans, knock out dents, make missing parts. They will make anything in
metal – you provide the drawing of what you want, they will make it up.

SUSSEX

**Robert Carden, 12 Namrik Mews, St Aubyns, Hove, E Sussex (Brighton
738892).** Repair and repolishing of brass and copper. Robert Carden does most
of his work for the trade, but will also refurbish private clients' fenders, bedsteads,
coal scuttles, chandeliers, fire irons. A coal scuttle would cost about £6 to repolish
and lacquer. He can arrange for sandblasting of old grates and fire dogs if necessary.

**Sam Fanaroff, Glynleigh Studio, Peelings Lane, Westham, Pevensey, E
Sussex (Eastbourne 763456).** Restorer of antique metalwork – brass, bronze,
gunmetal, copper and especially pewter, for which he is particularly well-known.
Sam Fanaroff also works to commission for churches and for individual clients. He
enjoys working on a large scale – copper canopies, weather vanes, altar crosses
– but also makes small modern decorative pieces.

Models and toys

CHESHIRE

June Butler Astbury, Dene-Hill Farm, Betchton, Sandbach (Sandbach 2294). Restorer June Butler Astbury has been collecting and restoring antique dolls' houses for more than twenty years, repairing walls, replacing doors and windows, renewing plaster mouldings and then papering the interior walls, often with her own handpainted paper. Fees are according to the complexity of the work. Often up to eight layers of exterior paint have to be stripped before reaching the original paintwork.

LANCASHIRE

John Woods, 180 Chorley Rd, Westhoughton, Bolton (Westhoughton 816246). A husband-and-wife team who restore old rocking horses from virtually any condition – even if they are in pieces. John restores the wood, carves new sections to fit, makes new saddles and replaces manes and tails with real horsehair. Dorothy handpaints in traditional dapple grey. Costs approximately £100 to £150 for a complete renovation.

LONDON

David Barrington Holt, Studio 211, 31 Clerkenwell Close, E C1 (01-250 1942). A restorer of mechanical antiquities with a particular interest in railway subjects – steam and electric trains. David Barrington Holt restores large and small mechanical antiquities from toy boats to enormous mechanical engines for the Science Museum, and is able to make or arrange for any part required. Prices vary according to the work involved, and if clients send a photograph and a brief description of requirements he will give a rough estimate. He also makes fine models or replicas to order.

MANCHESTER

Mo Harding, Wittering Court, 17 Ladybarn Rd, Fallowfield, Manchester (061-224 1621). Renovation of dolls. Mo Harding is a collector with strong views on how much or how little should be restored. She specializes in early wax and china dolls from 1840 to 1920 and refuses to repaint dolls' faces, preferring the original look of the doll. But she will replace fingers and feet, reset eyes and replace eyelashes. She makes new clothes from old fabrics which she adds to the existing garments. A full restoration job would cost around £25.

Doc Higgins, The Dolls Hospital, 28 Piccadilly, Manchester (061-236 6468). An eccentric old character who has repaired dolls in Manchester for over fifty years. He will tackle rag dolls, pot dolls, soft toys and teddy bears, replacing arms, legs and eyes and fixing heads back in position. Many of his doll 'patients' are anything up to eighty years old, handed down from mother to daughter.

MIDDLESEX

Margaret Glover, 42 Hartham Rd, Isleworth (01-568 4662). Restoration of wax dolls. Margaret Glover is one of the very few experts in this field and has only once been defeated by an irreparable face, left in the sun until it was concave. The finest wax dolls have always been made in England by Italian families, notably Montanari and Pierotti, who came here in the 1830s, but unfortunately did not mark their dolls, so identification is something of a detective trail.

SUSSEX

The Dolls Hospital and Collectors Shop, 82 Trafalgar St, Brighton, E Sussex (Brighton 681862). Repairs to antique and modern dolls and teddy bears. Jeff and Carol Jackman have a large stock of parts as well as dolls' clothes and shoes, and they also run classes in doll restoration. They deal with dolls from many parts of the country but will not accept antique dolls by post, as the dangers of damage are too great. A restring on a jointed doll costs about £6 to £10.

Chris Littledale, 65a Buckingham Rd, Brighton, E Sussex (Brighton 23891). Restoration of model trains. Chris Littledale is renowned for his artistry in refurbishing the paintwork of models going back to the 1880s, and collectors send him work from Switzerland, France and America. He began collecting old trains when he was a boy and began to do his own restoration. The work has occupied him full-time for fifteen years, restoring the bodywork and moving parts as well as repainting in authentic colours, and he does a lot of work for the Toy and Model Museum in London. Models of most kinds and rare toys are undertaken (one engine can cost £500 to restore), and smaller work is accepted too, including Dinky toys and lead figures. Chris Littledale's own collection and its unique 1930s working layout can be hired for special exhibitions. It is called 'The Great Vintage Model Railway Show'.

Photography

CHESHIRE

Christopher John Photography, 317 Hale Rd, Hale Barns, Altrincham (061-980 7601). Old photographs restored and copied. Christopher John will copy irreplaceable family heirloom photographs, even if the print is damaged, cracked or torn. The service includes retouching, and he can supply prints in black-and-white, sepia or hand-coloured. Charges are from £10 for a print to be copied to £50 for restoration of a damaged photograph with part of the image missing. He can also supply a handpainted watercolour miniature on mock ivory from a favourite photograph of a child or adult.

LONDON

Jim McFall, 4th floor, 102–108 Clerkenwell Rd, E C1 (01-251 4411). A photographic technician specializing in restoring, reprinting and enlarging old photographs. Faded and creased old prints can be restored to remarkable clarity. Price depends on the amount of work involved, but there is a minimum charge of £10.

YORKSHIRE

G. Whippey, Unit 40, The Piece Hall, Halifax, W Yorks. Family heirloom photographs copied, enlarged and sepia-toned so everyone in the family can have a print of great-grandma and her aspidistra. A framing service is also available.

Pianolas

SUSSEX

Mary Belton, 102b North Rd, Brighton, E Sussex (Brighton 607197). Pianola restoration. Mary Belton has closed her Original Pianola Shop but as pianola specialists are thin on the ground, she will still visit owners and give advice.

Pictures and sculpture

DORSET

Gordon Barrett, 23 Charles St, Dorchester (Dorchester 63422). A picture restorer of high quality and long experience. Gordon Barrett is a third generation of this family business, which has customers in Europe as well as in many parts of the U K. He specializes in all aspects of the restoration of oil paintings and watercolours, retouching, relining and reframing, and works for several museums and famous collections.

LANCASHIRE

Brian Cardy, 2 Portland Cottages, Buckholes Brow, Higher Wheelton, nr Chorley (Blackburn 830216, after 6 p.m.). Cleaning and repair of oil paintings, tempera paintings and wall paintings. Brian Cardy is in charge of the conservation department at Manchester City Art Gallery and will undertake private commissions at home. He repairs tears, relines, removes old retouchings and varnishes and fills and retouches missing areas.

LONDON

Trevor Cumine, 133 Putney Bridge Rd, SW15 (01-870 1525). A specialist in repairing pictures for restorers and dealers and collectors. He will mend tears or replace paint that is coming away from the canvas, which then goes back to the restorer for revarnishing. Prices from £30 to £2,000 – a useful contact for private clients if a picture is torn in a burglary, for instance. One client had hit his intruder over the head with one of his paintings!

Fortt and Bretherton, 40 Blandford Rd, Chiswick, W4 (01-995 3469). Restoration of oil paintings on canvas or panels. Rebecca Fortt and Anna Bretherton particularly enjoy the seventeenth-century Dutch period, although the work sent to them by galleries and private clients now is very varied. They clean, repair and restore, and each commission is estimated individually. As a guide, relining costs from about 5p per square inch, and cleaning of a small painting will be from £25 to £35.

Sebastian d'Orsai (A.B.) Ltd, 8 Kensington Mall, W8 (01-229 3888). Restoration of antique picture and mirror frames, gold-leaf gilding, resilvering of mirrors and restretching of old paintings. This company has specialized in frames for twenty-five years and also cleans oil paintings, watercolours and prints.

MERSEYSIDE

Wellington Crafts, 123 St John's Rd, Waterloo, Liverpool (051-920 5511). Mainly a recaning specialist, Neville Hymus also offers an additional service of stripping, restoring and polishing of old picture frames.

SURREY

Guildford Galleries Ltd, Cranley Court, 59 Cranley Rd, Guildford (Guildford 61646). Cleaning, restoration, conservation of watercolours, drawings, prints and some oils. Brian Mills is a specialist restorer who has recently developed an entirely new system for cleaning art works on paper. It uses ozone as an oxydizing agent, which means that fewer chemicals have to be used and which allows much greater control and safety. His first commercial model was installed in a private art gallery in 1982, and a further model is planned for Camberwell School of Arts and Crafts for use in conservation studies.

YORKSHIRE

Peter J. Hartley, 4 Warrington Terrace, Marsden, W Yorks (Huddersfield 842485). Conservation and restoration of all oil and tempera paintings, from medieval to modern. Peter Hartley will clean and repair pictures on canvas or panel, and provides a complete service.

Sports equipment

LONDON

Harrods, Knightsbridge, S W3 (01-730 1234). Sports equipment serviced in the Olympic Way department. Racquets restrung – tennis £7.50 nylon, £18.50 gut; badminton £15 gut; squash £17 gut. Also reshafting of croquet mallets in two to three days, £16.

Teeth

WARWICKSHIRE

Roberts the Tooth, rear of 35 Warwick St, Leamington Spa (Leamington Spa 27145). Dental and spectacle repairs by Ian Roberts, whose father started the family dental technician business forty years ago. At first they worked only for dentists, but now Ian provides a direct personal service for individual customers – he will repair metal- and plastic-framed spectacles that have broken across the bridge, for instance, and specializes in strengthening dentures. The nickname stuck about twenty years ago and now if he answers the telephone with 'Roberts Dental Technician' people think they have got the wrong number. Personal callers only – no mail order.

Textiles

CHESHIRE

Rosalind Holmes, Deepdale, Hague Bar, Strines, nr Stockport (New Mills 44197). Textile repairs and renovation, including cushions, embroideries, tapestry and upholstered furniture. Rosalind Holmes will tackle anything from a sedan chair to the drapes on a four-poster bed, and will also undertake invisible mending and relining and renovation of clothing and costumes.

The Textile Restoration Studio, 5 Oxford Rd, Altrincham (061-928 8289). Conservation, repair and cleaning of textiles. Jacqueline Pickford has conserved historic textiles for the North of England Museum Service, including the repair of Wordsworth's cape and frock coat, and will restore textiles ranging from family samplers and christening robes to dolls, wall-hangings and ecclesiastical vestments.

DERBYSHIRE

Irene Bobkiewicz, 111 High St East, Glossop (Glossop 3807, after 6 p.m.). A textile conservator who can tackle heirloom samplers, lace, tapestry, carpets, embroideries and costume. Old textiles are particularly susceptible to ageing, so cleaning must be done with care to preserve colours and materials. Irene Bobkiewicz will also strengthen damaged materials and will mount and frame embroideries and samplers. A sampler cleaned, supported and remounted would cost from £25, depending on condition.

LONDON

Atlas Display Co. Ltd, Atlas House, Commerce Way, Croydon, Surrey (01-688 9531). Repairs to scouting and other types of tents, recanvasing of deck chairs and repairs to awnings. This company also makes awnings and hires framed tents.

Anna Christian Textile Workshop, 18 Artesian Rd, W2 (01-229 2855). Repairs to all old textiles, wall-hangings, clothes, samplers and some tapestries (not fine restoration work). Anna Christian collaborates with a dealer in antique silks, velvets and embroideries and will make up cushions and other items from these to order. She will visit customers in the London area.

Jenny Lake Tapestries, 139a Sloane St, SW1 (01-789 0376). Conservation, not renovation, of antique tapestries, mainly from the fifteenth, sixteenth and seventeenth centuries. Eva Fraser trained in France (the name Jenny Lake comes from the name of the Hampshire cottage she shares with her partners, Marian Pearce and Clara Phillips) and is one of the few experts who can conserve very large tapestries. She will clean, repair, reback and then hang the tapestries in situ, and is prepared to travel any distance. Some of her commissions have come from Germany, Switzerland and Holland.

Philippa Scott, 30 Elgin Crescent, W11 (01-229 8029). Conservation and cleaning of textiles and tapestries, carpets and English stump-work, fans, feathers. Philippa Scott also deals in costumes and textiles, particularly from Ottoman Turkey and Central Asia, and in Roman, Greek and Islamic jewellery. She has embroideries from £15 and carpets up to £25,000. The collection is to be seen by appointment only.

MIDDLESEX

Janet Jowitt, 30 Alexandra Rd, Twickenham (01-892 3818). High-quality conservation of embroideries and woven textiles. Janet Jowitt prepares museum-quality textiles for display, cleans and conserves samplers, oriental brocades, re-moves mould and mounts pieces on cloth-covered boards, repairing areas damaged by previous tacks. She will raise the glass away from work that is already framed to avoid further pressure and condensation and will advise on new framing. Charges are £7 per hour – the cleaning of an embroidered picture might be between £30 and £50. She also does work on lace clothing and Persian rugs, but not on very large tapestries.

YORKSHIRE

W. R. Outhwaite & Son, Town Foot, Hawes, N Yorks (Hawes 487). Specialist rope-makers who will also undertake some repairs. Church-bell ropes, for instance, can be repaired from about 20p per ft.

Umbrellas

LONDON

Abdank Ltd, 5 Chiswick Common Rd, W4 (01-995 9718). Repairs to um-brellas and leather goods. Jan Gurawski will recondition, repair or re-cover umbrellas from about £2 minimum and will also repair all types of leather goods – suitcases, trunks, handbags, belts, remodelling bags if the condition of the leather is suitable, and putting right badly designed fittings.

T. Fox & Co. Ltd, 118 London Wall, E C2 (01-606 4720). Umbrellas repaired and made to order. Re-covering an existing frame costs from £9.50 to £18.50.

James Smith & Sons Ltd, 53 New Oxford St, W C1 (01-836 4731). Repairs to good-quality English umbrellas. New ferrules can be fitted from £1, new ribs £2 each, new handles from £2 in plastic, £6 in lacquered cane, £100 in ivory when available.

SUSSEX

Frances Leather Goods, 55 Upper Gloucester Rd, Brighton, E Sussex (Brighton 24492). Umbrellas, antique or modern, repaired. Before settling in Brighton twelve years ago, Albert Frances made umbrellas in Covent Garden – many for London stage shows. The cast of *Charlie Girl* got through four umbrellas a week, as they played sword games with them, and for *Oliver* he had to make *broken* umbrellas. He now concentrates on repairing and will also mend leather goods – handbags and travel cases.

Vehicles

KENT

Croford Coachbuilders Ltd, Dover Place, Ashford (Ashford 23455). Commercial vehicle body builders who will also restore horse-drawn carriages and vintage cars. They make 1,000 wooden wheels a year for horse-drawn vehicles and handcarts, and can build complete new ones if required. They also produce wheel chandeliers and coffee tables with glass tops – the simplest from about £85. There are few vehicles in the Brighton vintage car race that haven't had their attention at some time, they say, and they sell worldwide.

Prices were correct at the time of printing, but are only intended as an indication and means of comparison. Do not send cheques to any company without checking first by telephone on postal charges and availability.

---

4 | Getting Things Restored

Architectural supplies

AVON

Walcot Reclamation, 108 Walcot St, Bath (Bath 310182). A builder's yard full of individual workshops specializing in conservation. There are carpenters, wood-turners, furniture-makers, welders, stone and marble masons, a stained-glass restorer, sculptors, people who will strip pine, replace windows, make fire-bricks, mend vintage motorcycles. If they don't do a particular repair job themselves they will find someone for you.

GLOUCESTERSHIRE

Architectural Heritage, Boddington Manor, Boddington, nr Cheltenham (Coombe Hill 741 or Cheltenham 22191). Period house interiors from 1910 backwards. This company always has between ten and twenty entire panelled rooms in stock and 200 to 300 doors. The workshops will also make cottage doors to any size from period floorboards, with hand-rolled rails. They also stock stained-glass doors, Victorian bathroom fittings and replicas, and at the time of calling they had in stock an entire chemist's shop, a good pub interior and a board room from Lincoln's Inn Fields. Visits by appointment only – hours are flexible.

LONDON

London Architectural Salvage and Supply Company, Mark St, off Paul St, E C2 (01-739 0448). Spare parts for old houses from old houses. Just the place to find a run of eighteenth-century wood panelling, a marble fire surround or exactly the right bricks, tiles or slates to match a period building. LASSCO clear demolition sites and churches, so their stock is always different – one week a collection of washbasins from a wing at the Savoy, another a second-century oak beam from excavations in Pudding Lane. They have 1,000 doors from different periods in stock and will make seats from old pine pews.

OXFORDSHIRE

Hallidays, The Old Cottage, Dorchester-on-Thames (Oxford 340028); also at 28 Beauchamp Place, London SW3 (01-589 5534). Made-to-measure Georgian-style panelling and bookcases, and a large selection of carved pine mantelpieces. There are also fireplaces, grates, marble hearths and surrounds. Prices for mantelpieces start at about £99, and there is a good collection of antique fireplaces too.

TYNE AND WEAR

Abercrombie's, 140 Manor House Rd, Jesmond, Newcastle upon Tyne 2 (Newcastle upon Tyne 817181/2). Restoration in period style – a trend which has only recently become popular in the North-East. Architect and antique dealer Christopher Stell buys old fireplaces, wall panelling, door furniture, shop shelving and other architectural features from demolished buildings to use in his restoration work, or he will find craftsmen to make suitable reproductions. He will make plans for a restoration commission and supervise the work, including rewiring, heating and decorative work, all of which his company will undertake. Consultation and advice: up to one hour free; outline estimates and sketch plans: free. Detailed plans and drawings: approximately £15 per hour (payable only if the work is not eventually commissioned).

Awnings

LONDON

Atlas Display Co. Ltd, Atlas House, Commerce Way, Croydon, Surrey (01-688 9531). Canvas awnings made to order. The company specializes in hiring and erecting large framed tents and pavilions and provides awnings for grand-stands and exhibitions. Domestic awnings are available from 4 ft to 23 ft wide and cost from £103 (unfitted).

Bathrooms

CHESHIRE

The Bath Re-enamelling Company, 55 Main Rd, Worleston, Nantwich (Nantwich 626554). Re-enamelling of old baths whose surfaces have become pitted or discoloured. The process, involving four coats of air-dried enamel, takes about two hours and is available in white, all standard modern bath colours and the basic green, pink and primrose used in the fifties and no longer available. They will travel anywhere and the cost is the same regardless of distance – £46 in white, £52 in colour.

LONDON

A Bigger Splash, 119 Fulham Rd, SW3 (01-584 7454). Baths available in a variety of shapes, colours and sizes – round, square, metallic, sunken, double or whatever else you fancy – even a cloverleaf. There are 250 colours, and materials range from cast iron or fibreglass to marble. Prices start at £200 for a plain white bath and can reach several thousand.

Renubath Services (London), 108 Fulham Palace Rd, W6 (01-741 7307), and branches. The original bath renovation company, established eighteen years ago. They have a minimum charge of £28.75 for cleaning and renovation, can repair enamel chips from £8.35 each and will completely resurface the bath in white at £61 or in colour for £71.30. They operate nationally; the head office address will give you local branches.

Sitting Pretty, 131 Dawes Rd, SW6 (01-381 0049). Traditional wooden lavatory seats and genuine Victorian and Edwardian bathroom pieces. The seats are in solid mahogany or obeche in various colours and there are DIY kits too. Prices of handbasins and lavatories from £85 to £500; kits from £35; finished seats £49.50 to £65.

Woodentops, Wells Yard, Holloway Rd, N7 (01-609 5177). Wooden lavatory seats in mahogany at £47.50 or pine at £39.45 (also available by mail). There are bathroom fittings to match – soap trays and shaving stands, for instance, mirrors and toothbrush holders.

SURREY

Peter Fenton & Co., Fernhill, Horley (Horley 75357). Spa-bath conversion kits to turn almost any modern bath into a home jacuzzi. The package includes a motor pump, three to six jets, air controls and switches and can be added by a plumber to an existing suite or installed when a new bath is fitted. Called Whirlpool Conversion Kits, they cost from £287.50 to £805 through bathroom showrooms or direct from Peter Fenton, who specializes in bathroom and sauna equipment.

Conservatory extensions

CO. DURHAM

Amdega Ltd, Faverdale, Darlington (Darlington 68522); and at Zodiac House, 163 London Rd, Croydon, Surrey (01-688 0629). One of the largest specialists in conservatory-type home extensions. Amdega traces its history back to Richardson & Co., which began making conservatories in 1874, and their current designs are based on the Victorian originals. The frames are Western red cedar, which can be painted or left plain, and the shapes are mainly octagonal and lean-to. The standard range starts at £1,563 for 12 ft 1 in. × 8 ft 8 in. without installation, and special commissions can be undertaken.

LONDON

Machin Designs Ltd, 4 Avenue Studios, Sydney Close, SW3 (01-589 0773). Glass conservatory extensions with timber and aluminium frames in several styles, including one with a unique ogee-shaped roof. Francis Machin is an ex-architect who was frustrated by designing large buildings which took years to complete, and so he turned to designing complete small structures, including summerhouses and garden pavilions. The conservatories can be used as a roof-top extension or, more conventionally, as an attachment to the house at ground level, or they come in lean-to versions. The Gothic arched roofs, with the ogee double curve, have automatic ventilation. Prices about £7,000 for an extension 18 square metres, plus £1,500 for installation.

SUSSEX

Room Outside, Goodwood Gardens, Waterbeach, nr Chichester, W Sussex (Chichester 776563). Glass conservatory house extensions. A basic modular frame in wood and aluminium is available; panels come in 2-ft, 4-ft, or 4-ft 8-in. widths, 7 ft high or 5 ft 6 in. high set on a dwarf wall, so almost any shape is possible, including lean-to. A simple extension 10 ft 4 in. × 7 ft 2 in., 7 ft high, would cost about £2,100, without installation, but including the supply and fixing of the glass.

Fires, stoves and chimneys

CHESHIRE

The Fire Place, 24 Victoria Rd, Hale (061-941 2768). Individually designed fireplaces for period or modern houses, plus all the accessories. You can have dog grates from £55, 'real flame' gas fires from £130, fenders made to measure from £100. The company will install the fireplaces too, and can also supply plaster mouldings for cornices.

CUMBRIA

Tobias Fires, Barrow Hollin, Cartmel Fell, Grange-over-Sands (Newby Bridge 31231). Beautiful and unusual electrically powered cast-iron stoves in matt black or coloured lustre enamel. They are made by potter Toby Harrison, who hit on the idea when he needed an electric fire for his seventeenth-century cottage. He crafted one in earthenware in a Victorian design and used an element from an electric stove. Now he has them cast in iron in order to market them in quantity. They have a 1.25 kW heating element and a separate light to give glow when no heat is needed. Prices from £180 (matt black) to £230 (enamel), plus carriage. An illustrated leaflet is available.

LONDON

Acquisitions (Fireplaces) Ltd, 269 Camden High St, NW1 (01-485 4955). Carefully restored Victorian and Art Nouveau cast-iron and wood fireplaces, some with original tile surrounds. Most of the cast-iron ones are not rare, but the Art Nouveau carved wood fireplaces are often unique, having been made to order for a specific house. Prices are from £95 to £800. There is also a range of reproduction cast-iron fireplaces made from original 1860s moulds.

Jocelyn Burton, 50c Red Lion St, WC1 (01-405 3042). New solid-fuel or wood-burning stoves, designed by Jocelyn Burton along the old-fashioned lines but made to work well in modern houses. There are two styles available in four or five colours and they are priced from £450 to £1,000. A brief brochure is available.

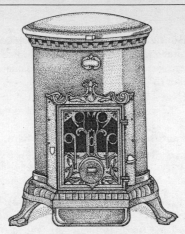

Old French Stove Co., 27 Clapham Mansions, Nightingale Lane, SW4 (01-673 7826). A wide selection of intricate French enamelled cast-iron stoves, all original and carefully restored and made serviceable. Some are wood-burning, some solid-fuel or mixed, and prices range between £180 and £500. Details are available by post.

Real Flame Log Fires, 80 New King's Rd, SW6 (01-731 2704/3056), and at 141 George St, Edgware Rd, W1 (01-402 8739/9006), 1181 Finchley Rd, NW11 (01-455 9473), and 29 Widmore Rd, Bromley, Kent (01-290 1548). Log- and coal-effect gas fires from about £85, designed if necessary to suit individual grates. There are also carved pine surrounds and brass fire irons and dogs. Brochures showing the different designs are available. Real Flame supply more than 100 stores throughout the country. Telephone the King's Road number for local suppliers.

Strax Distribution, 41b Brecknock Rd, N7 (01-465 7056 or 01-267 2660). For really difficult chimneys, this company supplies (but does not fit) an electric fan called the Exhausto to fit instead of a cowl. It is controlled from a switch near the fireplace and costs from £200 to £320.

Townsends, 81 Abbey Rd, NW8 (01-624 4756). A large stock of restored period fireplaces in wood, iron and marble. Prices start at about £150 for a restored stripped pine surround, or for a cast-iron insert. Townsends will accept restoration work and offer a fitting service in North London. They also have a range of stained-glass doors and other items for architectural restoration.

MIDDLESEX

Marble Hill Gallery, 72 Richmond Rd, Twickenham (01-892 1488).
Victorian firescreens and fenders and French marble mantels. The company also makes Adam-style firebaskets and hand-carved pine mantels. A brochure is available. Prices start at about £115 for a simple mantel.

STAFFORDSHIRE

Red Bank Manufacturing Co. Ltd, Measham, Burton-on-Trent (Measham 70333). Chimney pots to go with the stacks that go with the flues that go with the fireplaces that Jack's Dad built and bricked up and that Jack is now opening up as fast as he can. Red Bank have been specialists in chimney pots since 1919, and traditional designs are available in red terracotta, buff fireclay and blue black from £10 to £250. Commissions for special designs can be undertaken.

SUFFOLK

Chimney Specialists Ltd, Jubilee Works, Meekings Rd, Sudbury (Sudbury 75404); also at Units 3/4, Block 2, Woolwich Dockyard Estate, Church St, London SE18 (01-855 9009). The answer to a chimney that smokes, as so many do now that fireplaces are being opened up again. This company will advise and provide a service from the design to the supply stage. They don't install, but will recommend local contractors.

SUSSEX

Grate Restorations, 85 Gloucester Rd, Brighton, E Sussex (Brighton 699067). Restored period fireplaces for sale. John Hynam started his business three years ago because he couldn't find a suitable grate for his own house, and he now has about 300 in stock – cast-iron, marble, pine, mahogany, oak. Some wood surrounds are as little as £35; a restored Victorian or Art Nouveau grate with painted tiles would be about £150. No reproduction, and no restoration of customers' fireplaces.

WEST MIDLANDS

James Smellie Limited, Stafford Street Works, Dudley (Dudley 52320).
Specializing in metalwork for fireplaces, this company produces hand-hammered copper, brass, bronze or stainless-steel canopies, frames for hole-in-the-wall fires and cooker hoods, all to order in almost any size. Canopies and cooker hoods are from about £120, and there is a range of dog fires and firebacks in cast iron.

Fitted furniture and units

CHESHIRE

Greenwood of Oulton Mill, Oulton Mill, Little Budworth, nr Tarporley (Little Budworth 282). Custom-built kitchens in old pine. This company will supply basic units or do individual designs picking up the character of the property. They pride themselves on making use of every inch of space, which they claim can reduce costs of materials – a standard 600-mm base unit (pitch-pine door on beige melamine interior) costs from £218. Alternatively, solid timber units with timber carcase and framework can be supplied. A full design and planning service is offered, including the supply of appliances and all plumbing, plastering and re-decorating work. Antique pine dressers, chairs and tables are available from the showrooms. They also make fitted bedroom furniture, coping if necessary with unusual room shapes or cottages with sloping ceilings, and making pine bedheads, doors, skirtings, architraves and window sills to match. A 4-ft 6-in. wardrobe costs from £200, including fitting.

Martin Moore & Co., 28 Church St, Altrincham (061-928 2643). If you are looking for an alternative to a slick, streamlined kitchen, this small company will produce one that looks pleasantly 'warm and worn'. Their antique timber kitchens are made from recycled pine, which is better seasoned and has a nicer grain than modern timber. They will plan the layout, supply all the appliances and will even incorporate other antique pieces, such as a church pew or a pulpit. They also supply skirting boards, window casings, architraves and beam casings made to traditional styles from old timber. A 1,000-mm base unit for a kitchen costs from around £250.

LANCASHIRE

F S I Furniture, Kellet Rd, Carnforth (Lancaster 735076). Panelled or cane-work wardrobe doors supplied for you to fit yourself. Maximum width is 24 in.; the height is 6 ft 6 in. The cane panels can be reduced in height so that they can be used to box in central-heating radiators. Woven cane is also available by the metre in 14-in., 16-in., 20-in. and 24-in. widths, at £1.50 per square foot.

LONDON

Robert and Colleen Bery, 8 Rosehill Rd, S W18 (01-874 5542). Handpainted friezes, borders, screens and furniture. Robert Bery will design a complete room, making fitted furniture or one-off dressers, cabinets and coffee tables, and his wife Colleen will handpaint them to blend with the style of the house. Alternatively you can have your own furniture revamped with hand decoration – tables from £35, chests from £75, bedheads from £45. They also have a range of mirrors with decorated frames and can provide decorative blinds and screens in a range of seven designs, or to special commission. Prices from £60 per panel.

Greenwich Wood Works, 14 Royal Place, Greenwich, SE10 (01-858 1800 or 01-639 2178). Purpose-built kitchens and furniture. John Bradley's aim is to make imaginative furniture with traditional techniques, and he is adept at using every inch of space to advantage. He works in new and old pine, oak, mahogany, brick, tiles and marble, and makes built-in units to match existing furniture – dressers, cupboards in chimney breasts, units to cover washing machines in dining areas. Prices are very reasonable for hand work – for instance, about £130 to £170 for a pine double base unit.

Magnum Kitchens, Mercy Terrace, Lewisham, SE13 (01-690 1081). Custom-built kitchen units in anything from laminates to solid wood. The company began in a small way ten years ago and now provides a comprehensive service within fifty miles of London. They can supply units and fit them if required, will work with a builder, and can even undertake whatever rebuilding is needed. A brochure is available. The company is a member of the British Kitchen Furniture Manufacturers Association.

Alexander Sare, 33 Green Lane, N16 (01-226 5872). Fitted library units, television and other cabinets, all to commission and tailor-made for individual rooms. Modern or reproduction period styles can be made to measure in mahogany, oak, ash or beech solids or veneers, for private houses or office suites. The prices are reasonable for custom-built furniture; a 5-ft bookcase with a cocktail section, for instance, would be about £325.

Whitehead & Lightfoot, Block 4, Avon Trading Estate, Avonmore Rd, W14 (01-603 4237). Distinctive cabinet- and furniture-making and specialist joinery, from sash windows, doors and tables to fitted libraries and kitchens. David Bailie-Whitehead and David Lightfoot will design for clients or work to architects' specifications, and their work is beautifully made and finished in well-chosen combinations of timbers.

Woodstock, 23 Packenham St, WC1 (01-837 1818 or 01-837 3220). Personally designed kitchens, hand-built throughout, in solid maple, cherry or walnut. Alf Martensson has inherited his design talent and love of wood from his Swedish origins, and he and his co-designer, William Hodgson, provide a complete service, advising on appliances, tiling, lighting, flooring and ventilation as well as designing functional and very handsome units. The beautifully grained but rock-hard maple is used for the tops too, and any marks can be easily rubbed out. If you don't believe it, prove the point by spending £4 or £5 on one of their maple chopping blocks; you will never be satisfied with a plastic laminate again.

MANCHESTER

KMC Shopfitters and Fine Joinery. Showroom: 2 Cecil Rd, Hale Manchester (061-928 8410); factory: Bank Hall Lane, Manchester (061-928 5997 or 061-941 3129). Kitchen, bedroom or bathroom furniture made to order. Any sort of cabinet-making work, fitted furniture in wood or spray finishes, arches or doors in traditional or modern style. Designer David Caper will also draw up complete extension schemes. The preliminary consultation with estimate is free. There is a minimum charge of £40 for bedroom and bathroom layout plans with samples.

SOMERSET

Graham Colyer, Rose Cottage, Barrington, Ilminster (Ilminster 3007). Tailor-made kitchens and bathrooms to order. Graham Colyer will build kitchens to order in pine, oak, teak or whatever the client prefers, with the emphasis on creating a furnished look rather than just a series of units. He keeps a file of suggested equipment that will blend in well with this theme and is particularly good at solving awkward problems. If the budget is tight he will also fit commercial units, making them look as individual as possible with his use of tiles and surrounds.

WARWICKSHIRE

Hathaway Country Kitchens, Clifford Mill, Clifford Chambers, Stratford-upon-Avon (Stratford-upon-Avon 205517). Custom-built kitchens hand-made in English hardwoods – oak, walnut, ash, cherry and syca-more – and also in pine. Alan Moxon and Roger Jones will design anything to customers' requirements and have been doing so for fourteen years. They supply equipment – mostly Neff and Gaggenau – and will include leaded and stained-glass panels and copper canopies if that is what pleases. They also make one-off pieces of furniture to complement their kitchens, can restore antique furniture and offer a variety of paint finishes, including rag-rolling, dragging and stencilling. A very versatile and flexible company in a lovely old mill by the River Stour.

Gardens and paths

BERKSHIRE

Garden Consultants and Landscape Specialists, 28 Lower Cookham Rd, Maidenhead (Maidenhead 74484). Garden design service anywhere in the

U K. Gardens are surveyed and planned with particular attention to prolonged flowering periods, autumn colours and variety of winter foliage. The company also specializes in the reclamation and maintenance of lawns and grassed areas. There are local advisers in Staffordshire, West Sussex, Gloucestershire and Devon (addresses from head office, above).

CHESHIRE

Philip Swindells, Hill View, Whirley Lane, Henbury, Macclesfield (Macclesfield 22476). Garden fencing made to measure. Heavy-duty panels are well made, well finished and very strong. The main product is waney lap fencing panels, but other types, including vertical close board, interwoven and palisade, are available. A 6 × 6 ft waney lap panel costs about £11.27. The company can also supply and cut timber and weatherboarding for D I Y, and provide garden sheds, softwood posts and rails and garden gates to match the fencing panels.

David and Robin West, Garden Design and Construction, Birchtree Farm, Henbury, Macclesfield (Macclesfield 23270 or Alderley Edge 585348). Landscape gardeners who will draw up a plan of a garden appropriate to the amount of time you can spend looking after it. They will carry out all the work, including planting and decorative paving. They will also build walls, patios, rock gardens and ornamental pools. If required they can also introduce you to a reliable maintenance contractor to keep up the good work. They aim to match the garden to the house, so a Tudor cottage would have old stone flags, yew hedges and herbaceous plants, while the garden of a modern house would include bolder features. Average cost of a garden would be £1,000 to £2,000, and their £25 design fee is waived if the work is put in hand.

CUMBRIA

Coasthead Troughs, High Close Farm, Plumbland, Aspatria (Aspatria 20204). Handmade plant troughs with the appearance of stone but actually made of a mixture of sand, peat and cement, which weathers to an 'antiqued' finish. Prices are from £5 to £20 – usually the troughs are bought ready-planted with alpines, which are extra.

DORSET

Knight Terrace Pots, Manor Farm House, West Orchard, Shaftesbury (Sturminster Newton 72685). Specialists in cast stone work, including garden ornaments, urns, pots, troughs, balustrading and obelisks. Various colours are available, and prices for the standard range are from £10 to £75. Special designs or copies can be made to order, including coping stones, fireplaces, church altars, window mullions, in a selection of stones including Portland, Bath, Cotswold, Ham Hill and red and green sandstones.

GLOUCESTERSHIRE

John Rainbow, Badgers End, Fosse Way, Stow-on-the-Wold (Stow-on-the-Wold 31103). Garden architectural commissions in Cotswold stone, all designed to weather and mature and all one-offs – 'I don't make casts or concrete ghastlies!' A self-taught sculptor – the ram's head at Ramshead Art Gallery, London, is his – he is happy to tackle anything, including wall plaques, lamp bases, pedestals, sundials. He welcomes visitors to his studio workshop, where examples of his work can be seen in his garden. Prices are from £7.

KENT

British Gates and Timber Ltd, Biddenden, nr Ashford (Biddenden 291555). Traditional timber garden gates and fencing in a range of designs, two of which have Design Centre approval. They are mostly available in European redwood which is pressure-treated, giving a green tinge which can be stained or painted. The smallest garden gate is about 3 ft square, the largest 12 ft wide. Prices are from £15 for a cottage gate to about £100 for a large five-bar gate. The company does a considerable amount of work for National Trust properties and has a range of hardwood doors in period and modern designs from about £170.

Malling Pre-cast Ltd, Wouldham, Rochester (Medway 61017 or 61601). Artificial stone castings for churches and period houses, plus commissioned work in pre-cast concrete and stone. Their work includes balconies, columns, spiral staircases, mullions, flower and shrub containers as well as a variety of other products. Prices are quoted individually.

LEICESTERSHIRE

The Greensward Company, The Old Hall, Langham, Oakham (Oakham 2923). Fake lawns for roof gardens, artificial cricket pitches, practice putting greens, swimming pool surrounds and children's playrooms. Lazylawn Fungrass comes in 12-ft and 16-ft widths at £7.95 per square yard and is fixed with adhesive; Summertime has a heavier pile and can be loose-laid – available in the same widths at £10.95 per square yard. Both come in olive or emerald.

STAFFORDSHIRE

Rookes Pottery, High St, Ipstones, Stoke-on-Trent (Ipstones 606). Hand-thrown terracotta garden pots and planters, including wall pots. The range is standard, but individual commissions could be undertaken for, say, a large jardiniere. Small pots from 85p; jardinieres around £24.

SUFFOLK

Crawford Balch, Derrybrook Farm, Stowmarket (Debenham 860266, evenings). Traditional osier panel fences woven on site. Crawford Balch, having been in farming all his life, decided to grow his own osiers, and from them he makes attractive fences to the height and shape that will best suit the garden in question, sometimes making arches and special features to lead the eye to a point of beauty or special interest. Charges are about £1 per square foot, and the fences will last up to twenty-five years. He prefers to work within fifty miles of Stowmarket, but will travel further if necessary.

SUSSEX

Southern Tree Surgeons Ltd, Crawley Down, W Sussex (Copthorne 712215). Advice on ailing trees, backed up by a full service which includes planting, felling, pruning, feeding, and removing tree roots by stump-cutting machine. A complete arboreal service is provided throughout the UK, Ireland and Europe, and free estimates are given following inspection. There are offices in Berkshire, Gloucestershire, Staffordshire, Suffolk, Devon, Scotland and Ireland; a brochure listing addresses and telephone numbers is available from head office, above.

WARWICKSHIRE

Jim Keeling, Whichford Pottery, Whichford, nr Shipston-on-Stour (Long Compton 416). Handmade terracotta plant pots, from small ones at 50p to giant 25-in.-wide pots at £54.50. Jim Keeling says the best advice he ever had, from the fourth-generation potter who taught him, was never to go near a studio potter, but to learn to hand-throw. Plants like his pots because they are more porous than machine-made ones and they are frost-proof. Customers are welcome at the pottery weekdays and Saturdays.

Roadrive, Queensway Trading Estate, Leamington Spa (Leamington Spa 24236). Specialists in tarmac, this company will lay private drives and paths in other materials too – paving slabs, the block paving popular in Europe and now being done here, self-setting gravel and various finishes of tarmac. A civil engineering company, Roadrive has worked for local authorities for many years and has a small associate building company. Each job is estimated on site and the work is of high quality – 'Don't be misled by cheap prices, there are too many dodges in tarmac.'

Lighting

LONDON

N. Davighi, 117 Shepherds Bush Rd, W6 (01-603 5357). Chandeliers and light-fittings restored and rewired. Nevio Davighi, who has been a lighting specialist for thirty years, can undertake the restoration and making of all types of chandelier. The larger, important ones can cost as much as £2,000 to refurbish, but small domestic lighting is accepted too – conversion of bedchamber sticks to electricity, for instance, or small rewiring and polishing work from about £15.

Turn-On Ltd, 116–118 Islington High St, Camden Passage, N1 (01-359 7616). Original light-fittings from 1860 to 1920. Some of the rare ones are available for hire only, but there is a large selection of early Victorian and Art Nouveau chandeliers, wall lights and table lamps. Prices are from £56.

Christopher Wray's Lighting Emporium, 600 King's Rd, SW3 (01-736 8434), and branches. A huge stock of reproduction Victorian and Edwardian light fixtures and shades. There are wall lights, standard lamps, desk lamps, table lamps, some of them available by mail order. Christopher Wray also has one of the largest collections of original antique fittings, which are carefully restored and released for sale regularly in small quantities. The Lamp Workshop at 613 King's Road, almost opposite, sells spare parts for lamps, including globes and chimneys for oil lamps.

SUSSEX

Sugg Lighting, Massrealm Ltd, Napier Way, Crawley, W Sussex (Crawley 21874). Specialists in gas lighting, period and reproduction. The company, which was established in 1837, restores and refurbishes period gas lighting for private clients and for the Houses of Parliament and the royal parks and palaces. Their main business is the production of a range of handmade gas lights, most of which are designs taken from original Sugg catalogues of 1897. Prices are from £30; lamps in the style of gas lights but powered by electricity are also available, from £20. A brochure is available.

Woodall & Emery, Haywards Heath Rd, Balcombe, W Sussex (Haywards Heath 83608). Founded in 1884 this company prides itself on having as large and comprehensive stock of genuine Edwardian and Victorian lighting as any London specialist. The emphasis is on turn-of-the-century lighting and everything is excellent quality, from simple Dutch wall brackets at £85 to elaborate chandeliers at £6,000. They have their own craftsmen who will restore metal and glass fittings.

Metalwork and forged iron

AVON

J. A. Keenan, 3 Cranleigh Gardens, Stoke Bishop, Bristol (Bristol 682507). Specialists in making locks to order for period doors, incorporating modern techniques to give maximum security. John Keenan makes locks to fit existing keyholes so that handles can remain in their original positions and the features of the doors remain unspoiled. He has fitted locks to listed buildings and can deal with anything from a cottage to a castle.

CUMBRIA

Alan Dawson, Balnakiel Forge, Solway Estate, Maryport (Maryport 815320). One of a growing band of craftsmen who describe themselves as 'artist blacksmiths', producing decorative wrought ironwork of high artistic quality, from table lamp stands to an 8-ft-high tree for a wine bar. Alan Dawson's work has been commissioned by the National Trust and many international companies, and he exports to America and Europe. He will undertake any commission for private or architectural clients; pokers start at £10, fire screens at £45, fire baskets from £85.

Ian Rogers, Long Meg Mines, Little Salkeld, Penrith (Langwathby 264). A wide range of ironwork, from simple forging to the finest-quality ornamental black-smithing. Ian Rogers uses both traditional and modern methods and can cast original sculptures, decorative motifs, or reproductions of almost any object. He also makes iron wood-burning stoves, builds dry stone walls and works in silver, and he will accept commissions for any one of his skills. The attraction of his designs can be assessed by the fact that one lady was so determined to have a pair of his wrought-iron gates, which she saw at an exhibition, that she had to build a wall to justify buying them. Charges are £4.50 per hour, plus materials.

Stobart and Brown, Cumrew, Heads Nook, Carlisle (Croglin 279). Fire canopies, dogbasket grates, pokers and wrought-iron gates made to customers' own specifications. Also all types of metal agricultural equipment made and wagons and industrial trailers mended. Costs around £5 per hour, plus materials.

DORSET

Michael Malleson, The Trent Smithy and Studio of Contemporary Ironwork, 42 Rigg Lane, Trent, Sherborne (Marston Magna 850957). Hand-forged iron work. A member of the British Artist Blacksmiths Association, Michael Malleson concentrates on developing new designs rather than copying traditional ones, although he will do so if particularly requested. His own designs are simple and free-flowing and would look well in modern or period houses. He makes fire-screens from about £75, grates from £150 to £250, fire irons from £50 for a set of three, and he also undertakes sculptural ironwork for indoor and outdoor display.

ESSEX

Tim Wheeley, Water Lane Forge, Tylers Cross, nr Roydon (Roydon 2260). Tim Wheeley describes himself as 'very much the local blacksmith, prepared to tackle a variety of jobs'. He is not a farrier, but he will undertake work on farmers' machinery or for builders and private clients. He specializes in decorative ironwork, making ornamental gates from £100, fire baskets and fenders and weathervanes – his favourite commission – from about £75.

GLOUCESTERSHIRE

Austin Nicholls, The Old Smithy, Lower Swell, Stow-on-the-Wold (Stow-on-the-Wold 30041). Traditional wrought-iron work, brass and bronze work. In addition to iron firescreens and baskets, Austin Nicholls makes brass firescreens, Queen-Anne-style lanterns, Louis XIV wall lights, weathervanes and unusual wind dials – he was commissioned to design and make a replica of the one in Kensington Palace. He restores all types of antique metalwork and is one of the few craftsmen who can restore the equally rare spit engines fixed in the eighteenth century to beams over fireplaces. Prices range from £5 for a poker to £250 for chandelier fittings. He also makes 12-in.-diameter platters in nickel silver and, unusually, pinchbeck.

Michael E. Roberts, Anvil Barn, Miserden, Stroud (Miserden 244). A forge specializing in brass, bronze and aluminium. Michael Roberts makes many forged items, from brass paper knives at £14 to balustrades and bronze fountains and sculptures. His style is simple and functional, modern but not way-out, and typical of the contemporary British style of forging, which is quite distinct from its European counterparts. He is treasurer of the British Artist Blacksmiths Association.

HEREFORD AND WORCESTER

Simon Lawrence, Brook Cottage, Peterchurch, Hereford (Peterchurch 236). Decorative and functional domestic iron work. Simon Lawrence was a scientific technician turned odd-job builder when he decided to take a TOPS blacksmithing course. After shoeing horses for four years ('hard, dangerous, and customers always moan about the price'), he developed a power-hammer of his own invention and set up his studio. He now makes tools for fellow-craftsmen, does one-off repairs if parts can no longer be bought, matches antique iron work and undertakes creative commissions – among them have been a windmill for a friend and railings for the Herefordshire Society of Craftsmen's shop. Fire baskets are £80 to £170, candle holders from £14.

KENT

Melvin Pinnock, 4 St Martin's Avenue, Canterbury (Canterbury 63279).
Hand-forged ironwork to commission. Melvin Pinnock designs and makes modern fire baskets, architectural iron work, including screens and balustrades, and garden furniture, or he will reproduce traditional designs. A handsome poker costs about £8, a garden bench from £300.

LANCASHIRE

Ron Carter, Trapp Forge, Trapp Lane, Simonstone, nr Burnley (Burnley 71025). An artist blacksmith who will make 'anything that looks nice in iron', which includes dog grates, fire irons, wrought-iron gates for a cottage or a castle, spiral staircases, bootscrapers for the front door, lamps and lanterns and brackets for hanging baskets. Ron's ram's-head motif goes on much of this work, and his wife, who trained at the Royal College of Art, will help clients with designs; alternatively Ron will make to customers' own drawings. A ram's-head poker costs under £10. Dog grates are from £40 to £700, depending on design.

LONDON

Albion Design, 12 Flitcroft St, WC2 (01-836 0151). Spiral staircases and fixtures in cast iron and timber. There is a standard range based on Victorian designs, or special designs can be arranged to commission. The company offers a design service and will deliver anywhere. An illustrated brochure is available.

Brass Tacks Hardware, 50–54 Clerkenwell Rd, E C1 (01-250 1971). A wide range of decorative brass, plus a made-to-fit service. There are door fittings, knobs, knockers, bell pushes, letter plates and numerals, curtain rails and finials, decorative grilles to hide radiators. There is a catalogue, and everything is available by mail order.

Cornwell and O'Niell, The Forge, 21 Greenwich High Rd, S E10 (01-691 6595). Wrought iron, panel work, gates, balustrading, railings, spiral staircases, fire escapes, scroll work and restoration. Peter O'Niell and Roy Wilkinson undertake a good deal of work for stately homes, but they also welcome less baronial work and are happy to quote for individual commissions.

House of Steel Antiques, 400 Caledonian Rd, Islington, N1 (01-607 5889). Anything in ornamental and architectural iron – fireplaces, gates, railings, spiral staircases, garden furniture; this is said to be the biggest collection of metalware in the country – and it all started by accident. Judy Cole wanted to have an old sewing machine polished, found a 'little man who was a big villain' and decided to learn the business herself. Apart from stocking about 400 original Victorian and Edwardian fireplaces from £25 to £1,000, she also has workshops where customers' own fireplaces and any metalwork can be restored, and where anything can be made to commission.

Metalcraft, 6–40 Durnford St, Seven Sisters Rd, N15 (01-802 1715). Suppliers of gates, grilles, spiral staircases, fire escapes and many forms of metalwork. They have a range of about thirty castings designed to slot on to balustrades, so that a sturdy balcony can be made to building regulations and then made decorative with as many embellishments as you choose – they cost from £2.30 to £11.50 each. They are architectural metalworkers and structural engineers and do lots of restoration work. There is also a range of cast-iron reproduction Victorian bootscrapers in eight styles; from the sort with long tongues to press into the earth and ones that can be set in concrete to heavy, free-standing ones. Prices from £12.57.

NORFOLK

Minns Farm Forge, Minns Farm, Ranworth Road, Blofield, Norwich (Norwich 714378). Peter Rathbone is a survivor from the dole. After a two-year surveyor's course he was one of fourteen boys who couldn't find a job, and after a year took a three months' course in wrought-iron work. Through the Council for Small Industries in Rural Areas he contacted a retired blacksmith in Wroxham, who turned out to have been honoured with the freedom of the City of London because of the work he had done on St Paul's after the war. He trained Peter, who is now so accomplished he can boast on his brochure 'If it can be made in wrought iron – we can make it!' Gates, £60 to £600; fire baskets, £25 to £77; firescreens, from £34.50; traditional Norfolk pokers, from £3.45. Shop and hotel signs a speciality.

NOTTINGHAMSHIRE

Terry Martin, The Old Mission Forge, Main St, Newthorpe, Nottingham (Langley Mill 3868). Traditional village blacksmith, established for twenty-three years. Apart from shoeing horses and doing cartwork and builders' iron work, Terry Martin also restores and repairs gates and railings, produces hand-forged iron work and has a range of gates from £45.

SOMERSET

Tony Gane, Top-O-Hill, Percombe, Stoke-sub-Hamdon (Martock 822089). Traditional, hand-forged iron work designed to commission. Tony Gane has a range of fire baskets, lights, weathervanes and small items, and he also undertakes large commissions – among them the restoration of the 250-year-old railings at Mompesson House, Salisbury, for the National Trust. His standards are high, as he refuses to cut corners, so the minimum you can expect to pay for a small gate is £100; but the quality will be obvious.

Oakhill Forge of Wookey, Oakhill Forge, 39 St Cuthbert St, Wells (Wells 72984). Ornamental iron work, including one-off commissions. Oakhill's standard ranges include gates, garden furniture and plant holders, at competitive prices because they are produced in large quantities; prices for one-offs will depend on the amount of design work. Commissions have ranged from a bracket for a grandfather clock to gates for Wells Cathedral.

SUFFOLK

Stuart Hill, Claydon Forge, Old Ipswich Rd, Claydon (Ipswich 831000). Striking modern fire baskets, gates, balustrades and fences in forged metal. Stuart Hill is an innovative designer who took a one-week course run by the Council for Small Industries in Rural Areas in 1977, opened his forge at Claydon and set about learning the hard way – on his own. Unhampered by other people's notions of how things should be done, he has produced some of the most creative work of all modern blacksmiths, much of it forged from one piece, and he is a leading member of the British Artist Blacksmiths Association. Don't expect curly scrolls – his work is geometric and powerful. His fire baskets can be used with logs or with 'real flame' gas log kits. Prices from £100 for fire baskets, £80 for gates.

SURREY

Richard Quinnell Ltd, Rowhurst Forge, Oxshott Rd, Leatherhead (Leatherhead 375148). Specialists in wrought and cast-iron work who will restore period iron work and undertake one-off commissions in architectural and domestic metalwork all round the country and all over the world. The workmanship is of very high quality, and a gate might cost around £500. Because of the revival of interest in blacksmithing, Richard Quinnell, who is secretary of the British Artist Blacksmiths Association, has opened a gallery next to the workshops showing the work of leading craftsmen in forged iron, copper and stainless steel. Items for sale include lanterns and fire baskets, lamps, candlesticks, bowls and jewellery.

WARWICKSHIRE

Firmstone Safe Lock & Security Co., 4 New St, Warwick (Warwick 492809). All kinds of architectural ironmongery and brassware in a small shop with a very long history. The company was founded in Middlewich, Cheshire, in 1633, when the Firmstones were yeoman ironfounders. In 1790 they built the Iron Bridge in Shropshire (Abraham Darby was the biggest ironfounder in the area and got the credit, but actually subcontracted it. 'We let him have the glory and we took the money,' says the present owner, Frank Firmstone). In the 1820s they diversified into brassware because they had invented a polishing mop which they traded in return for brass, and now they specialize in all types of fittings to restore both property and furniture, and will advise on security locks too. They have the best selection of handles, hinges, bolts and knobs for miles around, and also sell fireplaces, lamps and decorative house-name-plates.

WILTSHIRE

Hector Cole, The Mead, Great Somerford, Chippenham (Seagry 720485). An ironworker specializing in old-established techniques of hand-forging. Hector Cole is an expert in Anglo-Saxon iron-working techniques and enjoys reproducing antique domestic ironware. His forge is blown by antique bellows, giving fine control of the fire for the making of small pieces such as candle snuffers and for fire baskets, screens, gates and railings. He works to commission; among his major undertakings were the gates to Highgrove House, Tetbury. Visits to his forge can be arranged by appointment.

Robacraft, The Forge, Kington St Michael, nr Chippenham (Chippenham 75585). Traditional village blacksmith's shop providing shoeing, farm repairs, restoration of gates and balustrades and making of decorative iron work. Robert Baker will work to customers' ideas and designs and also has a range of his own designs. Gates are available from £50. Work has included commissions for Wells Cathedral and local manor houses, but Robert has a very unassuming attitude to all that – 'I don't take much notice of things like that when a job comes in. I just do the best I can, wherever it's for.'

Plasterwork

AVON

Moran & Wheatley Ltd, Avondale Studio Workshops, Avondale Place, Batheaston, Bath (Bath 859678). Specialists in period plasterwork. Moran & Wheatley will restore and match old cornices and ceilings, retaining as much of the original plasterwork as possible. They can reinforce period ceilings from the back and replace timbers without damaging the decorative plasterwork. A range of standard items is also available.

LONDON

J. G. McDonough, 347 New King's Rd, SW6 (01-736 5136). Missing or damaged cornices matched exactly – sometimes it is less expensive to replace than to clean if the detail of the plasterwork is obscured by years of emulsion paint. The company deals with large suites of offices and banking halls, but will also undertake domestic repair work from £100. A large range of cornices is available, from £1 to £20 per foot.

MIDDLESEX

P D T Palgrave Brown, Norwood Wharf, Southall (01-574 4441). Authentic copies of period mouldings by a company which specializes in supplying builders of film and stage sets but will also deal with private customers on a cash-and-carry basis. They have a large range of period mouldings, including cornices, architraves, balustrades, dado rails, panel mouldings and rails and bars for sash windows. An illustration and price list are available; send a large stamped addressed envelope. The company is a branch of Powell Duffryn Timber, which specializes in timber mouldings and claddings. Telephone Basingstoke 59161 for addresses of their forty local branches.

YORKSHIRE

Simply Elegant, Hodkin & Jones Ltd, 515 Queen's Rd, Sheffield, S Yorks (Sheffield 56121). The largest range in the country of fibrous plaster cornices, fireplaces, niches, panel mouldings and thirteen centrepieces from 18 in. to 5 ft diameter. The company, established in 1868, will also design to suit the proportions of clients' rooms or will copy existing cornices. They clean and restore cornices caked with years of paint, although this is usually only worth while if the plasterwork has particular distinction, as it costs around £7 to £10 per foot; reproduction cornices are available at £1.18 per foot, so it becomes cheaper to replace. They will travel anywhere, but also have a network of distributors who are, or know of, craftsmen to fix plasterwork in local areas.

Rope

YORKSHIRE

W. R. Outhwaite & Son, Town Foot, Hawes, N Yorks (Hawes 487). Banister ropes made to order in five colours of hard-wearing staple fibre polypropylene with a wool-like texture and appearance. Two diameters – 24 mm and 30 mm – and available with solid brass support brackets. Prices are from £3 per metre. This company took over in 1905 from the Wharton family, who had been specialist rope-makers since 1841. The present range includes rope ladders, skipping ropes, lanyards, church-bell ropes, halters, cow ties and plough lines.

Stained glass

DORSET

Henry Haig, Home Farm, Fifehead Magdalen, Gillingham (Marnhull 820268). Stained-glass design and restoration, large and small, sculpture and murals. Henry Haig's commissions have ranged from stained and painted windows for new, modern churches, two dalle-de-verre windows for Clifton Cathedral, cast aluminium murals, and a group of five bronze seabird sculptures with 20-ft wing-spans to small windows and door panels for private houses. He also repairs and restores stained glass in houses of all periods. Visitors by appointment.

LONDON

Goddard & Gibbs Studios, 41/49 Kingsland Rd, EC2 (01-739 6563). Stained and leaded glass for all types of windows and doors. This is the largest stained-glass studio in Europe, founded in 1868, and they can cope with anything from a five-inch panel to a domed ceiling for a Middle Eastern palace. They will restore old stained glass or design new, and nearly all the glass they use is handmade. Prices are from £30 to £400 per square foot – a front-door panel, for example, might cost from £100, a more complex design, painted and fired, £500.

Annie Ross, Space Studios, Lower Rd, Rotherhithe, SE16 (01-237 4430 or 01-981 3575). Stained-glass repair and restoration, including releading and handpainting in traditional Victorian techniques. Annie Ross will also undertake designs for modern and reproduction windows and door panels for houses, hotels, pubs, and she will make arrangements for etching and sandblasting. Charges are from £25 per square foot. She will travel any distance.

Bronson Shaw, 1st floor, The Granary, Hope Sufferance Wharf, St Mary Church St, SE16 (01-231 0222, studio; 01-994 3212, home). Modern stained glass for anything from a small door or windowpane to a whole mural. Bronson Shaw will discuss any designs you have in mind – however fanciful – and has been commissioned by such colourful personalities as Diana Dors and Nigel Hawthorne. Prices start at £25 per square foot for, say, a small door panel. He sees clients by appointment only.

MANCHESTER

Charles Lightfoot Ltd, Brookside Glass Works, 81 Upper Brook St, Manchester (061-273 1134). Leaded lights and stained-glass windows restored or designed and installed, from a small replacement panel to a whole window, including the frame. The company also specializes in toughened glass doors, mirrors and Victorian-style etched glass windows.

Roger Mowl, Manchester Craft Village, Oak St, Manchester 4 (061-832 4274). Roger Mowl will restore and repair stained-glass window panels broken by accident or age. He will visit and remove a window, replace panes with stained glass that is as close a match to the original as possible, refit and relead where necessary and straighten any bowed leading. He also makes and designs stained-glass window panels, and stocks Tiffany lampshades (£40 to £300) and Art-Nouveau-style mirrors. Restoration work is from £5 per broken panel, plus travel expenses.

OXFORDSHIRE

Paul San Casciani, Stained Glass Activities, 11 North Parade Avenue, Oxford (Oxford 727529). A specialist in stained-glass panels for home decoration, Paul San Casciani also undertakes restoration and gives lectures, tours, demonstrations and one-day courses in traditional and modern techniques. The programme is available on request.

TYNE AND WEAR

Vitrail Studios, 9 Sidney Grove, Fenham, Newcastle upon Tyne (Newcastle upon Tyne 733530). Restoration and design of stained and leaded glass. Philip Crook repairs church and domestic stained glass and will also design windows and door panels to match the period of restored houses. New work in stained and coloured glass with no handpainting costs from £13 to £20 per square foot; more detailed panels are from £20 to £40 per square foot. Delivery and fitting extra.

WARWICKSHIRE

Holdsworth Windows Ltd, Telegraph St, Shipston-on-Stour (Shipston-on-Stour 61883). Specialists in leaded lights (manufacture and restoration) and in steel-framed windows, which are made on the premises to any size. This family-run business, established in 1967, can also supply wood or aluminium-framed windows to any size. Prices are from £15 for a simple steel frame 3 × 2 ft up to £1,000 for a double-glazed patio door 20 ft wide with special glass.

Stone and marble

CUMBRIA

Cumbria Stone Quarries Ltd, Crosby, Ravensworth, Penrith (Ravensworth 227). Polished limestone, sandstone, green slate, grey or pink granite or fossilized marble can be cut to sizes suitable for fireplace parts, window surrounds, floors or kitchen tops. There are some fireplaces already made up on the premises and many photographs available to stimulate ideas. Kitchen worktops are from £11 per square foot, fireplaces from £240. Delivery is extra.

LONDON

Konrad Stewart, 90 Fulham Rd, SW3 (01-581 3962). Marble supplied in any size, from pastry slabs to kitchen worktops. You can even have a complete bathroom fitted if you dream you bathe in marble halls – walls, bath panels, vanity tops, the lot. There are several qualities and many colours to choose from. A polished pastry slab, 18 in. square, $\frac{3}{4}$ in. thick, would cost from £34.50, according to the quality of the marble.

Thatch

CHESHIRE

John Burke & Son, Green Lane Farm, Timperley (061-980 7871). A family business specializing in the repair, maintenance and replacement of thatched roofs. They will reroof old straw thatch with Norfolk reed, mostly in traditional Norfolk and Cheshire thatching styles, and will undertake all types of estate buildings, manor houses and country cottages. Cost depends on current price and supply of reeds but is generally from about £250 for 100 square feet. John Burke & Son are members of the National Society of Master Thatchers.

SUFFOLK

Peter Davies, 13 York Rd, Sudbury (Sudbury 70911). One of only 500 thatchers in the country, Peter Davies works within a twenty-mile radius of Sudbury and has a three-year waiting list. The average cottage takes about one month to thatch in one of the three basic materials – long wheat straw, wheat reed and water reed, which is the longest-lasting. A cottage roof 30 ft long × 20 ft could cost about £5,500.

Tiles

CORNWALL

Jennifer Scott, Treluggan Manor, Landrake, Saltash (Landrake 291). An artist who has developed a technique of applying oriental brush painting to tiles, Jennifer Scott perfected her art in Malaysia, where she lived for six years. She paints directly on the biscuit tile, sealing the design with a transparent glaze and achieving the effect of a glazed watercolour – much more delicate than the oriental-style designs produced on tiles by transfer. She works to commission and will undertake panels and murals from £150 per square yard – interspersed with plain tiles at £10 per square yard.

CUMBRIA

Maggie Berkowitz Tile Decoration, 21/23 Park Rd, Milnthorpe (Milnthorpe 3970). Individually designed tile panels for conservatories, kitchens, bathrooms or fireplaces. Maggie Berkowitz uses six-inch unglazed tiles, paints the pictures in glaze and fires them herself. She does preliminary sketches on graph paper for discussion at a fee of 10 per cent of the final commission. Prices are from £15 per tile, with a minimum of fifteen tiles.

ESSEX

Sally Anderson (Ceramics) Ltd, Parndon Mill, Harlow (Harlow 20982). Handpainted ceramic wall tiles in modules which build up into murals. Sally Anderson's studio is an eighteenth-century water-mill set in three acres of pasture, and she surrounds herself with geese, ducks, chickens, sheep and a cow – all of which contribute to her designs, which are mostly based on animals and plants. Her Midsummer range, on rectangular tiles $8\frac{1}{2} \times 4\frac{1}{4}$ in., won a 1983 Design Council award. Square tiles are also available – 6-in. or $4\frac{1}{4}$-in. – and there is a choice of eleven designs to build up as you wish, and thirty-five colours. Plains are from £27.36 per square yard; painted, up to £40.

LONDON

Domus Ltd, 266 Brompton Rd, S W3 (01-589 9457). One of the largest ranges of plain Italian tiles, about eighty colours available. There are also seventy designs in stock, mostly bold, modern Italian, not the traditional floor tile. Prices are from £12 to £400 per square metre, with a good selection in the £20 to £25 range. For the top price you can have a handpainted mural in any of their range of colours. The work is done in Italy and sent back, carefully numbered, for you to have pieced together on site by your grumbling builder.

Christina Sheppard, 3 Doughty St, W C1 (01-405 9966), or Wood Farm, Leiston, Suffolk (Leiston 831131). Illustrated tiles to commission, from single tiles to be interspersed with plain ones to entire murals. Christina Sheppard was a book illustrator and uses a sgraffito technique – literally scratching the drawing through the glaze. Her range includes animals, birds, fruit, fish, landscapes and blue-and-white brushwork, like traditional Dutch tiles. Prices from £2 per 6-in. tile. She also makes decorative bowls and plaques.

Sloane Square Tiles, 4b Symons St, SW3 (01-730 4773). Tiles made to commission in any colour or design. There are various sizes for walls and floors, and individual tiles can be handpainted to match furnishings from £2 per tile. There is also a range of off-the-peg designs, including six *Alice in Wonderland* characters from £3.50 each.

Townsends, 1 Church St, NW8 (01-724 3746). One of the largest stocks of period tiles in the country. There are individual Victorian tiles from £2.50 to £6.50 each, picture tiles from £5 to £20, Art Nouveau from £5 to £10 each, and also sets and runs for fireplace surrounds. At this branch Townsends also have more than 300 stained-glass windows of various periods at prices from about £15 to £300. They also restore stained glass.

Anna Wyner, 2 Ferry Rd, SW13 (01-748 3940). One of the few specialist mosaic artists in the country. Anna Wyner designs and executes mosaic decorations for swimming-pool floors, bathroom walls, garden rooms, public buildings. They can either be pre-cast in her studio, ready for fixing on site (these can be shipped round the world), or the mosaic can be worked directly, and more expensively, on site. She uses mainly Byzantine smalti, obtainable only from Venice, which can be combined with other materials, including marble, vitreous glass mosaic and ceramics. A mosaic in Venetian smalti of about 16 square feet, pre-cast, would be about £2,500.

SUSSEX

Rye Tiles, The Old Brewery, Wish Ward, Rye, E Sussex (Rye 223038); also at 12 Connaught St, London W2 (01-723 7278). Handpainted, screen-printed and plain tiles, all to order and in colours to match furnishings. There is a special range of tiles to match Colefax & Fowler fabrics and more than 100 standard plain colours. Tiles are available in four sizes and start at £20.70 per square yard. Handpainted tiles are from £100 per square yard. A brochure is available.

YORKSHIRE

Clover Ceramics, Abbotsford, Thorpe Lane, Fylingthorpe, Whitby, N Yorks (Whitby 880346). Handpainted ceramic tiles for door panels, fireplaces and walls. Colin and Brenda Orrell will undertake commissions for private houses, hotels, pubs and shops, in modern and Victorian styles from small tile pictures to whole murals. They will work to clients' sketches and ideas and there is no limit to the size of murals. Tiles are from 70p to £4 each.

Wood stripping

LONDON

London Pine Stripping Centre, 223 Royal College St, NW1 (01-482 2584). Stripping of furniture, fire surrounds and inserts, doors and staircases. This company works mostly with pine and will also deal with window bays, ceiling beams and sanding of floors. Prices start at £8 for a standard interior door.

MIDDLESEX

Strippers, 10 Church Rd, Teddington (01-977 4740). Any type of wood stripped on their premises – chests, doors, fire surrounds, banisters. Prices are around 50p to £1 for each banister rod, £14 for a small chest of drawers. There is a same-day service for door stripping, so an exterior door doesn't have to be off its hinges for more than a few hours. Prices around £9 for an interior door, £12 for an exterior.

Woodwork and joinery

CHESHIRE

M. J. Twigg (Joinery) Ltd, Vincent Mill, Vincent St, Macclesfield (Macclesfield 610592). Mike Twigg is a specialist joiner who will make anything in wood in any period – a boon if you are renovating old property. He interprets customers' ideas to produce doors, window frames, kitchen units and bedroom fittings in sympathy with each particular house – anything from a small Gothic door to a large oak staircase (complete with barley-sugar or turned spindles). He also specializes in Strawberry Gothic-style windows and fitted units with a drag-painted finish. A standard replacement for a Victorian sash window costs around £150.

CLEVELAND

Amos Swift & Co. Ltd, Boathouse Lane, Stockton-on-Tees (Stockton-on-Tees 675241). A company of wood-turners who will match chair legs, finials, baluster rails, posts for four-posters, knobs, or whatever else you need for your restoration. They do not do the actual repair work.

HAMPSHIRE

Richard Elderton, 2 Lower Green Cottages, Hawkley, nr Liss (Hawkley 428). A specialist in wood-turnery who enjoys tackling design problems which require an analytical skill. He finds it difficult to classify himself, as he has made such diverse objects as a large double bed and a wooden mandrel to assist in the painting of road marker cones. Smaller items have included replicas of medieval chesspieces and a reconstruction of a Roman games board. He uses only hand tools, so large work can be expensive; but he considers himself very competitive on turnery prices and will copy knobs, chair legs, handles, newel posts, balusters. You could have a three-legged chair made functional again for about £8 for the extra leg, excluding fitting.

LONDON

Carlos, 131–133 Cloudesley Rd, N1 (01-837 9451). All types of fine carving to commission. Kyriacos Neophytou learned his skills in Greece and has been practising them in this country for twenty-seven years. He is expert in carving frames, figures, animals, chandeliers and fine panelling, and will undertake traditional and modern designs in all types of wood.

Dove Bell Ltd, Cloudesley Place, N1 (01-837 8151 and 01-278 6613). Purpose-made joinery for house renovation and conversions by this associate company of Dove Brothers, a family firm known particularly for their church work for 200 years – they were responsible for the refurbishing of St Clement Danes church in London after the war. Dove Bell specializes in joinery – windows, doors, bookcases, panelling. It has a permanent team at Hampton Court, which, in terms of woodwork, seems to be something akin to the Forth Bridge.

Prices were correct at the time of printing, but are only intended as an indication and means of comparison. Do not send cheques to any company without checking first by telephone on postal charges and availability.

5 | Getting Your Act Together

Entertainers

AVON

Bath Puppet Theatre, Riverside Walk, Pulteney Bridge, Bath (Bath 312173). Puppet shows at the theatre or at private birthday parties. Andrew Hume and Sue Smith run the tiny theatre, seating thirty, giving up to three or four shows a day during the summer (50p a seat). Punch and Judy is of course popular, and they also do other shows, such as a version of *The Hunting of the Snark*. Shows at private parties cost £30 for about forty-five minutes, including balloons and music. Andrew carves the puppets and they run workshops for schools where pupils can learn to make their own.

BUCKINGHAMSHIRE

Clockey and Watchy, Lincoln Lodge, Silver St, Newport Pagnell (Newport Pagnell 612912). An original act involving two artistic clowns – one glamorous one who paints pretty pictures and one naughty one who scribbles all over them. The act is suitable for children up to ten years old and lasts about an hour. The two clowns – both women – will travel any reasonable distance at fees from £60. It is advisable to book five or six weeks before the party. They also do a more sophisticated act for adults.

CUMBRIA

Over the Top Puppet Company, Mike and Eileen Hares, 1 Tindale Terrace, Tindale Fell, Brampton (Hallbankgate 373). An original show which uses an equally original form of transport – a converted ambulance. The stories are invented by Mike and Eileen Hares, who take their show on tour to schools, art centres and festivals all over the country. They offer two shows – one for 5–11-year olds, *Superweed and the Terrible Bulk,* and another for 3–8-year olds, *Willie the Wicked Wolf Show*. There are flying exits, flash powder, Cumberland wrestling, welly boot throwing and lots of audience participation and ad-libbing. They charge from £35 per show.

HAMPSHIRE

John Hart, The Spinney, Shalden, nr Alton (Alton 83239). A full-time magician specializing in children's parties for ages between three years and nine or ten. He offers a one-hour magic show with live doves, white rabbit and audience participation for £30 to £50, depending on travelling distance. Alternatively he will run the whole party apart from providing the tea; he arrives at the hostess's house before the children, brings his own suitable music, arranges games with prizes and after tea will perform his magic. This costs between £42 and £70. He is also available for more sophisticated magic shows for dinners or trade shows.

HERTFORDSHIRE

Patchy Peter, 29 Cowper Rd, Hemel Hempstead (Hemel Hempstead 61767). A clown, ventriloquist and magician, allegedly of very little brain, so that the children have to help him do the magic and 'have one big giggle all the way through'. £38 to £40 for a two-and-a-half hour show, including games, prizes – and a live rabbit. Any distance with expenses.

LANCASHIRE

Professor Wilf. Durham, 19 Woodbank Drive, Bury (061-764 5911). A Punch and Judy man in the old tradition who makes all his puppets and even his own swazzle (the device that produces Mr Punch's voice). He has three separate Punch and Judy shows and improvises according to the age of the children. He performs anywhere from small house parties to large galas and will also run games sessions at children's parties for ages up to thirteen. From £25 for a children's party to £50 for an all-day gala, plus expenses.

LINCOLNSHIRE

Doreen Slennett, Playday Puppet Theatre, 14 Seagate Terrace, Long Sutton, Spalding (Holbeach 362028). Playday Puppets are suitable for school performances for primary-age children from four to ten plus. Doreen Slennett makes all her own puppets, stage and lighting, and although the approach is traditional, with a dramatic plot and a comical sub-plot, the stories are all original. Audience participation is spontaneous and creative. Her fee for a one-hour show is normally £60, or £50 per show when she is able to visit several schools in one area. There is a reduction for two performances in the same school. A smaller drawing-room stage is now being made so that inexpensive shows for children's parties can be offered anywhere in the country.

LONDON

Polly Twiggle Parties, 25a Kensington Church St, W8 (01-937 3704).
Maria Bergamasco will run any children's party for ages from one to sixteen, including special decorations for the room and the table, an entertainer, film show or disco, plus going-home presents and food. 'Polly Twiggle' arrives two hours beforehand to set up and decorate the room, and will stay to help clear away afterwards. Costs are about £5.75 per head, including all decorations, food and balloons; for children under three about £4.50 per head.

MIDDLESEX

Derilea, 180 Grasmere Avenue, Wembley (01-904 5076). A dexterous magician and puppeteer with a trade-mark that never fails to amuse: he gets the children to stir a pile of shredded paper until – bingo – the birthday cake pops out. There is balloon modelling too during his two-and-a-half-hour show. From £39.50 for up to twenty children, including little gifts for them all. Any distance with expenses.

Oscar and Stephen, 9 Hillside Gardens, Edgware (01-958 8158). Two imaginative and informal entertainers with an understanding of children which helps them to involve everyone and not just ask them to be a passive audience. Magic, puppetry, film shows and junior discos are all part of their repertoire, and they run a two-and-a-half-hour party from start to finish, adapting themselves to the mood of the moment. Afternoon or lunchtime parties cost about £35 in London. Travelling expenses are charged if they travel further afield.

Bob Thingummybob, 48 Tenby Avenue, Kenton, Harrow (01-907 4606).
Bob Thingummybob, alias Robert Leven, has several shows suitable for children from three to eleven years old. He uses puppets, magic and guitar, and his original stories encourage audience response and involvement. He will perform for any size of audience and has devised a special puppet show, with very little speech and lots of action, for small groups of mentally handicapped children. He has appeared on BBC *Playschool* and the ATV *Magic Carpet Show*. Prices range from £32.50 to £55.

OXFORDSHIRE

Albert the Idiot, Clown Extraordinaire, c/o Mrs Casey's Music, Glorishears, Thame, Oxford (Thame 2231). Albert is a professional clown who will run the whole party for children aged between three and ten. He arrives as himself – Ian Scott Owens – and from the contents of a large suitcase the children help to transform him into Albert the Idiot, who creates magic, music, and mayhem. He also has a car called Henrietta in which he can travel to galas and fêtes, and he will run clown classes for budding clowns, if requested.

SOMERSET

Johnny Doel, Church Cottage, Church Rd, Sparkford, Yeovil (North Cadbury 40767). A magician and entertainer who also makes models with balloons. He performs for playgroups and schools as well as birthday parties (he does particularly well with ages four to seven), and large numbers are no problem, as he entertains at Butlin's holiday village during the summer. A private birthday party costs about £28 for an hour's entertainment.

TYNE AND WEAR

Dick McCullogh, 35 Addington Drive, Hadrian Park, Wallsend (Newcastle upon Tyne 622438). Traditional Punch and Judy man. Dick's show is based on the Punch and Judy described by Pepys 320 years ago outside St Paul's Church, Covent Garden. He uses the traditional swazzle for Mr Punch's voice but he does not include the coffin or gallows because he feels they are not appropriate for children in the 1980s. His puppets are specially made for him in Nottingham, but he makes his own booths for both inside and outside shows. His price for an hour-long show at a private party is £20 within twenty miles of Newcastle. For clubs, fêtes or summer shows with larger audiences, his charge would be approximately £60.

Johnny Neptune, 30 Ivanhoe, Monkseaton, Whitley Bay (Whitley Bay 529151). An entertainer who has been performing magical tricks and puppet shows almost every day for fifteen years. He specializes in magic and hand puppets for children, but also has a more sophisticated routine for dinners and cabarets. To entertain a party of up to fifteen children in a private house in the Tyne and Wear area his charge is £20. Dinners or evening shows cost between £25 and £50, depending on the time of night he is asked to entertain.

WILTSHIRE

Kooky Clown, 34 High St, Easterton, Devizes (Lavington 3658). An entertainer who provides clowning, balloon modelling and magic and will run the games at children's parties too. Kooky and his wife, Moira, also perform at local fêtes, where Moira does painted faces – making up children as clowns or animals – for 30p a time. Birthday parties are from about £25.

Fancy dress

CHESHIRE

Heather Jackson, 23 St Mary's Rd, Sale (061-973 5256). Special make-up devised for fancy-dress parties. Heather Jackson will turn you into Frankenstein, Dracula, Cleopatra, Spiderman ... or even Father Christmas. She will visit clients at home, and charges are from about £7.

LONDON

Bermans & Nathans Ltd, 40 Camden St, NW1 (01-387 0999). The largest film and theatrical costumiers in Europe, with one million costumes from all periods. The company began as military tailors in 1900, founded by Morris Berman, who had worked at one time at the court of the Tsar in Russia. He and his son Max started to expand their theatrical and film connections in 1912 but it was only after another sixty years that they merged with the even older costumiers L. & H. Nathan, founded in 1790. Today's company is still run by Monty Berman, grandson of the founder, and all types of costume are provided for theatre, film and television. They also hire fancy dress from Cleopatra to Wonder Woman and Henry VIII to Fozzie Bear, from £23 per week, with a deposit of £40.

The Costume Studio, 227 Eversholt St, NW1 (01-388 4481). Period costumes for parties or amateur dramatics, medieval to the twenties. They have a wide selection of costumes, including lions and gorillas, although their main business is in the dressing of large-cast amateur productions of, say, Gilbert and Sullivan. Fancy-dress hire charges are £10, animal costumes are £15 and Edwardian and Georgian costumes £15, all plus an equivalent deposit.

Escapade, 150 Camden High St, N W1 (01-485 7384). The craziest costumes around. You can be a gangster's moll, an ostrich, even a giant banana – all for around £9, with a returnable deposit from £15 to £30. There is a small selection of clowns, fairies and Supermen for children at around £8.63 to hire, plus £15 deposit. Party accessories too – streamers and poppers, and green make-up for those who fancy themselves as the Incredible Hulk (you have to tear your own shirt).

Magic, 36 Greenwich Church St, S E10 (01-858 0418). Fancy-dress hire for men and women. This shop specializes in animal fancy dress, which includes wigs and masks, £9 for a weekend, plus £25 returnable deposit. It also has a range of other costumes for £8, plus £15 deposit.

Party Parade, 868a High Rd, Finchley, N12 (01-445 6743). Animal and character costumes for hire to fit children from three years to the teens. Clowns, cats, foxes, princesses at £7, plus the same amount as a returnable deposit. Adult costumes range from £10 for simple ones to £20 for elaborate regalia, plus equivalent deposit. Lots of wigs, masks and general party paraphernalia.

Theatre Zoo, 21 Earlham St, W C2 (01-836 3150). A good selection of animal costumes to fit adults and older children (no tinies). For the minimum height, 4 ft 9 in., there are lion, dog, cat, rabbit or monkey costumes. If you are taller you could be a gorilla (one of the favourites), a panda, a wolf (who needs a costume?) or an octopus (for the office party). Hiring charge for two days is £8.85 for children up to 4 ft 9 in., £12.94 for adults. Also a big selection of masks and wigs – Bert Broe is the third generation of make-up artists and wigmakers who have worked with famous theatrical personalities from Lilian Baylis to Lord Olivier.

Wig Creations, 12 Old Burlington St, W1 (01-734 7381). Handmade wigs made to measure in European hair from about £287.50. This company and Simon Wigs Ltd, at 2 New Burlington Street, also hire all types of period and modern wigs for films, television, opera, ballet and fancy-dress parties. They have about 15,000 wigs in all sizes and styles. Hiring charges are from £23 per week, with a deposit of £50.

MERSEYSIDE

Harlequin Costume Hire, 172 London Rd, Liverpool 3 (051-709 8306). Fancy-dress costumes for all occasions, from a gangster to a girl guide or even a gorilla. Most cost around £7. The shop is run by ex-theatre costumier June Riley and is open Monday, Wednesday, Thursday and Friday, 11 a.m. to 6 p.m; Saturday, 11 a.m. to 3 p.m.

TYNE AND WEAR

Bea's, 7 The Side, Newcastle upon Tyne (Newcastle upon Tyne 616388). Fancy-dress hire and expert advice on party make-ups. Beatrice Atkinson is an ex-actress and ex-beauty consultant and will advise on the most suitable costume, the appropriate wig to go with it and how to make up to look like any character from a werewolf to a clown. Most of the costumes are made in washable fabrics and all are cleaned after each hiring. Charges are £7 per night, plus a £5 deposit.

Party catering

BERKSHIRE

Nuttall (Hampers & Catering) Ltd, The Annexe, Stubbings House, Henley Rd, Maidenhead (Littlewick Green 3261). Hampers for picnics and for Christmas from £22 for four people. For lovers, present or potential, a Love Basket – gold-lacquered wicker hamper lined in red and containing champagne, goblets, swizzle sticks, a red silk rose and one pound of handmade truffles for £35, delivered anywhere in the U K. They also provide a full catering service for small luncheons and dinners to full-scale receptions, including the marquee and dance floor. There is a courier delivery service at an extra charge for the hampers; otherwise there are collection points at Ascot, Henley, Wimbledon and the Derby where you can pick up your order at no extra charge.

CHESHIRE

Ruth Gore, 2 Birchfields, Hale (061-980 7596). Directors' luncheons and private parties. Ruth Gore specializes in traditional English and French provincial cooking and can lay on anything from a consulate cocktail party or a wedding reception to a tête-à-tête dinner. Imaginative menus and good food. A supper buffet (which includes two or three hot dishes, and no restriction on second helpings) for twenty people would cost around £10 a head. This includes serving staff, china and cutlery, everything washed up and your kitchen left immaculate.

Martyn Jackson Celebration Cakes Ltd, 51 Church Rd, Gatley, Cheadle (061-491 1893). Wedding and anniversary cakes in all shapes and sizes. Martyn Jackson is the only confectioner in the North-West specializing in celebration cakes – he has twenty three-tier cakes on permanent display. He matures his cakes for two months before decorating; monograms and coats of arms can be included and any colours can be used. Prices are from £10 for a cake serving twenty portions to £90 for a three-tier serving 140. He does not deliver and is closed on Mondays.

CUMBRIA

The Cookhouse, Ellers Mill, Dalston, Carlisle (Dalston 711058). Business or private luncheons or dinners, private parties and weddings and a 'fill your freezer' service. Felicity Coulthard can also arrange for all the necessary china, cutlery, glass, linen, staff, flowers, photographers, drinks and marquees, and she employs an expert cake decorator, who will undertake anything from a dozen iced buns to a tiered wedding cake. Example prices: from £1.50 per head for cocktail savouries; from £8 per head for a wedding luncheon; from £5 per head for a buffet supper for a dance. Distance is no object, but mileage is charged.

Dinah Scott-Harden, Mid Farm, Johnby, Penrith (Greystoke 616). Private parties catered for (up to 200 people), weddings, dances and other special occasions. Dinah Scott-Harden will also organize the flowers, photographers, china, glass and cutlery, drinks and serving staff. Prices range from £4 per head for a two-course meal to £7.50 per head for a more elaborate menu.

CO. DURHAM

Canny Cooks, East Wing, Colepike Hall, Lanchester, Durham (Lanchester 520794). Dinner parties and weekend catering to wedding parties for up to a hundred guests. June Machray will come to your house, lay the table, and leave a note for the hostess with last-minute details, or stay and serve the meal and wash up. She will even give the host or hostess her recipes so they can be spared any blushes if an enthusiastic guest asks how a dish was made. June specializes in the unusual assignment, like catering for a football team or an outdoor fundraising barbecue. But she will also undertake a wedding buffet from £3 a head or dinner parties with dishes like jugged hare or roast pheasant from £6.50 a head. Service charge for washing up and waiting is £2 per hour for each Canny Cook.

LONDON

Art for Eating, 43 Felsham Rd, S W15 (01-788 3934). Custom-built cakes for any occasion – and 'built' is the word for such elaborate confections. Denise Jarrett-Macauley's first cake in the shape of a company's logo (done as a favour for a friend) was so successful that she became a professional cake-maker overnight and will bake and decorate to any theme. Prices can be from £50 to £200 but, there is also an 'off-the-baking-board' cake for £28 (plus delivery) which has a built-in musical box playing one of a choice of tunes, from *Happy*

Birthday and *The Teddybears' Picnic* to *The Anniversary Waltz* and *Scotland the Brave.*

Caroline's Kitchen, 52 Pembroke Rd, W8 (01-603 9788). Cooking for business luncheons, conferences, private parties and weddings by Sally Purvis, who also offers a complete wedding organization service. She will provide as much or as little help as you need – hire equipment for you, arrange marquees, flowers, cars, and generally take the headache out of the planning. Charges for a fork buffet for 100 guests are from £4 to £15 per head, according to the menu.

The Cookshop, 16 Cale St, SW3 (01-589 8388). A dinner-at-home service which no one would know you hadn't prepared yourself. You can take your own dishes to Lavinia Janson-Smith and she will fill them with whatever you choose and return them, filled, in a taxi to anywhere in the Greater London area. Each order is priced individually, but as a guide, canapés would be about £2.50 per dozen, roast duck in black cherry sauce £2.40 a head.

Tessa Corr, 30 Beckwith Rd, SE24 (01-274 6196). A complete catering service, from children's parties to business luncheons and wedding receptions. Tessa Corr will cook and deliver the food of your choice and will supply flowers, tableware, tables and chairs and hire waiters and waitresses on clients' behalf. She is personally involved at every stage of the service she provides, so high standards are maintained throughout. There is a minimum charge of £20 for food, and a brochure is available describing the catering and also a very imaginative selection of foods prepared specially for the freezer.

Crackers (01-868 4883, 01-452 4447 or 01-573 1895). Tricia Reik will deliver individually boxed food for children's parties anywhere in the Greater London Area, at two or three days' notice. Arrangements can also be made for delivery in the Maidenhead area. For £1.95 per head each child will receive coloured boxes containing sandwiches with three different fillings, crisps, orange drink with straw, cracker, balloon, jelly and spoon, chocolate biscuit, gingerbread man biscuit (but not tasting of ginger, as she finds children generally don't like the taste), sweets, raisins and a Disney sticker. Special party boxes for children with bigger appetites also include a chicken leg and two beef chipolata sausages with roll and butter: price £2.65 each. Tricia Reik can arrange for a special birthday cake made in the shape of a cartoon character with appropriate number of candles, and can put party-givers in touch with an entertainer.

Duff & Trotter, 71 Palfrey Place, SW8 (01-582 8373). All sorts of catering, from children's teas with specially shaped cakes to anniversaries and 100th birthdays. Picnics too – for Glyndebourne (£8.50 to £13.50 a head), Ascot (£7.50 to £8.50) and the Racing Picnic (£5.50), which would do for any outdoor occasion at all. There is also a grocery delivery service six days a week in London; a list of the foods and wines they offer is available. Christmas hampers from £7.50 are available too – you can see them and a range of kitchenware, china and glass and delicatessen at their retail shop, 47 Bow Lane, EC4.

Lucinda Elborne, 33 Lysias Rd, SW12 (01-673 4858). Lucinda Elborne cooks from home for the freezer and for dinner parties of up to twelve people. Dinner parties cost from £5 to £7 per head, and a moussaka for four people for the freezer, for instance, is £9. She will deliver to the house in Central London. There is a charge for longer distances. Lucinda also makes the most delicious cakes.

Anne Fayrer, 66 Lower Sloane St, SW1 (01-730 6277). Decorative cakes incorporating flower themes are the speciality here, as Anne Fayrer trained first in catering and then in floristry. Wedding cakes are her favourite subject, as they give her the opportunity to design a cake painted with flowers to match the bridal bouquet, but she also does all sorts of novelty iced sponge cakes in the shape of telephones, typewriters and hamburgers – or what you will. Among her commissions was a full-size replica of James Hunt's broken leg in plaster cast, with graffiti, and a model Chippendale knee-hole desk in cake for Arthur Negus's eightieth birthday. Simple iced cakes start at £10 (no delivery, but she will send a taxi locally); a three-tier wedding cake would be around £85.

Liz Fielding, 173 Kensington High St, W8 (01-937 5998). Liz Fielding specializes in making 'cakes that don't look like a cake' – mountains, villages, cars, galleons, tabby kittens, fairy coaches and wedding cakes in the shape of tiered buildings. She uses a rich fruit-cake mixture for adults and a Victoria sponge for children. Liz will deliver 'fantasy' cakes two or three days before a celebration and assemble them on site, as they are too fragile to travel – she has even flown to New York for a very special party. She can show photographs of her work if you need some ideas. Prices are from £40 to £275.

Here is Food, 26 The Pavement, Clapham Common, SW4 (01-622 6818). All sorts of parties catered for, from small ones for you to pick up yourself to large ones with everything provided, including cutlery and dishes, on a distance-no-object basis – Wales, if you wish. Chicken dishes are around £2.75 a portion; pheasant with apple and Calvados is £3.75 to £4.50. Many dishes are ready to reheat or can be eaten cold. A brochure is available.

Ice Cubes Galore, 14 Stannary St, SE11 (01-582 9944). Ice cubes, crushed ice, ice blocks and dry ice available in the Greater London area twenty-four hours a day, seven days a week, including Christmas Day. Price £3.50 for 25 lbs.; £5 for 50 lbs. Out of office hours the minimum order is 50 lbs., with a £5 surcharge. Special deliveries can be made outside London by arrangement.

Leith's Good Food, 1 Sebastian St, EC1 (01-251 0216). One of the top names in catering. Prue Leith, of restaurant and school-of-cookery fame, now has an outside catering service for directors' luncheons, cocktail parties, hampers or weddings. Prices from £3.24 a head for cocktail nibbles to £20 a head for banquets, including waiting staff. Weddings from £6.75 a head.

C. Lidgate, 110 Holland Park Avenue, W11 (01-727 8243). Any type of catering undertaken by this fourth generation of an old-fashioned, courteous family business. Mixed meats with salads at about £2 a head, beef Wellington £9 to £10 a head. A particular speciality is barbecues, and they are prepared to travel up to 100 miles from London.

Partipaks, 5 Devon Rise, N2 (01-883 8128 or 01-455 3689). Home-made boxed children's treats at £1.90 a head. Each box contains bridge rolls, shaped sandwiches, butterfly cake, biscuits, crisps, jelly and drink. Biscuits iced with each guest's initials can be arranged in advance at no extra charge. Birthday cakes home-baked in any shape from £12 to £20. Bags of going-home presents from 80p can be arranged, as can entertainers. Catering for adult parties is also undertaken.

Pamela Price, 26 The Pavement, Clapham Common, SW4 (01-622 6818). Any kind of catering, from dinners at home and luncheons in the boardroom to picnics and discos. Pamela Price, who is Cordon-Bleu-trained, will cook anything you wish and provide tableware, waitress service and entertainment. A fork supper might cost around £7 a head. The shop is open seven days a week, from 10 a.m. to 9 p.m., so there is plenty of opportunity for those who live south of the Thames to try some of the home-made fare before deciding on a whole party.

Rhind & Lines, 55 Fullerton Rd, SW18 (01-243 6532; evenings and weekends: 01-874 4483). Special-occasion cakes in all sorts of amazing shapes. You can have any sort of 'theme cake' – underwater, tropical, space rockets or shops. A simple 8-in. 4-lb. fruit cake, decorated, costs £15, plus £2.50 delivery in London; space rockets and so on start from about £25. There is a catering service too – ex-architect Jonathan Rhind has an inventive yet practical approach, and for children's parties will ask if the food is required to be thrown or not. Tea parties for twenty children from £4 per head. Also food cooked specially for your freezer – all prepared by Amanda Lines, who trained as a cook and spent several years cooking directors' city luncheons.

NORFOLK

Hampers, 69a High St, Blakeney (Cley 740801). Cordon-Bleu cookery for children's parties, weddings and dances at very reasonable prices. Pizzas and quiches from about 30p a slice; children's parties from £1 a head; wedding buffets from £3 a head. Specialities include raised pies, meringues and truffles.

NORTHUMBERLAND

Lynn Gregory, Earsdon Hill, Morpeth (Felton 392). Cordon-Bleu catering, from directors' luncheons to large wedding receptions. Lynn does all of the cooking herself but has a battalion of waitresses and helpers to call on when necessary. Charges, which depend on whether the event is to be held in a private house, hall or marquee, and on the type of cutlery, china and linen and the number of helpers required, are from £2 per head for a finger buffet, £5.50 for a standard buffet.

SOMERSET

Tessa Woodhouse, Lawn Cottage, Stour Row, nr Shaftesbury (Templecombe 70233, daytime; East Stour 719, evenings). Highly recommended private dinner parties at home or larger functions (up to forty guests). Tessa has done receptions for 300 but prefers to keep the numbers small, so that she can do it all personally. She will undertake any type of catering, from picnics to directors' luncheons and freezer cookery. Dinners are around £3.50 per head, plus the cost of whatever food the client chooses.

SUSSEX

Party Picnics, 3 Brickhurst Cottage, Brickhurst Lane, Laughton, nr Lewes, E Sussex (Ripe 203). Picnics delivered to the cloakroom at Glyndebourne 1½ hours before the performance – everything done for you, including the china and glass, so that all you need to prepare is your best position for languishing on the grass. £12.60 a head. Similar picnics prepared for Ascot and Henley (mileage extra), and food for any other occasions.

Party equipment

NOTE

For older children, activity parties let off the most steam. Many local councils and leisure centres will hire halls for football, netball or basketball parties, or swimming pools for a splashing time. Many also can provide catering arrangements and hire halls for discos. Contact your local authority for details in your area.

CHESHIRE

Zeros Lighting, Christopher Toms, 41 Larchwood Drive, Wilmslow (061-430 2223, daytime; Wilmslow 532744, evenings). Special lighting effects for private parties and official functions. Christopher Toms also lights promotional parties and fashion shows and can provide dance bands and travelling discotheques. He can arrange lighting for parties in any location, inside and out, including boats. His most prestigious commission was to light Prince Andrew's twenty-first birthday party at Windsor Castle.

HERTFORDSHIRE

Curious Caterpillar By Post, 39 Benslow Lane, Hitchin (Hitchin 34156). Inexpensive stocking fillers and party presents by post. More than 200 ideas between 2p and £5. Brochure available.

LONDON

Balloons Over London, PO Box 124, SW11 (01-622 7566). Helium-filled metallic balloons printed with a special message for parties, anniversaries, promotions. Standard messages – 'Happy Birthday' or 'Good Luck', for instance – cost £18.50 for five, £24.50 for ten, or you can have a name added by hand at 5p per balloon. Special messages involving the making of a printing plate cost from £35, plus the cost of the balloons. Balloons are delivered free within three miles of Hyde Park Corner, and there is a charge of about 25p per mile beyond that. One balloon in a box with a six-foot length of ribbon can be sent anywhere in the country for £8.50.

Barnum's Carnival Novelties Ltd, 67 Hammersmith Rd, W14 (01-602 1211). Everything you need for a party, a fête, a carnival or a fund-raising event. Barnum's will provide carnival queens' crowns, flags and bunting, printed balloons, collecting boxes, novelties and prizes. They will also hire fairground games, side-shows, bazaar stalls and carnival heads. A catalogue and price list is available, and they will quote for special orders. They give cash-and-carry discounts.

BOC Ltd distribution centres. Head office: Great West House, PO Box 39, Great West Rd, Brentford (01-560 5166). Cylinders of balloon gas for hire. Organizers of fêtes and parties who need large quantities of balloons can keep costs down by pumping up ordinary rubber balloons instead of buying expensive metallic ones. A small cylinder of this by-product of refined helium will inflate 150 10-in. balloons and costs £23, including all the equipment, for seven days; a large one with five times the volume is £60.95. Be warned: helium is one of the thinnest gases and will escape from the smallest hole, so if you are using rubber balloons you must inflate them just before you need them. The service is available from about a hundred distribution centres throughout the country – telephone head office for your nearest.

The Cocktail Shop, 5 Avery Row, W1 (01-493 9744), and 30 Neal St, Covent Garden, W C2 (01-836 5772). All the equipment you need to make cocktails for two or a cocktail party for 200 – including the barman. Cocktail shakers, ice crushers, measures, glasses, 'how to' books, invitations – all you do is provide the people and the alcohol. An all-in party, including three cocktails per head, the barman, the glasses, accessories and transport, would be about £222 for fifty people. Or you can simply hire exotic glasses for 30p each for twenty-four hours and do the rest yourself. The Covent Garden shop sells difficult-to-find exotic liqueurs needed for some cocktails.

Juliana's Travelling Discotheque Ltd, 217 Kensington High St, W8 (01-937 1555). Discos and complete party planning. Juliana's started in 1966 as a travelling discotheque for private parties, and now runs nightclubs and discos all over the world in hotels, clubs, on cruise ships and at hunt balls, charity balls, private functions. They provide music, disc jockeys, sound equipment, lighting effects, arrange for the hire of marquees and portable dance floors, help with the arrangements and provide catering, photography and video. Prices are from £258.75, plus travelling expenses outside London and overnight accommodation if the party is more than sixty miles from the centre.

Oscar's Den, 127 Abbey Rd, St John's Wood, N W6 (01-328 6683). A mobile party shop offering an at-your-door shopping service. The Oscarmobile carries a wide selection of toys and party accessories for housebound mothers to buy on their own doorsteps. They also offer a complete party package comprising candles and holders, small and large decorated plates, napkins, tablecloth, cup, packet of coloured straws, trifle dish and spoon and going-home bag of hat, balloons, blowers, streamers and two gifts of the mother's choice, all for £1 per head. Matching plates and tableware are sold singly too, so odd numbers can be made up without having to buy unnecessary packets of eight.

The Party Place, 67/69 Gloucester Avenue, NW1 (01-586 0169). Everything you need for a party, with the emphasis on children's and theme parties – Valentines, Hallowe'en, Easter, Christmas and New Year. There is a huge selection of paper tableware and going-home presents from 1p, and there are crackers all the year round, some made specially for this company. For those who want to make their own crackers there are also supplies of the snaps to give them the professional finish – and make the party go with a bang. You can also hire animal cake-tins here, or have a special cake made to order, book an entertainer, and have balloons printed with a personal message of up to six words – £2 to make the block, plus 10p per balloon. Closed Mondays and all of August.

MIDDLESEX

Funfair, 60 Edgware Way, Edgware (01-958 6218). Complete children's party service. Marilyn Messik's idea when she opened this shop was 'to stop mums reaching for the Valium at party-time'. She creates a very informal atmosphere and makes sure that customers and children are relaxed, plying them with orange-juice and coffee and chairs to collapse into. In stock is everything you need to throw-it-yourself – she will even split packs of napkins and plates and so on to provide you with exactly the numbers you want – and she can provide shape cake-tins, going-home presents, and will put you in touch with caterers, entertainers and hirers of mini tables and chairs. Closed Saturdays; open weekdays 9 a.m. to 3.30 p.m., Sundays 9.30 a.m. to 1 p.m.

OXFORDSHIRE

Partymania, 179 Kingston Road, Oxford (Oxford 513397). Everything you need for a children's or adults' party, from paper garlands and party 'bombs' (which explode 100 little gifts all over the room) to decorative candles and cocktail paraphernalia. Jessica Dove will make up packages of chocolate dragees in special colours to match a scheme (from 75p a box) and will put customers in touch with caterers, entertainers and people who hire equipment, from china and glass to marquees. She also stocks a huge range of wrapping paper and is the only shop in the area to keep a range of ballet wear which relates to an enormous selection of wigs, masks and other fancy-dress items.

Stocking Fillas, Tennant House, Little Milton, Oxford (Great Milton 368). An annual catalogue of small toys, novelties, jokes and crazy ideas for parties. Lots of choice, from 15p and 50p up to proper presents at about £5.

Toastmasters and butlers

LONDON

Ivor Spencer, 12 Little Bournes, Alleyn Park, Dulwich, S E21 (01-670 8424 or 01-670 5585). Professional toastmasters, after-dinner speakers and butlers, with the emphasis on the word 'professional'. Ivor Spencer is an experienced and well known toastmaster with twenty-eight years' experience – hardly an important event takes place in London without him, and he has officiated at 650 royal occasions – and he is also an entertaining after-dinner speaker. His business is international, and his school for butlers, founded three years ago, has the highest possible standards; from 1,000 applicants he has accepted only twenty-eight, because, as he says, 'anybody can give good service for one day, but to be nice every day of your life takes a very special person'. Butlers today are also administrators and take charge of everything in the household (apart from the nanny and governess) – from buying the food to arranging restaurants and air tickets. The butler's fee, if you want a taste of such top living (for a private party, for instance), is £86.25; toastmasters' fees are from £57.50; after-dinner speakers start at £172.50; all plus fares and accommodation for long-distance engagements. Ivor Spencer will also organize special events and royal visits (municipal or private) and advise on protocol.

Bryn Williams Enterprises, 6 Gladstone House, High Rd, N22 (01-888 2398). Toastmasters, after-dinner speakers, cabaret artistes and orchestras. Bryn Williams is an accomplished toastmaster and after-dinner speaker himself and runs an agency which provides speakers for all types of occasion throughout the country. Tell him what type of event you are organizing and he will choose someone suitable – serious or get-the-party-going. Minimum fees will be £60 in London.

Prices were correct at the time of printing, but are only intended as an indication and means of comparison. Do not send cheques to any company without checking first by telephone on postal charges and availability.

6 Getting Personal

Glass engraving

AVON

Bernard York, 10 Tellisford Lane, Norton St Philip, Bath (Faulkland 318). Glass engraving in steel-point line and stipple, with diamond drills. Bernard York will undertake all manner of engraving, from a simple goblet with initial for about £5 to whatever complicated design the client wishes. He has in stock more than 120 shapes suitable for engraving, covering a wide price range; vases, decanters, jugs, paperweights, bells, stemmed glasses and line drawings are available with a price list. It is advisable to make an appointment.

CHESHIRE

Douglas Burgess, 4 Bramhall Drive, Holmes Chapel (Holmes Chapel 33347). A glass engraver with a very keen eye for detail, Douglas Burgess uses a diamond or tungsten carbide tip for his work, plus an eighteenth-century Dutch technique of 'stippling' or building up the picture with a series of dots. He alternates the engraving on the outside and inside of the glass, creating a three-dimensional effect which is particularly effective for landscape engravings. He works for large companies and individual clients; a presentation goblet with a picture of a house would be from £200, depending on size and complexity.

The Old Mill, Leighton Rd, Neston, South Wirral (051-336 1630). Presentation glass engraved to commission. Lesley Blackburne and Robert Ellison developed their own special method of wheel engraving over a period of three years and now use as many as sixty wheels on a design, from very coarse to pin-head fine for delicate detail. They specialize in wildlife, houses and crests (no portraits). They use English lead crystal for their tableware – a wine glass engraved with a wildlife study will be about £17.

CORNWALL

Calligraphics, 2 Royal Buildings, The Parade, Liskeard (Liskeard 44029); branches in Liskeard, Looe and Plymouth. Free-hand, one-off designs engraved on all types of glassware by a group of glass artists who say they are 'modestly proud' of the techniques and equipment which allow them to offer a very inexpensive service. You can have initials, inscriptions, coats of arms or whatever appeals. For weddings or births, designs incorporating bells or storks would cost about £1.50 to £3 in addition to the price of the glass. A coat of arms on a brandy glass is around £6.35, including the glass.

CUMBRIA

Patrick McMahon, 1 Birchwood Close, Ulverston (Ulverston 57719). Traditional, clear-cut glass crystal in eighteenth-century designs engraved to commission with names, initials or portraits. Patrick McMahon will provide suitable glass for engraving, or will decorate customers' own glass. One to three initials cost about £1.50.

James Denison-Pender, Denton Foot, Brampton (Hallbankgate 364). Stipple engraving on glass. This eighteenth-century technique builds up a picture with thousands of tiny dots of varying intensity; the engraving of a goblet can take four or five weeks. James Denison-Pender has developed the technique of using all surfaces of the goblet to form a three-dimensional picture. He particularly enjoys Northern English landscapes or African wildlife, but will undertake any pictorial subject, submitting scale drawings of proposed designs. He is a fellow of the Guild of Glass Engravers, with whom he exhibits regularly. He has also exhibited in London, Newbury, Texas, Johannesburg and New York. Prices are from £600.

Richard Hugo, Dent Glass, Unit 6, Dockray Hall Rd, Kendal (Kendal 31096). Anything decorative on any glass, from initials on a whisky tumbler at about £8.17 to a picture of your Scottish castle on a decanter. Quotes given for intricate work. You can also have window-panes decorated with your coat of arms or a view of your house from £50, depending on size.

DEVON

Patrick Heriz-Smith, 13 Lower North St, Exeter (Exeter 50474). Presentation and commemorative glass of the highest standard. Patrick Heriz-Smith creates special designs of houses, boats, flowers, birds, crests or initials and prepares full-size drawings for approval before starting diamond-point engraving on whatever glass is chosen – decanters, bowls, goblets, tankards. Prices range from £35 to £1,000.

DORSET

Nigel Pain Products (Wessex) Ltd, 2 Bailey Gate, Sturminster Marshall, Wimborne (Sturminster Marshall 7737). Glass paperweights to commission for special occasions – golf championships, company presentations incorporating logos, anniversaries. There is also a large range of off-the-peg paperweights which are sold in galleries, museums and cathedrals in a variety of designs, including wildlife, ships, old masters and portraits. A mail-order service is available; prices, including postage, are from £2.30 to £7.50. Nigel Pain also has a photographic department and can reproduce small runs of pictures in colour or black-and-white which can be made into paperweights.

GLOUCESTERSHIRE

Pettis Studio Glass Ltd, High Barn, Northleach, Cheltenham (Northleach 689). Handmade kiln-fired glassware. This studio, established by Margaret and Allan Monkhouse in 1975, has developed a technique for applying line drawings, halftone and full-colour artwork into glassware by deep-firing enamels into glass. They do tableware, plates, dishes, cake stands, paperweights, trays, scatter dishes, coasters and ashtrays; and heraldic crests, maps, landscapes and initials can be incorporated to commission for personal and company presentation. Personalized brandy glasses are about £3.50, 10-in. crested plates £7.50.

LEICESTERSHIRE

Elizabeth J. Charles, 534 Uppingham Rd, Leicester (Leicester 416319). Diamond-point engraving on a range of good-quality glass in a selection of shapes that are best suited to free-hand engraving. Elizabeth Charles is also a watercolour artist, and many of her subjects are taken from nature. She will prepare preliminary sketches for a client's approval – wildlife, crests, houses, almost any subject – and will undertake special-occasion commissions for anniversaries, weddings, birthdays or presentations. Prices are from £7 for a simply engraved paperweight. Mail-order commissions are welcomed; her work is in thirty-three countries as well as Britain.

John Finnie, c/o 10 Steyning Crescent, Glenfield, Leicester (Leicester 873075). High-quality glass engraving and sculpting for large companies. John Finnie has shown an outstanding talent since he first went to Stourbridge and 'started scratching on glass'. He displayed such promise that he was commissioned to engrave a piece for Harrods and hasn't looked back since. He uses diamond-point or stone wheels and specializes in architectural scenes – an engraving of Burleigh House, one of Althorp (home of Earl Spencer), a sculpted bowl for the Queen Mother with symbols of the sea interspersed with the coat of arms of the

Cinque Ports. His work is beautiful and expensive – not the place to go for a quick initial on a birthday decanter.

LONDON

Andrew Glass Engraving, 19 Walton St, SW3 (01-581 3963). High-quality hand-engraved crystal. There is a good range of goblets, tankards, jugs, decanters, paperweights, window and door panes, table tops and pendants which can be engraved to commission. Subjects include architecture, heraldry, monograms, inscriptions, natural scenes, portraits and company logos. Prices are from about £15 for a simple monogrammed goblet.

Thomas Goode, 19 South Audley St, W1 (01-499 2823). Very high-quality individual glass engraving by David Powell, one of the few engravers to use the fine copper-wheel technique. Elaborate free-hand designs include landscapes, houses and family crests to commission. Also smaller commissions – initials, zodiac signs.

Heal's, 196 Tottenham Court Rd, W1 (01-636 1666). Glass engraving on any of Heal's stock pieces and in any design. Charges are £1.80 per letter; special designs quoted individually.

Jean McBride, 61 Beechwood Rd, Sanderstead, Surrey (01-657 1531). An artist who is unusual in combining the two skills of glass engraving and jewellery making, Jean McBride particularly enjoys calligraphy on glass, using diamond and carborundum points. She has exhibited widely since she established her workshop ten years ago and in 1981 was made an associate fellow of the Guild of Glass Engravers. Apart from engraving goblets and bowls, she makes rings, bracelets, chains, pomanders, and has set semi-precious stones into an engraved paperweight. Prices are from £70 to £500.

Stephen Rickard, The Old Vicarage, Vicarage Park, Plumstead, SE18 (01-854 3310). Top-quality glass engraving, including heraldic designs, wild flowers, presentation pieces for anniversaries and retirement. Stephen Rickard started his career as a sculptor and won the gold medal for sculpture at the Royal Academy in 1939. He is now the Vice President of the Guild of Glass Engravers, having been made one of their first fellows in recognition of his excellence. Special commissions have included several pieces for the prime minister to present to heads of state on visits abroad.

Michael Virden Engraved Glass, 835 Fulham Rd, SW6 (01-731 3557). Almost any type of glass engraved with initials on the premises. Boxed crystal pendants, oval or heart-shaped, with one initial £6.95; plain glass thimble with one initial £3.25; also whisky tumblers, wine glasses, decanters. Special orders for more elaborate engraving to commission. Mail order available.

MANCHESTER

Kendal Milne, Deansgate, Manchester (061-832 3414). Glass engraving to commission for special occasions. John Dearden in the glass and china department will engrave glass bought in the department or customers' own pieces from about £1.65 for a simple initial to complicated designs, for which he gives a special quotation.

Richard Lewis, Studio 25, Manchester Craft Village, Oak St, Manchester 4 (061-832 4274). Acid etching, using a traditional Victorian method, on window or door panels, goblets, decanters, tankards or presentation bowls. Richard Lewis will etch names, designs, buildings, signatures or even portraits, which he copies from photographs. He prefers to work on his own glass; prices range from £10 for an engraved whisky tumbler to £70 for a cut lead-crystal decanter.

MIDDLESEX

Kate Richardson, Willow Tree Cottage, Longford, West Drayton (Colnbrook 2409). A specialist in calligraphy on glass for presentation. Kate Richardson is a versatile artist who was elected a craft member of the Guild of Glass Engravers in 1981. Any name, initials or message may be hand-engraved with diamond drills on a selection of crystal glass – decanters from £40, plates from £33, rosebowls from £30, goblets and paperweights from £20. A full price list and photographs are available.

SOMERSET

Sylvia Cave, Rambler Studio, Holford, nr Bridgwater (Holford 315). An artist specializing in the engraving of plant forms on glass. Sylvia Cave is also a water-colourist and teaches plant portraiture. She will accept commissions for any plant picture engraving in a style which is botanically detailed but has a free, individual expression. She is a craft member of the Guild of Glass Engravers and of the Somerset Guild of Craftsmen.

SURREY

Barbara Norman, 9 Downs Lodge Court, Church St, Epsom (Epsom 26570). A glass engraver specializing in birds, animals and plant life, Barbara Norman uses diamond-point and flexible-drill techniques and supplies suitable glass for specific commissions, so that the weight, shape and decoration all complement each other. Her designs can also incorporate a personal inscription. Prices are from about £40 for a goblet.

WILTSHIRE

Nicholas Anderson, Rectory Farmhouse, Britford, Salisbury (Salisbury 25811). Engraving of all types of glass for special occasions – anniversaries, prizes, commemorative gifts. Nicholas Anderson started his craft by chipping designs out of milk bottles and graduated to engraving a picture of the Lower Ward of Windsor Castle on a goblet for the Queen's Silver Jubilee. He will either copy a design or motif or will create one specially to fit the occasion, incorporating the client's special interests. Goblets from £50, decanters from £110, including the glass and the engraving. Illustrated leaflet available.

YORKSHIRE

Heather Barraclough, The Manor House, Lower Wyke Lane, Wyke, Bradford, W Yorks (Bradford 677064). Fine-quality copper-wheel engraving with a three-dimensional effect. Heather Barraclough uses traditional techniques with a machine made in 1856 and modernized by electricity. She specializes in flowers, insects and game birds (not people and architectural subjects) and uses heavy-quality crystal. Simple initials are £2 each, flower and bird designs from £10 on a goblet. An idea exclusive to her is a design of moths or other small insects engraved on to the globe of a candle-lamp. These are from £16.

Named gifts

AVON

Unicorn Glass Workshop, Tooses Farm, Stoke St Michael, Bath (Oakhill 840654). A selection of over sixty hanging stained-glass models for the home, including nurseries. Items include birds and flowers, as well as teddy bears painted with a child's name and hearts bearing an appropriate message for Valentine's Day, inscriptions being from 75p. Special Christmas and Easter subjects too and a range of *Wind in the Willows* characters. Commissions undertaken. Prices from £3.95 for a small rabbit 4 × 4 in. to £14.95 for a scarlet macaw 13 × 4 in. A coloured brochure is available.

Wellow Crafts, Kingsmead Square, Bath (Bath 64358). A variety of gifts made personal for special occasions – named towels, pillowcases, sweaters, children's mugs, furniture, bedlinen and delightful pastel pictures with the child's name intertwined with honeysuckle and woodland animals, £27 up to six letters, £30 over six letters, £32 over nine letters.

CHESHIRE

Hordern Farm Pottery, New Buxton Rd, Macclesfield (Macclesfield 612447). Handmade stoneware to order. Jane and Robin Hansell will undertake presentation pottery with logos or inscriptions for private customers and companies. They also have a standard range, handmade from materials blended to their own recipe; prices are from £1.95 for a mug to £8.80 for a cheese bell and £18 for a large casserole. They have a very helpful approach: 'If someone asks us to do something, we will have a jolly good try to please them,' they say.

Our Kid, 1–3 Bank Square, Wilmslow (Wilmslow 522385). Named wool sweaters and shoe bags, made-to-order cot and pram quilts, duvets, cushions and curtains. Prices from £14.95 for a child's sweater up to 26-in. chest. There are also three-legged stools which can be made with a favourite toy carved into the seat, plus a name and birthdate. These cost £15.95.

CUMBRIA

Birkhurst Pottery, High Birkhurst, Low Row, Brampton (Hallbankgate 397). Hand-thrown stoneware for sale and to commission. Six years ago Birkhurst Pottery was a dilapidated cow-byre; today it is not only a busy workshop but also has an attractive showroom where the range, including casseroles, quiche dishes, egg-cups and posy bowls, is on show. Richard and Barbara Wright also make christening plates in white with blue design and inscription to order. An 8-in.-diameter plate costs £12 to £14, and there are also personalized mugs and jugs.

Wetheriggs Country Pottery, Clifton Dykes, Penrith (Penrith 62946). Personalized earthenware to order. Wetheriggs is one of the last earthenware potteries in the country making slipware in the original nineteenth-century buildings. Visitors are welcome to wander round the workshops and see the potters using traditional techniques, including the application of slip decorations with cowshorn and goosequill. Christening plates in tin glaze (white) with cobalt blue oxide decoration cost from £15 to £40; chargers slip-decorated with pictures of animals, houses or pubs are from £35. There are also various garden pots and glazed planters.

DORSET

Cecil Colyer, Orchandene, Candys Lane, Shillingstone, Blandford Forum (Child Okeford 860252). Wood and silverware to commission. Cecil Colyer is a furniture-maker and silversmith, and among his special presentation pieces are handsome dishes in polished yew inlaid with silver initials in the centre and with silver bands round the rim (from £100). He also makes children's stools carved with a name and date of birth (from £40) and christening or caddy spoons in silver engraved with a name (from £20).

Crummles & Co., 2 Cromer Rd, Poole (Bournemouth 766877). Hand-painted enamel boxes made to commission for livery companies, hotels, businesses, even for private clients if they are not overfaced by the minimum order of twenty. Any design is possible, from simple monograms to landscapes at costs from £480 (£24 each box), with a discount for larger quantities. A name can be inscribed inside the lid for an extra £7 each box.

The Julian Workshop, 1 Cheap St, Sherborne (Sherborne 815473). Initialled, appliquéd cushions made to order. Jane Burden has developed a three-dimensional appliqué technique and makes cushions built out of layers of fabric with the initial in the centre. They cost from £16 to £20 each.

GLOUCESTERSHIRE

Celebration Clocks, 7 Chapel St, Stroud (Stroud 78125). Decorative wooden wall clocks for christening presents. Handpainted in primary colours with teddy bears all round the $10\frac{1}{2}$-in.-diameter dial, with a child's name, date and hour of birth inscribed on the base to order. The clocks have battery-powered quartz movements and are available in two colours at £29.50, including postage. Send a stamped addressed envelope for colour photographs.

Geoffrey Vivien, The Grange, Woolstone, nr Cheltenham (Bishop's Cleeve 2122). Names illustrated in the manner of George Cruikshank, the Dickens illustrator who designed a comic alphabet. Geoffrey Vivien rearranges the pictures according to the spelling of the customer's name, and inscribes the initials beneath – Will, for instance, would be Witty, Impish, Loyal, Loving, with appropriate pictures illustrating the characteristics. These are £2.30 per letter, framed; postage is extra. Also available at £10 a pair are bookends made to incorporate personal interests: favourite authors, family crests, initials of a bride and groom.

HEREFORD AND WORCESTER

Mary-Louise Hussey, Bredstone House, Burghill, Hereford (Hereford 760162). Children's names handpainted in watercolours on paper and decorated with their favourite fictional or cartoon characters; or with wild flowers and animals. There are five colour-schemes at £3.50 per letter, or special orders can be taken to match individual furnishings. Alternatively a name can be incorporated into a choice of three scenes – woodland, wildlife or steam locomotive – for £15, regardless of the number of letters. No framing; the names are sent rolled in a cardboard tube. A brochure is available.

LANCASHIRE

Croft Design, 1 Lincoln St, Cornholme, Todmorden (Todmorden 2795).
Handmade wooden jigsaws which offer children a pleasing and satisfying way of manipulating the chunky letters of their own name into place. Picture motifs can also be incorporated. Paul Croft uses non-toxic woodstains and charges £8 for the first three letters, plus £1 for each additional letter or motif. He will supply by mail.

LEICESTERSHIRE

Prezzies, Ivy Farmhouse, Greetham, Oakham (Oakham 812136).
Lots of initialled and inscribed gifts, from lead or coloured pencils printed with any name (up to sixteen letters), £1.60 a set of ten, to playing cards, book-matches, toys, leather goods. Prices are very reasonable, and a mail-order brochure is available.

LONDON

Alphabet, 23–27 Heddon St, Regent St, W1 (01-439 7660). Embroidered monograms on any fabric. Motifs from a furnishing fabric can be repeated as an embroidery; logos, crests, badges can be created; designs can be adapted from artwork or pictures. Many colours and styles are possible at prices from £1.75 per initial. A catalogue is available. Closed 12.30 to 1.30 p.m. and after 4.30 p.m.

Asprey & Co. Ltd, 165 New Bond St, W1 (01-493 6767). Monogrammed dinner services in a wide selection of colours and in any style – you can even have pictures of your various palaces in the centre of each dinner-plate. Crystal can be monogrammed to match. Strictly for the deepest pockets.

Eximious, 10 West Halkin St, SW1 (01-235 7222). A selection of mono-grammed accessories from hair-brushes and leather goods to glass goblets and dressing-gowns, with the emphasis on good quality and originality. The service includes miniature portraiture of pets on enamelled boxes – cats, dogs, horses – by a selection of artists. Prices for these are from £44 for a box 1-in. in diameter, £59 1½-in., £89 2-in. A brochure is available.

General Trading Company, 144 Sloane St, SW1 (01-730 0411). Your own pictures or prints, or even wedding invitations, mounted on heatproof trays or table mats, sealed on to a lacquered surface or put under glass. From £4.30 per mat. Also hand-engraving of glass at £4 to £5 per initial or from £2.50 if sand-blasted.

Thomas Goode, 19 South Audley St, W1 (01-499 2823). Monogrammed dinner services in a range of 150 designs. The cost is between £3 to £5 per piece, plus the cost of the china. They also have large stocks of discontinued china and may be able to obtain special items even if they don't stock them.

Harrods, Knightsbridge, SW3 (01-730 1234). Initials on luggage, £2 per letter, takes three days. Small leather goods initialled while you wait, in the stationery department, 50p per letter. Hand-inscribed wine labels, or a recipient's name inscribed free on Harrods' own whisky, or on whisky, brandy and port by Alexander Dunn. Prices from £12.50.

Veronica Noach, 4–23 Northwood Hall, Hornsey Lane, N6 (01-340 3029). Picture and photograph frames painted in watercolours and including names and dates of weddings or birthdays. You could also have the frames covered in fabric to match any colour-scheme or, as a romantic memento, the same fabric as your wedding dress. Prices from £2.95, about 3×2 in. The largest are 15×20 in.

Pet Presents, 35 Horn Lane, W3 (01-993 3804). A mail-order catalogue of personalized presents for pets. There are named towels, steel feeding bowls, car ventilators, cat scratchers, cat doors, at prices from about £2 to £27.

Selfridges, Oxford St, W1 (01-629 1234). Champagne, wine or spirit bottles engraved with any message – actually on to the glass, not the label – £2.75 for three words, plus 15p for each additional letter. Other items that can be engraved include pencils, pens, jewellery, sunglasses, walking sticks, umbrellas. In the Print-a-Gift section of the stationery department.

Ann Williams, 10 Barleymow Passage, W4 (01-994 6477). Table mats made from your children's drawings or your own. Send drawings on paper $10\frac{1}{4} \times 8\frac{1}{4}$ in.

(the size is important) and this will be reduced to 10 × 8 in. and given a heat-protective covering and cork backing. Oil paints and heavy wax crayons are not suitable; pencil crayons are good and felt tips are best. Only one mat can be made from each drawing – £2.30, including postage. Coasters are available too, at £1.10 each.

NORTHUMBERLAND

Errington Reay & Co. Ltd, Tyneside Pottery Works, Bardon Mill, Hexham (Bardon Mill 245). A family pottery established more than 100 years ago. It produces a variety of functional and decorative goods, from garden pots to vases made from the original Victorian moulds (these about £50). Any type of salt-glazed pot, plate, vase, jar, plinth, bread bin, or ornament can be ordered with a commemorative inscription if required, even when it is as idiosyncratic as that done by a partner for himself: 'David Reay gave up smoking. 1st February 1983'.

NOTTINGHAMSHIRE

Rockley Impressions, Rockley House, Retford (Gamston 271). Book-plates in the style of Victorian engravings incorporating your house, coat of arms or main interests – horses, wildlife, boats, for instance. Send a rough sketch or idea and Ann Procope and her partner Georgina Gamble will return designs for your approval. Prices from £45 for 1,000 plates. Smaller quantities are available if you have no library of your own, but a lot of forgetful borrowers as friends.

OXFORDSHIRE

Sidney Hardwick, Cedarwood, Stream Rd, Upton, nr Didcot (Blewbury 850263). Commemorative stoneware dishes and bowls for anniversaries. Sidney Hardwick makes slip-decorated stoneware in earthy colours and copper red, incorporating names and wedding dates in the flower designs. She also makes salt pots, casseroles, internally lit lamps, and decorative pots for flower arrangers and house-plant enthusiasts. Prices from £6 to £30.

SOMERSET

The Linen Orchard, Crowcombe Court, Crowcombe, Taunton (Crowcombe 247). An attractive selection of personalized gift items. Quilted teddy hotwaterbottle covers for children (£7.95), co-ordinating pillowcases and duvet covers (£6.95 and £21.95), cot-size bedlinen appliquéd and named, adult bedlinen and accessories initialled. A mail-order brochure is available.

STAFFORDSHIRE

Rookes Pottery, High St, Ipstones, Stoke-on-Trent (Ipstones 606).
Handthrown terracotta wedding platters decorated with the sgraffito technique –
14-in.-diameter £35, plus postage. David and Catherine Rooke also make 2½-
gallon home-brew flagons inscribed with the client's name – 'Brown's Brewery',
'Smith's Cellar' or whatever – £19.50. Tankards are also available.

SURREY

Alexander Dunn & Co. Ltd, 42 Walton Rd, East Molesey (01-941 3030).
Whisky, cognac, sherry, champagne or port, all available with the name of the
recipient hand-inscribed on the label, and sent anywhere on the UK mainland.
Prices from £5.04 for a bottle of amontillado to £24.78 for 1.75 litres of twelve-
year-old Scotch whisky – plus carriage. A brochure is available.

**Hobson's Bespoke Perfumery, 14a Guildford St, Guildford (Guildford
579095).** The 'bespoke' part of the name refers to special blends made up for trade
customers, but for those who can afford a money-no-object gift, this would be one
of the most flattering gestures of admiration – an exclusive scent made to order.
For about £1,000 a Swiss perfumer will fly in to create exactly the right blends for
the skin and personality concerned, and once approved the presentation package
will include 250 ml of perfume, six 125 ml eau de toilette, 1 lb. hand-collected pot
pourri, talc and 100 bars of soap. With the order comes a book which shows how
much of the original kilo of concentrate is left, so that further products can be
ordered until the mixture runs out.

**Mary Wondrausch, Wharf Pottery, 55 St John's St, Farncombe, Godal-
ming (Godalming 21812).** A highly individual potter specializing in the type of
folk designs which had a short vogue in England in the seventeenth century and
which reappeared in Hungary, Romania and Switzerland a century later. They are
hand-decorated on honey-glazed earthenware – jugs, egg stands, salt pigs, house
plaques – and commemorative plates for weddings or anniversaries can have
names and dates inserted round the rims. These cost from £20 for a 9-in. plate and
can be sent by post. Residential weekend courses are available at Mary Wondrausch's sixteenth-century cottage near Guildford; inquiries to Godalming 4097.

SUSSEX

**Crowborough Pottery, The Old Forge, London Rd, Crowborough, E
Sussex (Crowborough 63468 or Groombridge 814).** Handmade ceramic
name plaques thrown on a potter's wheel or moulded from traditional earthenware
or stoneware clays. Send a photograph, card or rough sketch and Andrew and

Georgina Cominos will design to your requirements. Simple house numbers with a decorative border are from £7.25, oval name plaques from £15.95. A price list is available, and quotes can be given for sizes other than those listed.

Rye Pottery, 77 Ferry Rd, Rye, E Sussex (Rye 3363). These well-established decorative tile makers also have a range of lettered ceramics for special occasions. They do ceramic wedding plates from £16 and two-handled loving cups from £10, all with floral decorations, names and dates. Children's mugs and tankards with one name only are available from £4 each, and house plaques decorated with fruit, flowers, birds, trees or just numbers are in various sizes from 6 in. at £18. Special designs can be ordered and will be quoted individually; the minimum extra charge would be £5. All are available by mail order; brochure and postal charges on request.

WEST MIDLANDS

J. & J. Cash Ltd, Kingfield Rd, Coventry (Coventry 555222). Personal labels for handmade knitted garments and needlework. There are five motifs – a ball of wool, a cone of wool, a lamb, a needle and cotton-reel, and a spinning wheel – three styles of lettering and four colour combinations with the wording of your choice – 'Blousy Blonde Knitwear' or 'Dorothea Designs' or whatever. Minimum order thirty-six labels, £4.95, including postage.

WILTSHIRE

Ken Meyer, 30 Boundary Rd, Chippenham (Chippenham 654563). Hand-carved house names. Ken Meyer started woodcarving as a hobby several years ago and turned it into a full-time job when he was made redundant. He specializes in hand-carved lettering, relief carving, trophies and plaques. Prices for house names £1 per letter, plus the cost of the wood according to size.

Portraits and houses

AVON

Peter Challen, Avonside, Limpley Stoke, Bath (Limpley Stoke 2547). Landscape artist in watercolours and oils. Peter Challen trained as an architect and particularly enjoys painting portraits of houses. He is a traditional watercolourist, and his paintings of waterscapes are extremely popular. Watercolours and oils are from £65. Conté drawings from £45.

Peter and Heather Jeffery, Glenfrome House, 280 Ashley Down Rd, Bristol (Bristol 421697). House portraits drawn in line for letterheads, invitations, table mats, coasters or in colour for use as framed pictures. Peter Jeffery is a versatile artist with a background in linguistics and publishing. He is also a silversmith and jeweller and enjoys inventing unusual presentation pieces – like the ruby-wedding model house in silver which played tunes when the chimneys were pressed. The personal stationery is printed on an old-style letterpress, and there is a basic charge of about £65, plus the cost of paper and printing.

Karen Mills, Bath (Bath 313444). A portrait artist with a traditional style – 'Rembrandt is my greatest hero and I like the Dutch school, so I could be over-old-fashioned in certain respects'. Karen Mills works in pencil from £10, watercolour from £30, oil from £250, and will only do portraits of children when they are old enough to understand why they are sitting. She is prepared to consider travel, which is negotiable.

CHESHIRE

Rita Lankuttis, 57 London Rd, Nantwich (Nantwich 628728). Picture portraits of your house or garden machine-embroidered on a handpainted background. The silky textured pictures are finely worked and glow with life and colour. Rita likes to work on a small scale from a photograph produced by the client or from one she takes herself. She usually uses a little artistic licence with gardens and embroiders everything in bloom. Prices for commissions are from £30 to £80, including a frame.

CUMBRIA

Una Thompson, The Old Rectory, Greystoke, Penrith (Greystoke 241). Tiles or plates handpainted with a picture of your house, your pet, a favourite view or any subject you choose. Una Thompson works either from life or from photographs or prints, and commemorative inscriptions can be included. Prices are about £20 for a 10½-in. plate, £15 for a tile.

HAMPSHIRE

Margaret Anderson, 314 Everton Rd, Everton, nr Lymington (Lymington 693932). A specialist in miniature watercolour portraits on ivorine, usually oval, 2½ × 2 in., in a gilt frame. Prices according to subject: people £150, animals £100 to £120 (she has even immortalized a goat). Pastel portraits available too, 14 × 17 in., people £120, animals £90, and portraits engraved on glass, around £45 on a ship's decanter, for example. Simple engraving on paperweights – initials or a picture from £8 to £12. Margaret Anderson will work from your own photographs if you live at a distance, but prefers to visit the sitter and if necessary take her own photographs to work from, as she finds meeting the subject helps her to give a truer likeness.

LONDON

Barbara Dorf, Montpelier Studio, 4 Montpelier St, SW7 (01-584 9667). An artist and teacher of the history of art, Barbara Dorf specializes in watercolours of private houses and landscapes with buildings. She always visits the site – never works from photographs and does not do pen-and-ink drawings. Pictures up to 15 × 20 in., mounted but not framed, from £75, plus travelling expenses out of London. Barbara Dorf exhibits regularly at the Royal Academy and has published several books on painting; her work is in many important private collections.

Gale Pitt, 32 Felstead Rd, Wanstead, E11 (01-989 7265). House portraits in watercolours to commission. Gale Pitt started to paint local shops, restaurants, pubs and hotels and has been selling these successfully at a pitch (226) on Bayswater Road, London W2, opposite the Lancaster Gate Hotel. So many people asked her to paint their houses that this has become a speciality. She has had work accepted for exhibition by the Royal Institute of Painters in Watercolour and by Libertys, yet her paintings are certainly not overpriced – around £75 for a framed picture 12 × 17 in.

Karen Usborne, 17a Great Ormond St, WC1 (01-224 7711). House portraits in line-and-wash. Karen Usborne is an artist and book illustrator whose work has appeared at the Royal Academy summer exhibition. She will draw houses for reproduction as letterheads – say 4 in. square, for about £50 – or larger pictures for framing at around £200. She is also an accomplished portrait painter; a head and shoulders in oils would require three sittings and costs around £250.

MIDDLESEX

Andrew Vass, The Hall Floor Flat, 35 Arragon Rd, Twickenham (01-892 0802). A watercolour painter and illustrator who also undertakes illustrated wedding cards and party invitations. He has a fluid and graceful style and a particular talent for landscapes. A drawing would cost around £25, a watercolour £50. He can also arrange for printing from the original drawing.

SUFFOLK

Jill Laurimore, Falcon House Gallery, Swan St, Boxford (Boxford 210238). Ceramic house portraits to commission. Jill Laurimore was a television scriptwriter when she first took up pottery as a hobby, but her houses were so popular they soon became a full-time occupation. Her aim is to capture the atmosphere rather than the brick-by-brick detail of a house and she usually works on a base 18 × 14 in. – very large houses will sometimes be made on more than one base. Each commission takes about four months to complete, as the clay has to dry out very slowly. Subjects have ranged from a Hampstead semi to Robert Carrier's Hintlesham Hall. Prices are from £450. She also makes Gothic follies and obelisks and ceramic eggs topped with flowers or fruit, and usually has a selection for sale in the gallery.

SURREY

Neil Godfrey, The Rectory, Woldingham (Woldingham 2192). A particularly sensitive interpreter of character (perhaps because of his previous career in community work), Neil Godfrey has made portrait heads and figures in cold-cast bronze a speciality. For heads, four or five sittings are required in order to make a clay master from which the cast is made; sittings can be at the studio or the client's house (with travelling expenses). The basic charge is £350, plus £15 for a standard mounting on a mahogany block. Successive heads each cost £200. Heads may also be cast in bronze, but this is necessarily more expensive. Small sculptures for table display and larger ones for the garden are also available. An illustrated leaflet is available for a stamped addressed envelope.

WILTSHIRE

Truda Panet, 161 Wilton Rd, Salisbury (Salisbury 3615). An accomplished artist well-known for her portraits of dogs. She works in pastels, which she feels are most suited to the texture of the fur, and 'sittings' take about two hours. Her clients include animals with famous owners and owners with famous animals. Fee for one dog.£50, two £85. She will travel any distance if expenses are paid.

Prices were correct at the time of printing, but are only intended as an indication and means of comparison. Do not send cheques to any company without checking first by telephone on postal charges and availability.

7 | Getting What You Want

Needlework and Craft Supplies

Basketware and timber

HERTFORDSHIRE

Centre of Restoration and Art, 20 Folly Lane, St Albans (St Albans 51555). Rattan cane for basketwork at £2.13 per quarter-kilo, £3.70 per half-kilo; plastic rattan, for those who don't want to work with cane that needs to be wet, £2.65 per half-kilo. There is also a wide range of artists' materials.

OXFORDSHIRE

Kate and Tony Handley, Country Chairmen, Home Farm, Ardington, nr Wantage (East Hendred 362). English rush home-grown, harvested and cured. The top quality is about £5 per kilo (discounts for quantity), and occasionally there is a second quality suitable for basket-making, but not for chair seats.

WARWICKSHIRE

Nicholas Joyce, Alscot Estate Yard, Alderminster, nr Stratford-upon-Avon (Alderminster 345). Timber supplies for cabinet-makers and amateur DIY enthusiasts who are not able to prepare and cut their own wood. Nicholas Joyce is a cabinet-maker who offers a variety of timbers, dried in his own dehumidifier and cut into lengths suitable for making small furniture and fittings. He also sells other restoration supplies, including shellac at very competitive prices.

Dressmaking

HAMPSHIRE

Tessa Maynard, Forge House, Wolverton, Basingstoke (Kingsclere 298294). For those making their own wedding dresses, Tessa Maynard has a selection of 80 Thai silks in white, ivory, cream colours and prints. There are two weights, light at £7.95 a metre, medium £9.25 (plains) and £8.95 (prints).

LONDON

The Button Box, 44 Bedford St, WC2 (01-240 2716). Old and new buttons in all sorts of materials – plastic, pearl, wood, nylon, handpainted novelties in animal shapes for children. Also glass buttons from the 1930s, some still on their cards. They will dye specially in quantities no less than 100. Send a stamped addressed envelope for the mail-order leaflet.

Elegance Fabrics (UK) Ltd, 650 Holloway Rd, N19. Mail-order cut-length fabric service for dressmakers. A catalogue containing hundreds of swatches is produced twice a year; each page includes colour photographs of clothes created by leading designers to show how different materials can be worn together. As little as half a metre of fabric may be bought at a time. All the fabrics are exclusive to Elegance, who have operated a similar service on the Continent for thirty years. They also produce a Multicolor Classics Collection catalogue, which contains more than 400 plain colour classic fabrics, plus linings, threads, zips, thimbles and pins – everything to complete a garment. The seasonal catalogue costs £23.95, the Multicolor £14.95, and the two together £33.90, all including postage. The costs, of course, could be divided between several dressmaking enthusiasts in the same area.

A. Taylor, 1 Silver Place, W1 (01-437 1016). Specialists in covered buttons for more than 100 years. In this tiny shop in an alleyway off Beak Street (it isn't even on the map in the *A to Z*), buttons are made for the top couture houses and for private customers by the wife of the present owner, Leon Rose, who bought the business thirteen years ago from the founder's son. They can also arrange for belts to be covered, buttonholes to be made by hand or machine, and alterations and invisible mending to be done. White buttons can be dyed to special colours – and there is a huge selection of all types of button in stock – and fabric can be pleated to order. Man-made fibres, mixtures and silks are the best for pleating – allow two-and-three-quarters times your hip measurement and send the fabric hemmed at one end. It will cost from about £10 to £12, and you can have flat, accordion or crystal pleating.

MANCHESTER

William H. Bennett & Sons Ltd, 79 Piccadilly, Manchester (061-236 3551). A large and remarkably inexpensive range of pure silks 36 in. to 45 in. wide. There are fifty-three shades of Habotai at £2.50 per metre, twenty-seven in crêpe de Chine (£7.50), thirteen in Macclesfield silk (£4.50), plus a large range of prints and silk shirting. Minimum order – three metres. Swatches sent on request.

SUSSEX

Trisha Rafferty, 54 Byron Street, Hove, E Sussex (Brighton 773855). Handmade ceramic buttons, earrings, pots and pictures. Trisha Rafferty is a potter who started making buttons because she couldn't find anything ready-made that she liked. They are either handpainted or made in many-layered coloured clay. There is a small range of designs readily available; others are done to special commission. Prices from £5.95 for a card of six buttons.

YORKSHIRE

Duttons for Buttons, 32 Coppergate, York, N Yorks (York 32042); branches at Harrogate, Ilkley and Otley. Millions of buttons, they say, from modern Italian handmade ones, French glass, mother-of-pearl, leather to men's glove buttons from the Boer War. Send them a swatch of fabric and they will do their best to provide suitable samples by post. They also do general haberdashery and are selling lots of antique and reproduction lace since the Princess of Wales set the vogue. The York shop has a restored medieval room devoted to crafts and craftwork.

Embroidery

CHESHIRE

The Handicraft Shop, 5 Oxford Rd, Altrincham (061-928 3834). Needle-craft supplies of all kinds. Mary Bealey and Marie Jackson specialize in tapestry and embroidery kits and yarns and also have large stocks of beads, felts, threads, gold and silver kid, rush, seagrass and materials for candle-making, rug-making and marquetry. They will also make up their customers' own work, will stretch and mount tapestries, and frame pictures. Send stamped addressed envelope and 20p for a catalogue.

CUMBRIA

Roy and Christine Page, Edenfield, Armathwaite, Carlisle (Armath-waite 222). Pictures and tapestries mounted and framed in a converted barn/

studio. Christine Page uses the old-fashioned method of tapestry-stretching by steam-pressing the canvas over a semi-flexible board and lacing the back rather than pinning it with tacks, which can rust and rot the fabric. To stretch a 15-in.-square relatively unbiased tapestry she charges £2.90; to frame a picture 12 × 16 in. with 1-in. mahogany frame, £9.50.

DORSET

Mary Gostelow, Sew-a-Sampler, 43 Milton Abbas, Blandford Forum (Milton Abbas 880654). Useful Line-Finder to make it easier to follow embroidery and knitting charts. It is a simple 11 × 8¼ in. white-enamelled metal board, with two bright green magnetic strips. You place the board under your chart and adjust the strips to make a guide along the line you are following, thus avoiding crossed eyes to go with your crossed stitches. £3.75, including postage. Also a good range of counted-thread samplers.

Joan Payne, Great Down Farm, Marnhull, Sturminster Newton (Marnhull 820217). Wall-hangings, chair seats and heraldic needlepoint canvases designed to order. Joan Payne won a Design Centre award for her Royal Wedding commemorative cushion, and she has now produced another cushion kit, hand-screenprinted with classical cherubs. These are available by post at about £16.50, or £25 for a pair. Individually designed canvases are handpainted, mostly with crests or in the French Empire style – intended for drawing-rooms full of family antiques. If you don't want to work them yourself, you can have a design created to suit your decor and it can then be completed for you.

GLOUCESTERSHIRE

Jane Rainbow, Badgers End, Fosse Way, Stow-on-the Wold (Stow-on-the-Wold 31103). A designer in canvas embroidery and crewel who will create cushion kits to suit individual furnishings and individual expertise, so if you are a beginner or an expert you can work something specially tailored just for you. Any size of work can be designed, from chair seats to carpets; the minimum cost is about £12 for a 10-in.-square cushion. When you have finished the work it can be stretched and made up too. Jane Rainbow also designs kits under the Needle Art House label, available from her or from stockists of Paterna yarn. There are four cushion designs, a pincushion and needlecase kit, and a chair seat in stripes in four shades of one colour, which will fit most sizes of chair seat and goes well with modern or antique furnishings.

LONDON

Ells & Farrier Ltd, 5 Princes St, Hanover Square, W1 (01-629 9964).
Beads, sequins, diamanté, clips and clasps – everything you need for embroidery,
collage and jewellery-making. This company has supplied the trade for fifty years
and is now selling to private customers too. The selection is vast but if you are
unable to visit the shop there is a catalogue, hand-sewn with sample beads and
braids, available for £2 from their mail-order address, Creative Beadcraft, Unit 26,
Chiltern Trading Estate, Earl Howe Rd, Holmer Green, High Wycombe, Buckinghamshire.

**Glorafilia, The Old Mill House, The Ridgeway, Mill Hill Village, NW7
(01-906 0212).** Tapestries designed to co-ordinate with your furnishings, wall-
hangings, chair backs and seats, cushions, bedheads. Prices from £45 for a specially commissioned cushion design, with all the materials to work it. Also a large
range of needlepoint kits designed by Jennifer Berman and Carole Lazarus. A mail-
order catalogue for these is available. Prices from £8 to £95.

Luxury Needlepoint, 36 Beauchamp Place, SW3 (01-581 5555). The only
shop in the world, they claim, to deal exclusively in hand-prepared tramé tapestries.
The tramé idea is said to have come from Mary Queen of Scots' lady-in-waiting,
Mary Seton, who brought her mistress details of a book illustration intended for
embroidery and 'markkyed a linnene with colord threads' to show how the design
would look. There are designs suitable for every furnishing period, from £10 to
£1,500, and when you have finished a tapestry you can take it back to be stretched
or made up. They will even fill in the background for you if you get bored after you
have done the design. Their computerized mail-order system works worldwide.

**Anna Pearson School of Needlepoint, 25 Kildare Terrace, W2 (01-727
9696).** To match a favourite outfit, Anna Pearson's Needlework by Post catalogue
includes an evening clutch bag in black suede or leather with a removable
'window' in the front into which you can slide your own needlework panel. The
bag is £49, the panels, petit-fleur or trellis, each £11. For an extra £2 you can send
a piece of fabric and have the stranded cottons selected to tone. Postage extra, but
free over £50. Needlepoint classes for beginners or advanced students available
in London or, by arrangement, in the country.

The Royal School of Needlework, 25 Princes Gate, SW7 (01-589 0077).
Embroideries and tapestries to commission. Your own ideas can be handpainted
on canvas, and they will also stretch your work when it is finished. They undertake
the restoration of antique tapestries and lace, and their shop stocks all the equipment and yarns. Courses on embroidery are available.

Women's Home Industries Tapestry Shop, 85 Pimlico Rd, SW1 (01-730 5366). Any type of hand-printed needlepoint canvas designed to commission, from handpainted initial cushions to rugs and carpets. Also a large range of designs in stock. A chair seat will cost from about £30 for the canvas and sufficient wools. WHI stock Appleton crewel and tapestry wool, Anchor tapestry wool, and Paterna Persian yarn, and will stretch and make up customers' own work.

TYNE AND WEAR

Le Prevo Leathers, Blackfriars Craft Centre, Stowell St, Newcastle upon Tyne (Newcastle upon Tyne 617648). Whole sheepskins and other leathers. Stuart Hails is a leather-worker producing finished goods, but he also sells to customers who want to make their own clothes. The skins are priced in square feet – a sheepskin works out at £5 to £7, a pigskin between £10 and £15, a cowhide between £20 and £35 a side. There is an excellent selection of skins in natural colours and of dyed suedes, and a leaflet is available giving advice on sewing leather, size of needles, length of stitch and placing of patterns.

WILTSHIRE

Mace & Nairn, 89 Crane St, Salisbury (Salisbury 6903). Everything for the embroiderer. This specialist shop has a mail-order service and will supply a large selection of linens, cottons, tapestries and canvases, wools and threads, including metal threads for ecclesiastical work. You can also have embroideries and tapestries designed to commission. A mail-order brochure is available.

Jewellery

CORNWALL

Kernowcraft Rocks & Gems Ltd, 21 Pydar St, Truro (Truro 573888). Jewellery supplies by mail order. There is a large range of semi-precious stones, natural and synthetic stones, settings, silvercraft and enamelling equipment and tools. An illustrated catalogue is available.

HEREFORD AND WORCESTER

Janet Coles, Eastham Grange, nr Tenbury Wells, Worcs (Tenbury Wells 79472). Many shapes and sizes of beads and necessities for jewellery-making and embroidery. There are glass fruits and flowers, cubes, lozenges and bugles, round beads from 2 mm to 12 mm, shapes in plastic and wood. Janet Coles also supplies various kits for beginners from £2.25 to £7. A brochure is available for two first-class stamps.

SUSSEX

Southern Handicrafts, 25 Kensington Gardens, Brighton, E Sussex (Brighton 681901). Mail-order suppliers of thin sheet copper and pewter for jewellery-making. The copper is £5.75 per yard and the pewter is in two thicknesses at £6.68 and £9.13 per yard. There are also fifty-eight types of fur fabric for soft-toy making from £2.45 to £9 per yard. Those who can visit the shop will find large stocks of supplies for needlework, lampshade-making, lacemaking, cold enamelling, plaster of paris and many other crafts.

Knitting

LONDON

The shops mentioned here stock mainly widely available brands well-known to knitters, but for those who are house-bound, the mail-order services could be useful.

Browns Woolshop, 79 Regent's Park Rd, N W1 (01-586 2160). George Picaud yarns, including interesting cotton blends. Rachel Brownson designs her own knitwear or can arrange for Picaud patterns to be made up for about £20, plus the cost of the yarn. Mail order available.

Laines Couture, 20 Bedford St, W C2 (01-836 1805). Pure wool alpaca and wool/mohair mixtures by Laines Plassard and Tiber. Yarns and patterns by post.

Ries Wools of Holborn, 242–243 High Holborn, W C1 (01-242 7721). A wide range of fashion yarns and designer kits, including brands not widely available. These include Sandy Block mohair kits, Kaffe Fassett sweater packs and Susan Duckworth designer kits in cotton and wool.

Patricia Roberts, 1b Kensington Church Walk, W8 (01-937 0097). One of the best-known names in British knitting. Her own patterns and yarns are available by mail. Some patterns can be made up in different yarns – wool, cotton, silk – so you can achieve a variety of effects with the same instructions.

The Yarn Store, 8 Ganton St, W1 (01-734 4532). Icelandic wools and patterns and natural British wool. The store also has its own patterns.

TYNE AND WEAR

Woollies, 21 High St, Gosforth, Newcastle upon Tyne (Gosforth 852848). Shelf upon shelf of multi-coloured wools and yarns to tempt even the most hamfisted knitter. Audrey Blakey and Barbara Netts stock well-known British and French yarns; Patricia Roberts, Anny Blatt, Tiber and Laines Plassard are exclusive to them in the North-East. They also stock craft items, Danish thread-work, ready-trimmed tapestries and soft-toy and quilting kits, and they have a complete range of D M C tapestry wools. They will knit anything to order from any pattern in the shop, and they stock ready-knitted samples for their customers to see and try on. Prices according to the wool and degree of difficulty for the finished garment. They also offer a postage and telephone service for out-of-town customers.

Spinning and weaving

CUMBRIA

Susan Foster, 9 Windermere Rd, Kendal (Kendal 26494). A large range of spinning and weaving supplies, including Glimkara Swedish looms and equip-ment, spinning wheels and a good range of yarns, including Borgs, Craftsman's Mark, William Hall cottons, Genesis 31. There are fleeces, natural and chemical dyes and dyeing equipment, macramé supplies and craft books; help and advice are enthusiastically given. The showroom is open Wednesday, Friday and Saturday from 10 a.m. to 5 p.m.

LONDON

The Handweavers Studio and Gallery Ltd, 29 Haroldstone Rd, E17 (01-521 2281). Specialists in spinning and weaving with all the equipment from cotton and wool to silk, cashmere and alpaca for hand-spinning. Apart from the yarns there are several types of looms and spinning wheels, and courses in tapestry, spinning and weaving are available. A brochure is available if you send a large stamped addressed envelope.

YORKSHIRE

Olicana Crafts, Unit 27, The Piece Hall, Halifax, W Yorks (Bradford 681930). Spinning wheels and accessories, and the owners offer free tuition in spinning to any customers who buy a spinning wheel. They also stock combed wools and speciality fibres, spindle spinning kits and Danish hand-looms. Hand-tufted rugs can be made to order. Open Thursday, Friday, Saturday, 10 a.m. to 5 p.m.; Sunday, 11 a.m. to 5 p.m.

Shops for Collectors

Antiquities

LONDON

Charles Ede Ltd, 37 Brook St, W1 (01-493 4944). Specialist dealers in antiquities at prices which encourage inexperienced collectors to extend their knowledge. Charles Ede, who founded the Folio Society, began to sell antiquities in the mid-sixties and by 1971 had to devote all his time to them. He and his son James have probably the largest collection in the middle price ranges of Greek pottery, Egyptian sculpture, Roman glass and near-Eastern antiquities, all between £30 and £5,000. They have flints from at least 10,000 BC and their latest pieces are seventh century A D. Each piece is issued with a descriptive authentication. They produce nine specialized catalogues a year – send £5 annual subscription for them all; or individual subjects and the Christmas catalogue can be obtained free. Viewing outside shop hours can be arranged by appointment.

Arms and military

LONDON

Blunderbuss, 29 Thayer St, W1 (01-486 2444). Military memorabilia from Cromwell to the present day. Tom Greenaway started the shop fifteen years ago and is now one of the few specialists left in the country. He has everything from buttons and badges to pistols, swords and suits of armour and '39–'45 uniforms. Prices are from 20p for small items for schoolboy collectors to a great deal more for rarities for serious military buffs.

WARWICKSHIRE

The Arms and Armour Museum, Poet's Arbour, Sheep St, Stratford-upon-Avon (Stratford-upon-Avon 293453). Antique swords, pistols, blunderbusses, muskets and armour from the sixteenth to the nineteenth century. Mainly a private museum, but there are genuine pieces for sale in the shop similar to those in the museum. Pistols are around £200, swords from £100, blunderbusses £600 to £1,200, half-suits of armour from £650.

Books and newspapers

CHESHIRE

Garrick Book Shop, 8–10 Wellington Rd South, Stockport (061-480 4346). Antiquarian books from the eighteenth and nineteenth centuries. Peter Aird specializes in natural history (birds, horses, flowers, wildlife) and books and directories of local interest on Manchester, Cheshire, Lancashire and Derbyshire. He also stocks children's books from 1850 to 1950, will trace out-of-print books and provides a full bookbinding service. Postcards, particularly local views from 1900, are available from 10p to £20.

GLAMORGAN

Out of Print Book Service, 17 Fairwater Grove East, Cardiff, S Glamorgan (Cardiff 569488). A time-saving book-search service without obligation to buy. Each week a list of books wanted by clients is distributed throughout the second-hand book trade and if a dealer has a sought-after copy a description is sent to the client quoting the price. There is no charge for inclusion on the list and no obligation to agree to the price. The minimum price is £5, even for paperbacks, and you can reckon on the price a hardback would cost to publish today, even if it was originally only 3s. 6d. All subjects are covered. Please send first-class stamp with inquiries or requests.

LONDON

The Basilisk Press, 32 England's Lane, N W3 (01-722 2142). A specialist in private-press productions – probably the only shop of its kind. Charlene Garry opened it in 1977 (having been no nearer to bookselling than running a discotheque in Hong Kong) to deal in all the private-press and limited-edition books in print from Britain and other countries. The beautiful hand-bindings and hand-made papers are a delight, and there is a detailed catalogue for £4, describing all the presses and including details of Basilisk's own publications. The shop also sells hand-marbled papers, bookplates and other book-related items, including calligraphy and wood-engraved illustrations.

Robert Heron Original and Rare Newspapers, 46 The Market, Covent Garden, W C2 (01-379 7779). Newspapers, news-sheets and the earliest news-books from the seventeenth century to present-day curiosities, such as *Not The Times* (when the paper was on strike) and the *Guardian*'s Island of San Serife April Fool's spoof, although, by Robert Heron's definition, newspapers cannot be described as rare after 1855, when the tax stamp on them was abolished. Prices are from £3 to £50 for newspapers, from £75 for newsbooks. There is also a selection of old American newspapers. By the time you have browsed through the pleasantly airy gallery you will agree with Macaulay that 'the only true history of a country is to be found in its newspapers'. There are also twentieth-century editions of *The Times, Financial Times* and *Daily Express* to present for birthdays – from £10.

Vintage Magazines, 39–41 Brewer St, W1 (01-439 8527). 'Anything in paper that you would expect to be thrown away' – newspapers, magazines, posters, programmes, comics, fashion plates, Victorian sheet-music; you name it, Danny Posner has got it. He has been collecting for years and now has two floors packed with literally millions of papers and magazines – a Mecca for researchers and film and television props departments. Prices are from £3 or £4, but for a first issue of *Playboy*, which has Marilyn Monroe as a centrefold, you can expect to pay £750 – everybody ripped out the picture and stuck it on the wall, so there aren't many complete issues left. More modestly you can have issues of newspapers which show what happened on the day you were born, with an attractive presentation folder to put them in, from £3.

TYNE AND WEAR

Steedman, 9 Grey St, Newcastle upon Tyne (Newcastle upon Tyne 326561). An antiquarian bookshop run by three generations of the Steedman family since the beginning of the century. Apart from rare books at four-figure prices, they also sell first edition signed copies of living writers – Lawrence Durrell's *Alexandria Quartet*, for instance – and have a fine selection of early recipe books and a comprehensive North-East collection, including several rare and fine copies illustrated and written by the local engraver Thomas Bewick.

Buttons

LONDON

The Button Queen, 19 Marylebone Lane, W1 (01-935 1505). Unusual antique buttons bought by collectors throughout the world, plus a huge range of modern buttons. Pearl shirt buttons come in twenty-six colours, and there are many shapes and sizes in all sorts of materials. If you send a piece of fabric and three first-class stamps, the Button Queen will send a selection of suitable samples in the sizes you specify.

Cartoons, maps and photographs

LONDON

The Cartoon Gallery (formerly The Workshop), 83 Lamb's Conduit St, WC1 (01-242 5335). The only gallery in the country to specialize in original cartoons. It was opened in 1971 by Mel Calman and has a selection of work by him and by Heath, Larry, Honeysett, Marc and Posy among other leading cartoonists. Prices are from £10 to £100. The gallery also holds monthly exhibitions of watercolours and illustrations by new as well as established artists.

The Map House, 54 Beauchamp Place, SW3 (01-589 4325/9821). Rare and beautifully illustrated maps from 1486 to 1850. Established in 1907 in St James's, the Map House moved to Beauchamp Place in 1973 and collectors all over the world noted the move in their diaries. Prices for the most unusual maps are in the collectors-only class, but there are more modest offerings from £5 to £60.

The Photographers' Gallery, 5 and 8 Great Newport St, WC2 (01-240 5511). Photographic prints by internationally known names and new photographers, on exhibition and for sale. The gallery opened in 1971, when photography as an art-form began to be recognized in this country, helped along by David Bailey and the film *Blow Up*. (The Museum of Modern Art in New York has had a department of photography since the late 1940s.) It holds sixteen major exhibitions and ten smaller shows a year and sells posters, postcards, books, including out-of-print publications, and photographs from nineteenth-century prints at £25 to £200, examples of the work of Bill Brandt and Brassai at £275 to £750, and modern British photographers, including Fay Godwin and John Blackmore, from £100 to £170.

The Vision Gallery, 30 Museum St, WC1 (01-636 9519). A gallery specializing in photographic prints for decoration. Among them are landscapes by John Hedgecoe, wildlife by Peter Johnson, abstracts by Nicholas Rowe, sepia prints from original glass negatives by Donald McLeish, who specialized in landscapes and portraits taken in Europe and the Middle East between 1880 and 1935. Prices are from £25 to £175, some in limited editions. The gallery, part of a photographic agency and library, has regularly changing exhibitions of contemporary work.

Clocks and barometers

CHESHIRE

Peter Bosson, 10b Swan St, Wilmslow (Wilmslow 525250). Antique clocks of all shapes and sizes, from 1700 to the early electric clocks of the 1930s.

A gentle soothing ticking sound greets you as you walk through the door, so it's a relaxing shop to visit. As well as long-case clocks, wall clocks, bracket clocks and carriage clocks, Peter Bosson also specializes in scientific instruments, barometers, shipping instruments and barographs (recording barometers). Mercury barometer tubes are always in stock, also barograph charts, nibs and ink. He also undertakes repairs and restoration of antique clocks, including cabinet work. Clocks from £20 to £10,000.

KENT

Nigel Coleman, High St, Brasted, Westerham (Westerham 64042). One of the country's leading specialists in barometers. As well as dealing with all aspects of restoration, Nigel Coleman has an interesting collection for sale – and some choice pieces of eighteenth- and early-nineteenth-century furniture.

YORKSHIRE

Clocks and Things, Unit 4, The Piece Hall, Halifax, W Yorks (Halifax 66571, evenings). A good selection of small antique clocks, all in working order and with a six months' guarantee. Monica Clay is a language teacher who began to collect clocks as a hobby and found that they became a full-time occupation. She specializes in mantel clocks, carriage clocks and small wall clocks – long-case clocks are too large to carry up to her first-floor showroom – and she deals in all periods up to the 1940s. She also sells clocks in need of restoration. Prices are from £5 (unrestored) to £500 for an interesting, fully restored model.

Commemoratives

LONDON

Britannia, 101 Grays Antiques Market, 58 Davies St, W1 (01-629 6772). Commemorative china from the early nineteenth century to Prince William's birth, at prices from £4 to £200. Not every royal occasion has been marked by a commemorative pottery mountain; just one pottery mug was produced for the marriage of the then Princess Elizabeth to the Duke of Edinburgh, and a cup and saucer produced for Princess Margaret's wedding is now so rare that there is a waiting list of people anxious to pay whatever is asked. Ian and Rita Smythe have been specialists in this field for sixteen years and now combine it with majolica, English art pottery and Art Deco ornaments and tableware.

J. & J. May, 40 Kensington Church St, W8 (01-937 3575). Commemorative items of museum quality. John May has been a specialist in antique commemoratives for fifteen years and has pieces from the early eighteenth century. Among the rarities in his shop recently was a drawing of Napoleon by Sir Henry Bunbury, the only person who actually saw him at close range at the beginning of his exile, and so the most authentic drawing of the period. You will find interesting historic items here, from about £100 for a jug commemorating the marriage of Edward VII to Alexandra. John May has written books on his subject; the most recent is *Victoria Remembered*, the first of a two-part volume on Queen Victoria's life seen through the eyes of her commemorators.

Craft shops and galleries

DERBYSHIRE

The Gallery, 4 West End, Wirksworth (Wirksworth 3557). Michael and Marguerite Howard opened this gallery three years ago in a converted sixteenth-century cottage. They run four major exhibitions a year, showing and selling work by selected East Midlands artists and leading British potters, including Michael Casson, Joanna Constantiniolis and Mary Rich, and there is a constant stock of high-quality pottery and original prints. The gallery is open from Wednesday to Saturday 10.30 a.m. to 5 p.m., or by appointment with the Howards.

DEVON

Dartington Craft Shop, Dartington Cider Press Centre, Shinners Bridge, Dartington (Torquay 864171). Pottery, textiles, jewellery, knitwear, leatherwork, toys, prints, studio glass and woodwork, well displayed in a spacious gallery complex. Prices from £5 to £1,000. You can also buy seconds of current Dartington glass ranges at about one third less than the price for perfects.

LONDON

Coleridge, 80 Highgate High St, N6 (01-340 0999). The most representative collection of modern British glass in the country. Adam Aaronson has a sensitive appreciation of glass forms and enjoys sharing his knowledge with his customers. He has something to appeal to all pockets, from nuggets of coloured glass for children (3p and 5p each) to superb examples of leading glass artists, including Peter Hanauer, Margaret Alston, Dillon Clarke, Sam Herman, Brian Blanthorn and Anthony Stern.

J. K. Hill, 151 Fulham Rd, SW3 (01-584 7529). Handmade pottery at very reasonable prices. Jan Hill and Stuart Mansell always have a selection of practical pots – mugs, soup tureens, bread crocks, in earthy colours from about £1.85 – and every six weeks or so they present an exhibition of one-off designer pots by up-and-coming potters as well as by well-known names such as David Leach, Emmanuel Cooper and Robin Welch. Even prices for these are rather less than you will find in other galleries.

Living Art, 35 Kenway Rd, SW5 (01-370 2766). A pleasant, airy gallery run by John and Izzy Harrap, who hold regular exhibitions of hand-work, sculpture, art, clothes and glass. Each exhibition lasts for eleven days and gives craftspeople with no London base an opportunity to show to a metropolitan market. Several artists who first showed here have gone on to expand their businesses nationally. Prices are modest – you can find small items from £2.50 – and there is also a room devoted to antique silver, where very early spoons are a speciality.

Victoria and Albert Museum Craft Shop, Cromwell Rd, SW7 (01-589 5070). New and experimental work in ceramics, jewellery, glass, textiles and wood by leading contemporary craftsmen. Also at the V & A is a selection of high-quality replicas of works in the museum, including porcelain, netsukes and pewter. Prices are from £2.50 to £6,000. Closed on Fridays.

OXFORDSHIRE

The Oxford Gallery, 23 High St, Oxford (Oxford 42731). An always interesting collection of jewellery, textiles and pottery by leading makers, including Wendy Ramshaw, Roger Oates and Bernard Leach. Glass and wood are also represented, and Joan Crossley-Holland shows a large and international collection of prints in the lower gallery. There are regularly changing exhibitions of work by groups of new as well as by established craftsmen.

SUSSEX

Hands Craft Gallery, 150 St Pancras, Chichester, W Sussex (Chichester 787645). Permanent displays by leading designer/makers of ceramics, studio glass, metal, wood and textiles, shown in the converted ground floor of a seventeenth-century house on the main road from Chichester centre to Brighton. The owner, Hilton Ambler, also puts on three or four group exhibitions of new work each year. Individual craftsmen may be commissioned through the gallery. Closed Mondays and from mid-January to mid-March.

TYNE AND WEAR

Hopper Williams, Designers Gallery, 46 Dean St, Newcastle upon Tyne (Newcastle upon Tyne 615336). A focal point of good design, offering craftsman-made furniture and objects to commission, a range of off-the-peg furniture, lighting and fabrics, and a consultancy on architectural and interior design. You will find Magistretti chairs, hand-blown Cowdy glass, and one-off vases by local glass-blower Paul Manson. Furniture designer/makers include John Colman, whose tables are from £189, and David Cowell, whose leather folding chair is £129. The gallery is closed on Mondays, open Saturdays; the consultancy works a normal Monday-to-Friday office week.

WARWICKSHIRE

Peter Dingley, 8 Chapel St, Stratford-upon-Avon (Stratford-upon-Avon 205001). One of the best craft galleries in the country. When he opened in 1966 in Meer Street, Peter Dingley was probably the first to devote a privately owned shop entirely to the work of British artist craftsmen. His appreciation of quality in design and workmanship helped to give artistic status to many crafts previously dismissed as folksy, and he still encourages young talent by exhibiting the work of new craftsmen side by side with well-established international names – Lucie Rie, David Leach, Anthony Stern among them. Prices are from £2.50 to £1,000 – you will find pottery, woodwork, glass, hangings and fabric pictures, and Peter Dingley is always happy to discuss and advise. You can also learn a lot by studying the display and lighting of the objects by designer Guido Marchini, and you can be sure that there is not an ill-chosen piece in the gallery.

Dolls

CUMBRIA

Carol Black, Sun Hill, Great Strickland, Penrith (Hackthorpe 330). Carol Black's fascination with miniatures, coupled with her artistic training, has been the basis for this shop in her house, which provides everything imaginable for the dolls' house. Carol Black makes many of the items herself, and in the 1982 Edinburgh Dolls' House Exhibition she and her husband Robert won first prize for their miniature black kitchen range, complete with 'hookie' mat and sampler over the mantelpiece. Prices start at 85p for a mini-mousetrap; a brass bedstead is £5, an old-fashioned kitchen sink with wooden draining board and copper geyser £21. A catalogue is available for 75p in stamps. Customers are seen by appointment.

LONDON

The Dolls House, 29 The Market, Covent Garden, WC2 (01-379 7243). Enchanting handmade miniatures, from strings of onions and Brussels lace table mats to Chinese screens and four-poster beds. There are kits and mass-produced furniture too, and about twenty different designs of modern dolls' houses, from

£52.90 in kit form to more than £1,000. For children there are plenty of inexpensive items, and for collectors a selection of highly covetable antique houses and beautiful scale models, all 1 in. to 1 ft.

The Singing Tree, 69 New King's Rd, SW6 (01-736 4527). Dolls' house furniture and furnishings, exquisitely made to a scale of 1 in. to 1 ft. The styles are mainly Victorian and Georgian, and many pieces are handmade. Apart from the furniture there are all the accessories, from miniature tableware to pictures and wallpaper. Sample prices: a dining table with brass feet is £12.95, an upholstered dining chair £5.95. A mail-order catalogue is available (£2).

MANCHESTER

Mo and Steve Harding, Wittering Court, 17 Ladybarn Rd, Fallowfield, Manchester (061-224 1621). Doll dealers who generally stock up to 100 old dolls, specializing in early wax and china dolls from 1840 to 1920. There are also dolls' houses, dolls' prams, and other associated toys. Dolls are from £60.

SUSSEX

The Dolls Hospital and Collectors Shop, 82 Trafalgar St, Brighton, E Sussex (Brighton 681862). Specialists in dolls' house furniture, with an exclusive line of their own in miniature metalwork and glassware. Their handmade tiny brass fenders, copper kettles, drinking glasses and decanters are exported all over the world.

Fifties and Deco

LONDON

Cobra and Bellamy, 149 Sloane St, SW1 (01-730 2823). Tania Hunter and Veronica Manussis began to notice a strong feeling for fifties furniture on buying trips to France, where the period is taken almost as seriously as Art Deco. They are now major specialists and have an excellent – not cheap – collection which includes the big fifties names – Heal's, Olivetti, Kosta, Bertoia, Venini, Mollino. Small items such as ashtrays from £10; major items in the hundreds.

John Jesse and Irina Laski, 160 Kensington Church St, W8 (01-229 0312). Keep an eye on John Jesse and you will always be ahead of the trend. He started collecting Art Nouveau in 1963, long before it became fashionable, and since then has been the first to deal in Deco, Fifties and now costume jewellery and plastics. Irina Laski joined him in 1978 and they now specialize in all these periods at prices from £10 to £10,000. 'We like to buy things no one else has got,' says John Jesse, 'We do the whole of this century, although of course we can't do the nineties yet.' If anybody could, he would.

Limited editions

WILTSHIRE

Limited Edition Club, PO Box 17, Marlborough (Marlborough 52176). An exchange-and-mart club for collectors of limited editions who want to realize some of their assets in order to make room for more. It was set up in 1981 by a trio of collectors who found there was no properly structured secondary market for limited editions of any kind, including prints, ceramics, silver, sculpture or glass; they are worth only what a buyer is willing to pay at the time, and if you need to sell in a hurry, a dealer may offer much less than you paid. Members receive regular For Sale and Wanted lists for an annual subscription and strike their own bargains with each other.

Pewter and silver

LONDON

Richard Mundey, 19 Chiltern St, W1 (01-935 5613). An expert and specialist in the rarest and finest pewter. Richard Mundey has been collecting for fifty-five years, and is a liveryman of the Worshipful Company of Pewterers. He has rare examples in the shop from the seventeenth and eighteenth centuries, but also has more accessible nineteenth-century items at prices between £20 and £100.

S. J. Phillips Ltd, 139 New Bond St, W1 (01-629 6261). Specialists in antique silver, jewellery and objets d'art. The company was established before 1860 – the records don't show exactly when – and is still in the same family. They have some superb seventeenth- and eighteenth-century English and Continental silver, and their collection of eighteenth-century snuff boxes is one of the finest in the world. They also have some very important jewellery, but prices for all these are strictly in the collectors' and investors' category (they don't like the word 'investors' because, as they say, 'the minute you want to sell in a hurry everybody looks the other way'). There are, however, some beautiful pieces of jewellery at more accessible prices, and for those who have from £200 to spend, this is a shop which will give genuine advice and expertise, ensuring good value and doing it all with immense courtesy.

Records

ESSEX

Adrians Records, 36 High St, Wickford (Wickford 3318). Large stocks of difficult-to-find modern records – the ones which have been recently deleted and which you need to complete a collection. Specialists in 12-in. singles and rare imports – there are singles from £1.40, LPs from £2.25 to £16. A list of their 16,000 records is available if you send a large stamped addressed envelope and 75p.

LONDON

Dress Circle, 1st floor, 43 The Market, Covent Garden, WC2 (01-240 2227). Rare records and sound-tracks of stage shows and films. Patrick Martyn aims to keep one example of every show and soundtrack ever issued anywhere in the world, including rare, deleted records. At the time we spoke he had seventy different LPs of Sinatra, fifteen of *Showboat*, eight versions of *The King and I*. He isn't at all surprised when collectors come in for the Japanese and Mexican versions of *Evita*, and he has unusual issues of shows that folded quickly, like Rodgers and Hammerstein's *Me and Juliet*. Prices are from £2.99, with quite a number of examples in the £25 to £30 category. He is also a source of information for amateur shows and whatever is going on in the business – he knows it.

Mole Jazz Record Shop, 374 Gray's Inn Rd, WC1 (01-278 0703). Not the oldest, but, I'm assured by a jazz expert, the best. They specialize in West Coast and modern, post-war jazz, with some swing and big-band. There is a large selection of imports and second-hand rare records, all discounted, and they also have their own jazz label. A mail-order list is available; please send stamped addressed envelope.

Reckless Records, 79 Upper St, N1 (01-359 0501). Exchange your old records for something even older. This shop will take any record and offer you money or an exchange of similar value. They have a good selection of deleted and rare records and their price range is from a modest 10p to £30.

Rugs and textiles

LONDON

David Black Carpets, 96 Portland Rd, W11 (01-727 2566). One of the first shops to specialize in kelims when it opened in 1967. David Black and Clive Loveless stock antique and old dhurries, embroideries, textiles and rugs from Persia, Turkey, Russia, Turkestan and the Caucasus. Prices are from £100 for saddle bags; kelims are from £350 to £3,000, 12 × 9 ft carpets from £1,500. They also restore kelims on the premises and publish specialist books on textiles and rugs.

Caroline Bosly, 13 Princess Rd, NW1 (01-722 7608). A broker in all types of oriental rugs and carpets who will take clients to the bonded warehouses in north London and, from her extensive knowledge of the thousands of possibilities, point them in the direction of the right rugs within their price range. Unlike other brokers, she will also take rugs back if they prove unsuitable once the customer gets them home, bearing the cost herself of the duty, which is payable once the rug leaves the warehouse. She will arrange for repair and cleaning of rugs, will value clients' own rugs and will even undertake to sell them for a 10-per-cent commission. If you have ever tried to raise the value of an oriental rug through a dealer, you will know how useful that service could be. All clients seen by appointment only.

Carmine Carpets, The Kilim Warehouse, 28a Pickets St, SW12 (01-675 3122). Kelims, berbers and other tribal rugs at very reasonable prices. Jose Luczyc-Wyhowska and David Green also have a few 'investment' pieces, but, through astute personal buying in Turkey and North Africa, they try mainly to offer attractive decoration from £50 to £600. All the rugs are handmade; some are up to seventy years old, others modern. The warehouse doesn't exactly attract a lot of passing trade, as it is in a residential street, but it does have plenty of devotees willing to brave the depths of Clapham between 10 a.m. and 4 p.m. on Mondays to Saturdays and 11 a.m. and 2 p.m. on Sundays. Or you can make an appointment.

Lunns Antiques, 86 New King's Rd, SW6 (01-736 4638). Exquisite Victorian and Edwardian lace and embroidery. Stephen and Juliet Lunn were among the first to specialize in lace when they started six years ago, and they now have one of the largest collections in the country. They have lace from 1600 to the present

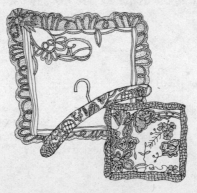

with reproductions of period garments. There are bedcovers, curtains, cushions, pretty Edwardian nightdresses, camisoles and christening robes, and they will make feather pillows to any size, including square continental pillows – £16 in feather, £28 in feather and down. They will also advise on the restoration and laundry of clients' antique lace.

Shells

LONDON

The Eaton Bag Company Ltd, 16 Manette St, W1 (01-437 9391). Special-ists, although you wouldn't think so from the name, in seashells, minerals, fossils, cane, bamboo, seagrass, raffia and jewellery. The name came from the company's founder who had a leather-goods business in Vienna and was warned by one of his staff to leave the country before the Nazis confiscated everything. He came to England and was so grateful to find refuge here that he called his company by the most English institution he could think of – Eton. His only mistake was that he couldn't spell. The shop is also known as the Shell Shop, as it is one of the country's main suppliers now, and it will also make cane roller blinds to whatever measure-ments you require from £5.85.

Thimbles

LONDON

Bees, Stand 378, Grays Antique Market, 58 Davies St, W1 (01-493 0560). Thimbles from the fourteenth century to the present day. Bridget McConnel and Betty Huntley-Wright became fascinated by thimbles and sewing accessories when, as general antique dealers, they bought a large private collection. They soon gave up selling other antiques to concentrate on sewing instruments – probably the only people in Europe specializing in the subject. They run a Thimble Society and produce a quarterly magazine which goes to many parts of the world and gives interesting snippets of social history, among them the story of the ladies who used to take their tatting to parties and surreptitiously unravel the gold epaulettes of their male companions. The practice became so prevalent that an Act of Parliament had to be passed in the 1820s to restrain such immoral behaviour. Collectors can find thimbles in ivory, silver, gold, glass and porcelain. A Meissen one, if you could find it, might cost £8,000, but mostly the examples at Bees are between 50p and £500.

Wine antiques

AVON

Robin Butler, 9 St Stephen's St, Bristol 1 (Bristol 276586). A dealer in eighteenth-century antique furniture, glass and silver, who became the first specialist in wine-related English antiques when he put on his first show five years ago for the British Antique Dealers Association's jubilee. Robin Butler now has one of the largest collections in the country, ranging from £3 for a simple bin label to £10,000 for the finest eighteenth-century wine-cooler. Most of the stock is between £50 and £500, and one of the most unusual pieces was an ivory hydrometer to measure the specific gravity of wines.

LONDON

Richard Kihl, 164 Regent's Park Rd, NW1 (01-586 3838). A wine shipper with a very fine old claret list. Richare Kihl began to collect wine accessories several years ago and accumulated so many he had to open a shop. He now also has a very varied and interesting collection ranging from the most ingenious corkscrews (from £5) through hunting flasks and wine labels to wine-coolers (from £50 to £1,000). You might even be lucky and find a spittoon – a rare curiosity these days.

Specialist Shops

Books

HERTFORDSHIRE

Watford Technical Books, 105 St Albans Rd, Watford (Watford 23324). The only shop in the country devoted exclusively to books on computing and electronics. Jeremy Dicks was in publishing and had so many problems trying to persuade book retailers up and down the country to stock this not only up-and-coming but here-and-now subject that he opened his own shop. He has everything in it to suit the beginner, the teenage genius and the expert professional, and also operates a very quick and up-to-date mail-order service – by computer, of course.

LONDON

Robinson & Watkins, 21 Cecil Court, WC2 (01-838 2182). Books on spiritual, mystical and occult subjects. John Watkins, who founded the business in 1893, was persuaded to devote a shop entirely to this subject by Madame Blavatsky, one of the originators of the Theosophical Society. At one time it was conducted like a small club, with visitors such as Jung dropping in for a philosophical discussion. Now run by Richard Robinson and his family, it deals worldwide and also has a publishing company. Subjects also include fringe medicine, astrology and the esoteric and hidden sides of religious beliefs.

OXFORDSHIRE

The Country Bookshop, Bear Court, Burford (Burford 3495). A small and charming bookshop at the bottom of the hill behind Bear Court Gift Shop. Caroline Wright specializes in books on country lore, natural history, gardening, cookery and craft, and has an excellent selection of children's books.

TYNE AND WEAR

The Bookhouse, 13 Ridley Place, Newcastle upon Tyne (Newcastle upon Tyne 616128). Iris Penny concentrates on literature and the arts, prides herself on a quick and efficient book ordering service and has one of the best collections of children's books in the North. There is a small coffee shop which helps to create the friendly atmosphere, and occasionally there are evening readings, musical events or Saturday-morning children's entertainments.

Food

BUCKINGHAMSHIRE

Burgers of Marlow Ltd, The Causeway, Marlow (Marlow 3389). A Swiss family confectionery business which has been trading for forty-one years and still makes bread, cakes and chocolates on the premises. Marie and Eric Burger will send boxes of delicious handmade chocolates or truffles anywhere by post; soft centres (cream, fudge, caramel and marshmallow) and hard centres (marzipans, pralines, nuts) are from £2 ($\frac{1}{2}$ lb.), £4.40 (1 lb.), £8 (2 lbs.); truffles (rum, plain, coffee, milk and orange) are £2.40 ($\frac{1}{2}$ lb.), £4.80 (1 lb.), £9.20 (2 lbs.), plus postage.

CHESHIRE

Durig Swiss Pâtisserie, 4 Broomfield Lane, Hale (061-928 1143). A family bakery and confectioners making bread, cakes and chocolates to traditional Swiss recipes and without preservatives. They also have their own flavoured vinegars (for which they grow the herbs), special curry-powder mixes and selections of spiced rices, as well as interesting and unusual chutneys and preserves. They don't do mail order, but they have a selection of gâteaux and savouries specially prepared for the freezer, so a bulk-buy visit could save a lot of stove-slaving later. Not cheap, but very high quality.

CUMBRIA

New Mills Trout Farm, New Mills, Brampton (Brampton 2384). Either catch your own trout – £5.75 per day, for which you can keep four fish – or buy fresh rainbow trout from £1 per lb. Smoked trout available at £2 per lb. and frozen pink New Mills trout £6 for 5 lbs. Lunch boxes and refreshments are available during fishing. Open Wednesday to Sunday from October to May; daily June to September.

The Toffee Shop, 7 Brunswick Rd, Penrith (Penrith 62008). Home-made butter toffee, treacle toffee and three flavours of fudge made on the premises by owner Sadie Fearon. Everything is made with butter to closely guarded traditional recipes. The shop also sells Romney's Kendal mint cake. A postal service is available; send a stamped addressed envelope for the price list.

The Village Bakery and Licensed Restaurant, Melmerby, Penrith (Langwathby 515). Bread and local specialities made with wholemeal flour milled at the watermill in Little Salkeld nearby. The bread is baked in a wood-fired brick oven, one of the last of its kind in the country. There is also Cumberland Rum Nicky, a traditional Cumbrian delicacy made with dates, rum butter and stem ginger: £1.20 for an open flan with enough for eight. Flapjack is 45p, butter shortbread 55p, Borrowdale Tea Bread made to a traditional recipe for slicing and buttering 60p. Closed Mondays and Wednesdays. All this also available from the Village Bakery Foodshop, Angel Lane, Penrith (Penrith 62377).

Ye Olde Friars, Market St, Keswick (Keswick 72234 and 73872). A former tea-room with a delicious selection of Lakeland specialities. Established in 1927, it still retains the same gentle pre-war atmosphere and aura of quality. John Webster and his family sell local delicacies, including Quiggins brandy butter and Cumberland rum butter, home-made preserves, Kendal mint cake and a tempting selection of chocolates and toffee, mostly made in Cumbria. Loose chocolates and truffles with thirty different fillings are from 55p to 65p per $\frac{1}{4}$ lb. Genuine Kendal mint cake with or without a chocolate covering is from 20p per slab. Brandy butter or Cumberland rum butter: $3\frac{1}{2}$-oz. tub 40p, 7-oz. 80p

GLOUCESTERSHIRE

Andie and Juliette Broadhurst, The Epicurean, New St, Painswick (Painswick 812092). Holidaymakers in the area can order picnics in advance or pick them on the spot from a selection of tempting delicatessen from 40p a portion – quiches, pies, salads, pates, cheesecake and half-bottles of wine. Paper plates, knife, fork and spoon available for 10p.

LONDON

Fortnum & Mason, Piccadilly, W1 (01-734 8040). *Tea:* Special advice on the right tea for the water supply in your area. Ring and tell them where you live and what sort of water comes out of your taps (preferably without slandering your local authority), and they will blend a tea specially for you and it.

Wine: Your cellar assessed and valued, advice given on laying down and an annual assessment sent out to tell you how your wines should be progressing. They will also decant old port and return it to its bottle for you to take home if you need it in a hurry for that evening's dinner-party.

Pasta Pasta, 52 Pimlico Rd, SW1 (01-730 1435). All sorts of fresh pasta – the idea imported from New York, the expertise from Italy, where Robin Gage and Derek Jones learned all about the techniques. Choose pasta in many shapes and the sauces to go with them, or buy ready-filled pastas such as ravioli, lasagne and tortellini. There is even a wholemeal pasta for those who insist on wholefoods (tried to find a generic term and could only come up with 'wholefood nuts'). Also a large range of other Italian foods.

The Tea House, 15a Neal St, W C2 (01-240 7539). Everything you associate with tea – apart from the cucumber sandwiches. Twelve blends of tea, plus herb teas and fruit flavoured teas, plus beautiful teapots, funny teapots, grotesque teapots, infusers, lemon squeezers, strainers, cosies, caddies. Even honey still for tea, but not, as yet, tea and sympathy.

MANCHESTER

On the Eighth Day, 111 Oxford Rd, Manchester (061-273 4878/1850). An exceptionally good wholefood shop, with a wide range of grains, pulses, whole-wheat pastas, nuts, dried fruits, herbs and spices, all at rock-bottom prices. Because the shop is run as a co-operative by a well-organized group of young people, overheads are kept to a minimum. In the student area of the city, the shop is a short bus ride from the centre. There is a vegetarian restaurant next door serving home-made soups, salads, stews and rice dishes.

Herbs and plants

LONDON

Culpeper Ltd, 21 Bruton St, Berkeley Square, W1 (01-629 4559), and branches. Mail order: Hadstock Rd, Linton, Cambridge. Specialists in naturally grown herbs and spices. The company was founded in 1927 by Mrs Hilda Leyel, a herbalist who thought that natural cures were about to be swamped by the then new chemical remedies. She took the name from Nicholas Culpeper, the seventeenth-century herbalist who translated the Latin pharmacopoeia into English, giving ordinary people their first chance to understand just how they were being treated. Doctors were as furious then as some still are today when challenged by a questioning patient. The shops sell cosmetics and toiletries, herbs and spices for cooking, herbal remedies, herbs in pots, gardening and cookery books. Their mail-order service is worldwide. Price lists are available for a stamped addressed envelope.

LOTHIAN

Equatorial Plants, 35 Broughton St, Edinburgh (031-557 0725). Orchid seedlings by post. Richard Warren has 150 varieties grown from seeds he brought back from Brazil, and he now supplies many professional growers with rare species. The seedlings arrive in tubes, where they may be allowed to grow before transplanting; they take from two years to flower, so impatient gardeners should stick to Busy Lizzies. A price list is available, plus a back-up service of advice, seed kits and potting materials. A Beginner's Kit, including two seedlings, costs £3.50.

YORKSHIRE

Yorkshire Herbs, The Herb Centre, Middleton Tyas, Richmond, N Yorks (Barton 686). The largest growers of herbs in the North. From May to November they will send fresh-cut herbs by post. There are twenty varieties at £1.50 per pack plus postage, and throughout the year there are half-day courses in the use of herbs – growing, cooking and using for cosmetics. There is also a small range of herb pillows and other craft products.

Household

AVON

Wellow Crafts, Kingsmead Square, Bath (Bath 64358). Traditional British crafts, including Aran and Fair Isle sweaters made to customers' requirements, hand-smocked children's dresses, crocheted bedspreads, handpainted jewellery and local pottery. They also specialize in local services and will find craftsmen to repair bellows, recane chairs, or make almost anything to commission.

BUCKINGHAMSHIRE

Peter Knight, London End, Beaconsfield (Beaconsfield 5561/2/3/4); also at 5 High St, Esher, Surrey (Esher 64122). Everything you need to furnish a house, plus a complete interior design service if you prefer an expert to do it for you. Peter Knight has always had an appreciation of good design – he was London's youngest furniture buyer when he was twenty-three – and from small beginnings in Esher he has not only developed the shop there, but has also opened a much larger one in Beaconsfield, where he offers a highly individual range of furniture and furnishings in a charmingly converted Victorian house. The range includes gifts, table linens, furnishing fabrics, oriental and modern carpets and high-quality furniture.

DEVON

Good Ideas, Moles Cottages, Exminster, Exeter (Exeter 833019). Futons and cotton bedding supplied by post. The futons are the traditional Japanese ones, a 3-in. thick slab of cotton in a cotton covering finished with silky tassels. All are 6 ft 6 in. long; single sizes £45 (30 in.), £50 (36 in.), doubles £70 (50 in.), £75 (56 in.); all plus £5 postage. Colours are black, red, white or brown. There are also cotton quilts and pillows.

LONDON

Judy Afia's Carpet Shop, 123 Fulham Rd, SW3 (01-589 3681), and 154 Tottenham Court Rd, W1 (01-387 4466). Specialists in all-wool berber carpets at very reasonable prices. Judy Afia's 'not quite patterned, not quite plain' two-tone berbers come in an excellent range of twenty-eight colours – among them peppermint, silver grey, peach, navy, all with off-white, at £11.45 per square yard. The two-tone nubbly effect is very good for not showing marks. There are fringed rugs too, in eight plain colours to go with the carpets, from £24.95 for 2 ft 8 in. × 4 ft 6 in.

Anything Left-handed, 68 Beak St, W1 (01-437 3910). A self-explanatory shop started twelve years ago by a left-handed proprietor, but now run by two right-handed but understanding owners who are sympathetically aware of the problems experienced by people who use the 'wrong' hand. Children are specially catered for, and there are scissors, gardening tools, kitchen utensils, even boomerangs and a sail-maker's palm. The mail-order service operates worldwide. Send two second-class stamps for catalogue and price list.

Casa Catalan, 15–16 Chalk Farm Rd, NW1 (01-485 3975). Three floors of Spanish design. Spencer Elster hand-picks his stock in Spain – hand-thrown terracotta is a speciality; there are pots from £4.50 to £85 and even some antique ones. There is wicker too and some handsome handpainted ceramics, including wall plates, cache-pots and jardinieres. The shop is open seven days a week.

The Copper Shop, 48 Neal St, Covent Garden, WC2 (01-836 2984). Anything made or mended in copper or brass. The Copper Shop specializes in selling British-made copperware and has a large range of pans, jelly moulds, fish kettles, mixing bowls, plant troughs and coal-scuttles. They have skilled craftsmen who will make cooker hoods and copper table tops, repair and retin copper pans, and make anything to commission. A mail-order catalogue is available at £1.30.

Elizabeth David Ltd, 46 Bourne St, SW1 (01-730 3123), and Covent Garden Kitchen Supplies, 3 North Row, The Market, Covent Garden, WC2 (01-836 9167). Specialist kitchen supplies, from professional knives to baking equipment and tableware. The original shop in Bourne Street was established long before the cookshop revolution which resulted in similar shops in every major town and department store. Although the world famous cook is no longer associated with the company, the spirit of the doyenne of 'foodies' lingers, and you feel the purchase of just one terrine will turn you into a master chef. Many items are available by mail order. They are not cheap, but there is an annual sale at Bourne Street with some worthwhile bargains.

Ganesha, 6 Park Walk, Fulham Rd, SW10 (01-352 8972). Specialists in imports from South-East Asia. You will find Indonesian spices here that you can't get anywhere else in the country – laos root and kencur root, for instance, plus recipe books to tell you, in the nicest possible way, what you can do with them. There are textiles too, Balinese carvings, masks, shadow puppets, jewellery, incense and records of oriental music.

The Gas Log Fire Emporium, 141 George St, Edgware Road, W1 (01-402 8739/9006). Specialists in barbecues of all shapes and sizes, plus a large range of accessories. Prices range from £10 to £500. The Emporium is part of the Real Flame Gas Log Fires group. They have brochures and can arrange mail order.

The Futon Shop, 267 Archway Rd, N6 (01-340 6126), and 654a Fulham Rd, SW6 (01-736 9190). Futons made in the traditional Japanese manner by a company specializing in natural, organic materials. The futons are $3\frac{1}{2}$ in. thick (they roll up easily for storage); there are five sizes, from 3 ft 3 in. × 6 ft 6 in. to 6 ft 6 in. square, and they cost from £43.75 to £89.75. Cotton covers are available in seven colours from £25 to £49, and there are lambswool duvets at £47.50 (single),

£67.50 (double) and £87.50 (king-size). The range is also available from the workshop, 10–12 Rivington St, EC2 (01-739 5007).

Leon Jaeggi & Sons, 232 Tottenham Court Rd, W1 (01-631 1080), and 124 Shaftesbury Avenue, W1 (01-434 4545). Kitchen equipment for caterers and private cooks. Leon Jaeggi was a chef and set up the company in 1919 to import the best knives from France because he couldn't find anything to match them here. They still specialize in Sabatier and Gustav Emil Ern knives and have their own ranges of copperware and black iron.

Just Mirrors, 181–183 New King's Rd, Fulham, SW6 (01-736 8586). Specialists in framed mirrors, including gilt, pine, fabric, aluminium and stained finishes. There is a selection in stock ranging from £10 to £300 or £400, or special orders can be undertaken. There is a selection of tinted mirrors – grey, brown, and 'antiqued' – which can also be supplied without frames.

The London Sofa-Bed Centre, 185 Tottenham Court Rd, W1 (01-631 1424); and at 236 Fulham Rd, SW10 (01-352 1358), and 223 West End Lane, NW6 (01-794 5166). The most comprehensive range of sofa-beds available. This company was the first sofa-bed specialist when it opened in 1978, and it has twenty designs which can be bought off the peg or made up in any fabric, including customers' own. The average price is between £400 and £600.

Naturally British, 13 New Row, by Covent Garden, WC2 (01-240 0551). A feast of well-designed and well-made British goods. When John Blake and Charles Harris opened the shop in 1978 they wanted to offer handmade items at all price levels, so that tourists could have an alternative to 'mass-produced tat'. They now have more than 300 suppliers of leather goods, pottery, glass, knitwear, toys, textiles, jewellery, cosmetics, jams, honeys and decorative woodwork, including tables made from reclaimed pine. Prices are from £1 for a pair of earrings to about £400 for the tables. A mail-order catalogue is available for a stamped addressed envelope.

Neal Street East, 5 Neal St, WC2 (01-240 2128). All things oriental. The bookshop area has all the reference books you need on Japanese and Chinese art, including architecture, gardening, cookery, philosophy, calligraphy, the martial arts, zen and acupuncture, carpets and textiles; the gallery shows prints, ink paintings, screens; the antique department has jewellery, ceramics, embroideries, scrolls, objets, boxes and chests from China; the fashion department shows old Japanese kimonos and haoris, summer yukatas. Prices from 1p to £1,000.

Paperchase, 213 Tottenham Court Rd, W1 (01-580 8496), and 167 Fulham Rd, SW7 (01-589 7839). Everything to do with paper – wrapping, writing, artists' materials, stencils, greetings cards, coloured paper by the pound, decorations. Paperchase was the first specialist stationery shop in London when it opened in 1967 in Brompton Road, moving to Tottenham Court Road a year later. They will send anywhere by mail.

Propaganza, 92 Nether St, N12 (01-446 2176). Weird and wonderful props for interior design, displays and exhibitions, television sets and even extravagant parties. Before opening his own company, Ivan Monty specialized for twenty-five years in creating fantastic displays for windows and exhibitions, and he now offers a variety of amazing and amusing items, from a velvet hamburger-shaped floor cushion to a giant toad hideous enough to frighten away the most predatory garden gnome. A team of specialists offers fibreglass props, soft sculpture, mirrors, lighting and murals; prices are mostly between £100 and £400.

The Russian Shop, 278 High Holborn, WC1 (01-405 3538). The largest range of Russian and Bulgarian goods in any Western country. The shop was opened twenty-three years ago and the most popular line is still the famous Matrioshka nested dolls in threes at £2.30 and in nines at £19.55. There is also some attractive porcelain, pokerwork and straw-inlay and, best of all, beautiful lacquer boxes handpainted with miniatures of Russian legends and landscapes. Each traditional picture differs slightly, according to the artist's particular talents, and they are collected by connoisseurs all over the world. Prices are from £14 to £500.

Scribbler, 170 King's Road, SW3 (01-351 1173), and 29 James St, Covent Garden, WC2 (01-240 7640). Smartest selection of wrapping paper, greetings cards and trimmings. Not the place to go for hearts and flowers – but if you want to make an impact with shiny black-and-white stripes or polka dots, this is where you start.

NORTHAMPTONSHIRE

Jenny Blair Designs, Vine Cottage, Guilsborough Rd, West Haddon (West Haddon 202). Hand-blown glass scent bottles, bowls and vases decorated with silver. Jenny Blair trained as a silversmith and developed a technique of electroforming metal on glass. She designs the glass and has it blown and, usually, sandblasted to give a frosted texture. She then decorates it in silver, silver plate or gold plate in a variety of botanic and geometric designs. She also uses the same technique on white, unglazed china. Prices are from about £35 for a small bowl to £70 for a large vase.

YORKSHIRE

Illume, 285 Ecclesall Rd, Sheffield, S Yorks (Sheffield 683501). A large selection of lighting, including many fittings which are exclusive in the North of England. Styles are modern in appeal, Art Deco, modern Italian and high tech, with a large range of ceramic table lamps from £12 to £50 and an excellent selection of brass lamps and wall fittings.

Leisure – indoors

CUMBRIA

The Model Shop, 11 Poet's Walk, Penrith (Penrith 65378). This model shop attracts customers from the Borders to Lancashire. Everything for the model enthusiast, from a 50p plastic kit to the shop's own exclusive model of the old Arab dhow 'Sohar' (£28). They sell kits for model wooden boats (priced from £18) and aircraft, castings and authentic enamel paints for steam engines, all types of railway accessories, tools, hardwood for boatbuilders and a range of books on modelling.

LONDON

Hadley Hobbies, 131 Middlesex St, E1 (01-283 9870). *The* place for a small boy to buy his father's Christmas present – a shop full of model railway sets. They cater for the enthusiast, offering everything from 30p accessories to gauge-one steam locomotives at £1,400. Many items are exclusive to them; they have a second-hand counter and part-exchange, as well as a repair shop. They also stock model cars, aircraft and ships.

Just Games, 62 Brewer St, W1 (01-734 6124). The first specialist games shop in London when it opened ten years ago. It has everything from executive puzzles to traditional chess, backgammon, cribbage, nine men's morris – and would you believe Monopoly in Chinese? A brochure is available.

Optimago, 43 Perrymead St, SW6 (01-736 2380). Hand-cut wood jigsaw puzzles packed in hinged boxes designed to be placed on a shelf like a book. Each box contains a drawstring bag of the puzzle pieces. Subjects include the sixteenth-century English maps of Christopher Saxton, a Great Sea Chart of Europe from the first compilation of sea charts ever printed, and a series of twelve flower prints for each month of the year by Robert Furber, gardener at Kensington Palace in 1730. Prices are from about £18 to £26, and the puzzles contain from 300 and 700 pieces.

YORKSHIRE

Dee and Kevin Howley, Bullace Trees Pottery, Triangle, Sowerby Bridge, Halifax, W Yorks (Halifax 832356). Modern doll kits which include china heads, arms and legs with a pattern for the body. Priced from £4 to £10 per kit, plus postage and packing (£1.25 for one up to £3 maximum). Kevin Howley models the dolls' heads with faces based on local children, so they have a really 1980s look about them. There is also a range of woodland creature dolls – hedgehogs, rabbits and fieldmice.

Leisure – outdoors

CHESHIRE

John Dutton, Beech Farm, Chester Rd, Mickle Trafford, nr Chester (Chester 300456). A well-stocked archery shop, run by an enthusiast with a real love of the sport and an interest in encouraging children to take up the hobby. John Dutton specializes in inexpensive beginners' equipment in the shop he has set up next to a fruit and vegetable shop on his farm, and as he is a professional coach he is well qualified to advise. Bows are from £54 for an imported one to £200 for a Nottingham-made Marksman bow. Also available are sights, stabilizers, strings, nocks, piles, flights, crestings, quivers, clickers, bow gauges, rule books, and handicap tables. Open two days a week. Telephone to check opening times.

CUMBRIA

Survival Aids Ltd, Morland, Penrith (Morland 307). Everything you need for survival outdoors. When Nick Steven left the army four years ago, he was so appalled by the total lack of personal survival equipment on the market that together with co-directors Freddy Markham and Chris Hardwicke-Davies he opened Survival Aids. There are bags and blankets, compasses, torches and flares and many items invented by the directors as a result of their own experience. Send £1 for a catalogue, including details of their Survival School.

LONDON

The Kite Store Ltd, 69 Neal St, W C2 (01-836 1666). All sorts of kites, selected by three enthusiasts, Andy King, Mark Cottrell and Martin Lester, who can show you at least 120 models and advise on the best choice for the price you want to pay. They all fly well – they refuse to keep any that won't. Prices are from £2.95 to £100 and they have all the accessories too – line, reels, books, even materials for you to make your own kite. If you want a kite with your name, or a message, on it, you can have that, handmade, from £8.55.

James Purdey & Sons, 57 South Audley St, W1 (01-499 5292). *The* name in sporting guns. The first Purdey to become a gunmaker was born in 1732, and his son James founded the present company in 1814. Nobody just makes a gun. After a five-year training a craftsman becomes a barrel-maker, an ejector-maker, an engraver, a finisher; and guns in the finest French walnut are still made to measure in the traditional manner. There is a two-year waiting list and you can expect to pay more than £10,000. There is also an accessories shop selling sporting clothes and gifts.

SOMERSET

A. W. Rule, 8 Parrott Close, Langport (Langport 250649). Specialists in guns and fishing tackle. This Purdey-trained gunsmith sells high-quality guns, from secondhand ones at £80 to custom-built at £3,000. He also services and repairs quality guns, and stocks all types of rods and fishing accessories.

SUSSEX

John Cookson, Taunton's Lofts, Guildford Rd, Rudgwick, W Sussex (Rudgwick 2276). A specialist breeder of racing pigeons and one of the few in the country to have white Logans. J. W. Logan's pigeons, established in 1870, were the best of their time and when he retired in 1924 his entire stock was sold at record prices. John Cookson's father bought at that sale and John started selective in-breeding to produce white pigeons. He supplied pigeons to the armed forces during the Second World War and now sends the birds to customers all over the world. He has a stock of about 300 birds at prices from £50 and is happy to give free advice to customers who are new to the sport.

TYNE AND WEAR

L.D. Mountain Centre, 34 Dean St, Newcastle upon Tyne (Newcastle upon Tyne 323561). All equipment for ski-ing, climbing, walking and mountaineering available personally or by mail order. There are anoraks, sweaters, salopettes, knee breeches, hats, gloves, boots, shoes, sleeping bags, dehydrated meals, Kendal mint cake, ropes, crampons, ice axes and rucksacks. The Centre hires skis and clothing (£18.50 per week, £20 deposit, for ski-pack of boots, skis and sticks; jackets and salopettes are £12 per item per week) and equipment for walking and climbing: tents (£9 per week for a two-man tent, £20 deposit), walking boots, rucksacks and ice axes. There is a ski workshop for repairs, fitting and tuning; everything except resoling is done on the premises. They also give details of snow conditions in North-East England and Scotland each day during the season.

WARWICKSHIRE

Hogan & Colbourne Ltd, Phoenix Works, Alscot Park, Alderminster, nr Stratford-upon-Avon (Alderminster 764). Made-to-measure guns 'at prices people can afford'. John Hogan and Peter Colbourne trained as gunsmiths in Birmingham and set up their workshop a year ago to make 'honest-to-goodness' sporting shotguns. They don't pretend to compete with London gunsmiths, but they tailor each gun to the individual client at prices from £1,000 to £6,000, depending on the weight, quality of walnut and amount of engraving. They also repair and service sporting guns.

Prices were correct at the time of printing, but are only intended as an indication and means of comparison. Do not send cheques to any company without checking first by telephone on postal charges and availability.

8 | Getting Service

Children

Nannie Knows Best ..., and Occasional & Permanent Nannies, 15 Beauchamp Place, S W3 (01-584 5700, 01-584 0232 or 01-589 3368). A complete service for mother and child, from the crib and layette to the trained nanny. Jan Govett has run the agency for twelve years, supplying nursery staff worldwide, and has now branched out into handmade items for the baby and nursery. Special orders can be undertaken. Expensive but very high quality.

Poppinjay Nannies Ltd, 2a Hasker St, SW3 (01-581 3278). Nannies, maternity nurses, mothers' helps, emergency mums and, most recent, child escorts arranged. The child escort service is run as a separate department within Poppinjay by Rachel Campbell and Joy Foottit, who will send a representative to collect children from airports or stations on their way to and from school and escort them to their destination. There is a standard charge of £30, and this includes liaising with the schools, checking trains and so on. Arrangements can also be made simply to meet children from day school or other locations.

Northumbrian Nannies, 5 Cattle Market, Hexham (Hexham 605071). Sheila Bell, who runs this agency, is a trained nursery nurse herself, with seven years' experience as a nanny in the UK and abroad. She can supply nannies for permanent jobs on a full-time basis at home or abroad, daily nannies or mothers' helps and maternity nurses. Registration fee is £10; fees for a permanent placement are £100, for a part-time nanny or mother's help on a regular basis £50, daily £2.50 and weekly £15. The wages for the nannies are negotiable, depending on circumstances and experience.

China matching

DEVON

China Matching Service, Fern Lea, Frogmore, Kingsbridge (Frogmore 372). For those who have odd cups languishing in cupboards, without saucers, this is a sort of lonely-hearts service which will get the two together. For £3 you can become a member and Miriam Clark will log the china and stoneware items you want to get rid of or need to find to make up a set, and when she tracks down the right match she will put buyers and sellers in touch by post or telephone. She has about 1,000 people on her register and likes to encourage those who have only one item to sell by charging them no registration fee – that one piece might be just what someone is looking for. Lots of Royal Doulton, Derby, Wedgwood and Denby change owners, and sometimes pieces up to sixty or seventy years old are matched.

SUFFOLK

Chinamatch, Nutwood, Fen Walk, Woodbridge. A similar service is run by Anne Garrett, who charges £1 registration fee from buyers (sellers register free, as do clients buying and selling). There is a 'match fee' from each party (£1 for three items, £5 for thirty items, and pro rata), which is payable when a match is found and is refunded if it is not satisfactory. Mrs Garrett's was the first service of its kind and since she began in 1980 she has built up a register of more than 4,000 clients from all parts of the world, so you may even get the chance of matching old and valuable sets. She will send more details for a stamped addressed envelope.

Family trees

LONDON

College of Arms, Queen Victoria St, EC4 (01-248 2762). Genealogical research, the identification of existing arms and the granting of new arms. Those who believe they are entitled to arms should first do as much preliminary research as possible before approaching the College. Arms do not automatically apply to anyone bearing the same surname as an armigerous family. Entitlement descends in a direct male line from a grantee of arms, and a very small percentage of families qualifies. New arms may be granted to eminent public figures. The College has the best collection in existence of records of the heraldry and genealogy of English, Welsh, Irish and Commonwealth families. Fees depend on the complexity of each case.

Society of Genealogists, 37 Harrington Gardens, SW7 (01-373 7054).
Membership of the Society entitles you to use the extensive library to research your
family history. The records include 50 per cent of the parish registers in the country,
a document collection containing 11,000 surnames, research, family histories,
wills and pedigrees contributed by genealogists and an alphabetical register of surnames to help, for instance, those who don't know the exact place or date of an
ancestor's marriage. Membership costs £20 for London residents, £14 for those
beyond twenty-five miles of the city; there is a £7.50 entrance fee. Non-members
may use the facilities on payment of a search fee of £2 for one hour, £4 for up to
three and a half hours, and £6 for a day.

SUSSEX

Heraldic Design, 8 Newport St, Brighton, E Sussex (Brighton 601161).
Surnames researched and coats of arms illustrated on a coloured scroll. Many
surnames have had a coat of arms historically associated with them, and these are
arms used in the last 700 years. Rita Fogarty will research a surname and find its
origin and meaning, however differently spelled, and her husband Kevin will
prepare a hand-coloured scroll for £14.95, 13¼ × 9 in., laminated and framed, or
in the form of an etched copper plaque, up to £51.50. This is not genealogical
research and does not entitle a family to use the arms – a fact which is emphasized
when you receive your scroll.

Fashion and beauty

CHESHIRE

Heather Jackson, 23 St Mary's Rd, Sale (061-973 5256). Remedial make-
up lessons to camouflage birthmarks and scars. Heather Jackson gives an hour's
consultation, advising on products and colours and teaching the best methods of
application, for £9. She does not sell the products, so there is no pressure to buy;
you go away with a list of products, recommended colours and suppliers, and make
your own decisions.

LINCOLNSHIRE

Carl Linden, 6 Gordon Rd, off Bailgate, Lincoln (Lincoln 42589). Handmade herbal shampoos, toiletries and scents. Carl Linden has a range of his own
preparations, including pot-pourri and herbal gifts. He will also create limited
editions of scents for companies, including handmade bottles signed by the
craftsman.

LONDON

Katherine Corbett, 21 South Molton St, W1 (01-493 5905 and 01-629 6136). A top skin-care expert with particular skills in the treatment of spider veins and similar skin blemishes. Katherine Corbett, who trained as a nurse, researched the removal of spider veins on the face and legs by sclerotherapy and evolved a technique which became internationally known and highly regarded. She also treats bright red spots or spider naevi, brown patches, warts, moles, chickenpox pits, whiteheads and blackheads. She keeps close contact with the medical profession still and has a range of her own skin-care preparations which are particularly suitable for sensitive skins, as their emphasis is on purity and freedom from chemicals and scents. A mail-order list is available. All treatments are preceded by a free consultation and fees are from £35 per treatment.

Cosmetics à la Carte, 16 Motcomb St, SW1 (01-235 0596). Cosmetics made on the premises by two young chemists, Christina Stewart and Lynne Sanders. They have a large range of colours – more than 100 eye-shadows and lipsticks, for instance – and will blend instant foundations to suit individual customers. They give make-up lessons and customers can come in and play with various colours until they are satisfied. Prices are around £5 for a lipstick, £5 cream rouge, £8 blusher, £10.50 foundation.

Joan Price's Face Place, 33 Cadogan St, SW3 (01-589 9062), and 31 Connaught St, W2 (01-273 6671). Two cosmetic shops which are more like beauty playgrounds where you can try all sorts of cosmetics until you find exactly the right one for your skin type – and without any of the biased sales pressure you get over the big store beauty counters. Lessons in make-up are £7.95.

Norman Ricklow, 13a Crawford St, W1 (01-935 9181). A very personal choice, but it is sometimes useful for visitors to London to know of a hairdresser who is highly skilled but totally unpretentious and not outrageously expensive. Many hairdressers have to see clients several times before managing their hair really well – and in London they often contrive to make you feel as if yours would look better on a Yorkshire terrier. Norman Ricklow, who was manager at Vidal Sassoon before opening his own salon, cuts superbly and does it without any affected airs and graces. Prices from £7.50 for a blow-dry; £13.75 cut and blow-dry with a stylist, £17.50 with Norman. Men's cut and blow-dry £9.95, all stylists.

MANCHESTER

Ganymede Perfumes, Manchester Craft Village, Oak St, Manchester 4 (061-834 6447); also Cherry Tree Cottage, Foxcovert Lane, Lower Peover, Cheshire (Lower Peover 2892) for mail order only (no visitors).

Perfumes blended specially to suit the colouring, personality and preferences of the customer. Andrew and Sheila Berwitz will develop a fragrance for you, test it on your skin (or send a sample by mail) and package it in a ground glass apothecary's bottle, about £10 for $\frac{1}{2}$ oz. They also make herbal cosmetics to traditional recipes (from £2 to £5) and sell pot-pourri, orris root, hops and natural beeswax. Their natural remedies include comfrey and thyme ointment for strains and sprains and marigold antiseptic for cuts and grazes. They started as a cottage industry in their own cottage at Peover, and rapidly had to find other premises when coach-loads of visitors wanted to watch them at work. The Craft Village is in a converted fruit and vegetable market – worth a visit – but mail order is operated from the cottage; send in details of your skin type and colouring and a sample will be made up for you to approve.

NORTHAMPTONSHIRE

Martha Hill, The Old Vicarage, Laxton, nr Corby (Bulwick 259). My favourite skin-care preparations. I have to be as personal as this because beauty is such a subjective matter – if you believe that something costing three times as much will do you more good, then go ahead and buy it. These creams do not come in flossy packages, so all the goodness is in the preparations, made from pure ingredients – no animal by-products. Best of all for dry and sensitive skins is the No. 4 night cream, and for those who believe in the cleanse, tone, moisturize routine there is an excellent four-product pack. A leaflet is available.

OXFORDSHIRE

Carola Skyrme, Style Supply, Britwell House, Britwell Salome, Oxford (Watlington 3255). Fashion counselling by a designer and ex-model. Carola Skyrme advises on what to wear with what, which clothes to choose to make the most of your figure and colouring, how to use the latest accessories. 'Often women are only aware of their bad points and need help in making the most of their good ones,' she says. She will see clients by appointment or will visit them at home, taking a selection of photographs from which they can choose, with her help, an ideal outfit. As she also owns a shop in Ireland she knows what is being planned for the coming season and can have items specially made. Designers include Jasper Conran and Bellville-Sassoon at prices from £80 to £500, and in some cases a discount is offered on the usual shop prices.

Hire services

BUCKINGHAMSHIRE

Rosehill Instruments Ltd, The Old House, London End, Beaconsfield (Beaconsfield 71717). Musical instruments rental service. Strings, woodwinds and brass, percussion, even bagpipes for hire on a three to six months' basis. Fifteen per cent of the cost of the instrument covers rental for three months, at the end of which the client is given the opportunity to buy, less the rental already paid. Useful for small bands, teachers and parents who want to find out if they have an infant Menuhin or Acker Bilk on their hands before investing. A flute costing £180, for example, is £27 for three months' rental.

KENT

The Ladder Hire Company, Scotts Rd, Bromley North (01-460 9111), and branches. Large and small equipment for hire or sale, from cement-mixers, mechanical diggers and car trailers to garden cultivators and drycleaning equipment for floors and carpets. Established for twenty-seven years, they now have branches in Sidcup, Lewisham, Shirley and Bromley South and can send a list of the 400 items they hire.

Flag Hire Centres, 39 High St, Sittingbourne (Sittingbourne 78795), and branches. Any tools and equipment for building and house and garden maintenance. There is a large selection, including concrete-mixers, water pumps, ladders, chain saws, scaffolding, carpet cleaners, lawnmowers, rotivators and one-ton road-rollers. They have five branches in London, four in Kent and many others throughout the country. A brochure and price list is available.

LONDON

Atlas Display Co. Ltd, Atlas House, Commerce Way, Croydon, Surrey (01-688 9531). Large frame tents for hire for exhibitions. Atlas put up all the entertainment chalets for Goodwood and the pavilions for Epsom and the Derby. They also hire frame tents for weddings and will travel anywhere.

Black & Edginton, 29 Queen Elizabeth St, Tower Bridge, S E1 (01-407 3734). Strictly large-scale hirers of tented structures for exhibitions, not the small private function. They do the marquees, flooring and furniture for Wimbledon, Henley Regatta, Farnborough Air Show. Provincial branches deal with smaller events.

Blackman Harvey Ltd, 29 Earlham St, Covent Garden, W C2 (01-836 1904), and 11 Masons Avenue, Coleman St, E C2 (01-726 2502). Pictures for hire to hotels, offices and advertising agencies. Anything in stock can be hired under one of three arrangements: short-term hire for a photographic session, for instance, £5 per picture; long-term hire, 99p per week per £100 of the picture's value; hire purchase, £1.40 per £100, and after eight consecutive quarterly payments the pictures become the property of the lessee.

Donmar Hire, 39 Earlham St, W C2 (01-836 3221). Everything in lighting equipment for professional and amateur stage shows, exhibitions, concerts, private parties, plus smoke guns, bubble machines, falling snow machines, theatrical drapes, all sorts of stage gear, apart from props. They hire nationally and internationally.

Gerrard Hire, 85 Royal College St, N W1 (01-387 2765). Stuffed animals for hire for film, television, window display and private parties. If you have a jungle theme party, for example, Gerrard will provide the exotic birds to sit in the branches (no jokes about the ones sitting in the laps, please). The charges are according to the value of the skin; a small item could be £6.90 for seven days, and a tiger will cost £97.75.

Halsey Marine Ltd, 22 Boston Place, Dorset Square, N W1 (01-724 1303). Yacht brokers and charterers who supply yachts from 30 ft for self-sailing holidays to 350 ft with crew for cruises and business conferences. Prices for crewed vessels range from £190 per person per week for 47-ft motor sailers on the southern coast of Turkey to over £4,000 per person for the 169-ft *Southern Breeze*. The company also supplies yachts for meetings, conferences and exhibitions and arranges charters for the film industry.

London Borough of Camden: Libraries and Arts Departments. Many libraries have reproduction paintings for local residents to borrow. Camden is unusual in that its collection is of originals. There are 1,000 paintings, many by local artists, and a small selection of modern sculpture. The works are on display in all Camden libraries and are available free, for three months at a time, to those who live, work or study in the area.

Moss Bros, Bedford St, WC2 (01-240 4567). Men's formal wear, as everybody must know, with all the accessories, including shirt and shoes, but also lounge suits for college students who have a job interview but nothing to wear except jeans; and there are silver-grey lounge suits for weddings for those who feel uncomfortable in the full traditional bit. Highland wear (for men with good knees, say Moss Bros) and Highland outfits for pages; ski-wear for men and women. Prices from £20 a day, formal wear; £28 per week, ski-wear.

Pelling & Cross, 104 Baker St, W1 (01-487 5411), and branches. All you need to hire for studio photography or film making. Pelling & Cross have still and ciné cameras, audio and video equipment, lighting, loudspeakers, film and accessories. Rental is charged on a twenty-four-hour basis, but if you collect after 3 p.m. on Friday and return the equipment before 10 a.m. on Monday you get it all for one day's charge. Branches in Birmingham, Bristol and Manchester.

MANCHESTER

Glina Props Hire, Harrison St, Ancoats, Manchester (061-273 8888). Plants and greenery to hire for special occasions. Exotic and tropical plants and palms, ball bay trees, rubber plants, bucket ferns or an instant jungle by the yard. For weddings, marquee garden parties, fund-raising events. Also real and silk flower arrangements. A bay tree in a pot costs from £8 a week, a large palm tree £10 a week.

MIDDLESEX

Rentatent, Third Way, off South Way, Wembley Stadium Trading Estate, Wembley (01-903 3473). Everything you need to hire for camping – except the sleeping bags. Frame and ridge tents, tables, chairs, crockery, water carriers, grills – you name it, they can camp it up, and have been doing so for twenty-five years. A price list is available, a package deal of a tent and all the equipment for a family of four is, for example, £87.30 for two weeks in the high season.

SURREY

Hire Service Shops Ltd, Warenne House, 31 London Rd, Reigate (Reigate 49441), and branches. Specialist tools and equipment for house maintenance and building. HSS has a large range, including ladders, scaffolding and equipment for lighting and welding, mechanical handling, woodworm and dry-rot treatment, injection damp-proofing, wallpaper steam-stripping, plumbing, drilling, sanding, gardening. There are thirty-seven branches in London and the South-East, twenty-two in the Midlands and North-West, and others in Bristol, Wales, the Solent and the North-East. A brochure gives their addresses.

SUSSEX

George Hobbs Trailers, Lydwick Farm, Hayes Lane, Slinfold, nr Horsham, W Sussex (Slinfold 790675). Horse boxes and trailers for hire, plus car transporters, Land Rovers, van trailers, tipping trailers for builders, and non-tipping trailers for those who wouldn't be seen anywhere near a trowel. Charges from £10 per day or £42 per week for a horse trailer, rear-unload, to £30 per day or £120 per week for a Bedford two-horse box. All vehicles are available for overseas use by prior arrangement.

WEST MIDLANDS

Embess (Hire) Ltd, 129–131 Stratford Rd, Sparkbrook, Birmingham (021-772 7031). All kinds of tableware for hire. Embess have china, glass, silver or stainless-steel cutlery, silver candelabra and punch bowls, cakestands and centrepieces, electric carving knives, damask tablecloths and folding chairs and trestle tables. There is a minimum hire charge of £5 and a £10 returnable deposit.

Household services

BUCKINGHAMSHIRE

Homesitters Ltd, Moat Farm, Buckland, nr Aylesbury (Aylesbury 631289). Domestic caretaking while you are away by mature people with long-standing references. Charges are by the day, £5.50 for basic home-sits, from £7.25 with pets, and the home-sitters adhere to strict rules – no parties, no long-distance phone calls, no visitors after 10 p.m.

CHESHIRE

J. P. Connolly Ltd, 29 London Rd, Alderley Edge (Alderley Edge 583672). Valuations of all types of jewellery and silver, including rare stones, by Cheryl

Blackshaw, a Fellow of the Gemmological Association of Great Britain. The company also makes jewellery at a branch in Knutsford and will undertake special commissions.

Help (Household) Agency, 43 Stamford New Rd, Altrincham (061-928 4154). An extraordinarily helpful agency that can fix anything, from someone to water your tomatoes while you're away to a full-time nanny or a Mrs Mopp. They supply temporary or permanent help on a resident or non-resident basis, house-sitting and pet-sitting while owners go on holiday, gardeners (from odd-jobbers to experts who can advise on layout and undertake planting and pruning), house-keepers, mothers' substitutes and school-meeting for working mums. There is a share-a-nanny scheme for mothers who want to work part-time or job-share. Babysitting lists cost £7.50 (forty sitters, whose references have been checked). Agency fees are from £1 for temporary non-resident help to twice the week's pay for a permanent non-resident job.

Keyways Master Key Systems Ltd, 18 The Square, Hale Barns (061-980 6655). General locksmiths and safe engineers who will open, fit or repair all types of locks. If you have locked yourself out of anything or anywhere, these are the people to call. They will change your locks if you have your handbag stolen, fit locks to the doors and windows of your house, and repair antique locks on furniture. A front door mortice lock (to BS 3621) costs from about £17 to £23, a window lock £3.45, plus fitting. Supplying and fitting an underfloor safe is about £150. They will visit clients' houses and give free advice.

DERBYSHIRE

Intervac, International Holiday Exchange, 6 Siddals Lane, Allestree, Derby (Derby 558931). A home-swapping scheme can offer not just a holiday on the cheap but a chance to sample a whole new lifestyle. Organizer Hazel Nayar founded Intervac in Britain twenty years ago for other teachers. Now anyone can join. An international directory three times a year lists 6,000 homes in more than thirty countries. It costs £20 a year to be listed or £18 a year if you just want the directory. Being guests in each other's homes creates a special bond of trust, and people swap cars, gardening duties and even children!

HERTFORDSHIRE

Sheelagh Lewis Ltd, 10 Stockings Lane, Little Berkhamsted, Hertford (Cuffley 875044); and The Old School House, Bury, Dulverton, Somerset (Dulverton 23715). A consultant on oriental rugs, Sheelagh Lewis now concentrates largely on restoration work, but will value rugs for insurance and will undertake to find special rugs or to sell clients' rugs on commission.

LONDON

Abba Security, 817 Raleigh Drive, Whetstone, N20 (01-445 9667). All types of locks supplied and fitted. In an emergency they will be with you within an hour. They cover central, north and north-west London, and the cheapest lock they fit is £38.

Divertimenti, 68 Marylebone Lane, W1 (01-935 0689). Knife sharpening from 40p per knife; grinder calls on Thursdays. Scissors too, 50p. copper pans relined from about £3. Takes three weeks.

Edwards & Wake Ltd, 35 Mysore Rd, SW11 (01-228 8440). Specialist packers and carriers of antiques and fine arts. Jonathan Edwards and Philip Wake will undertake all types of removals, anywhere in the country, from individual items to the contents of a stately home. All their vehicles are fitted with security alarm systems, and the service is available seven days a week. Charges are £15 per hour in the London area, more for long distances.

Featherston Transport Ltd, 274 Queenstown Rd, SW8 (01-720 0422). Specialists in antique furniture removals, mainly for antique dealers moving goods from London to the Continent, but also for private clients. They have a weekly service to North Germany but can go anywhere, and the service is door-to-door. They also do freight forwarding to anywhere in the world, with regular services to the US, the Middle East and Australia.

The London Fine Art Valuation Consultancy, 7th floor, 50 Pall Mall, SW1 (01-935 6826). A comprehensive and confidential valuation service covering jewellery and silver, furniture, paintings, drawings and objets d'art. Rates are one per cent of the first £100,000, and half a per cent thereafter. Advice also given on insurance, probate, family division and capital transfer problems.

David Mellor, 4 Sloane Square, SW1 (01-730 4259). Knife sharpening for 35p for a small knife, 60p large, 70p scissors. Takes at least two weeks; minimum charge £1.50.

Problem Ltd, 44 Lupus St, SW1 (01-828 8181). A members-only agency which will come to your rescue in almost any emergency. They will find people to mend your pipes if they burst at midnight, to walk your dog if you are ill (or just plain lazy), clean the house, answer the mail, open your door if you lock yourself out. They have even provided a kangaroo for the BBC. They supply food for the freezer and funny-shaped cakes and take their members on shopping trips to Calais and Paris. A year's subscription costs £25 and their services are available twenty-four hours a day, every day of the year.

Thuro Steam, 55 Bondway, SW8 (01-582 6033). Flood and fire rescue service. Thuro Steam will come within a couple of hours of being told of a disaster, extract the water from furnishings or clean them if fire-damaged, repolishing smoke-damaged furniture. If burst drains have caused sewage pollution they will fumigate, and they can get rid of the smell of smoke from a whole block of flats – all under insurance. They normally work within twenty miles of central London, but will travel further for a full day's job.

Universal Aunts, 250 King's Rd, SW3 (01-351 5767). 'Advice and aid in all emergencies' has been Universal Aunts' slogan for many years. There are only four exceptions, laid down by Miss Gertrude Maclean when she founded the agency in 1921 – no matchmaking, no legal or medical advice and no money-lending. But through the Aunts you can hire your party staff, get your freezer filled, engage a babysitter, have your travelling children escorted and accommodated, get your passport or visa collected, be put in touch with experts on valuations or arrange a holiday in an English home. A brochure is available.

TYNE AND WEAR

Flowers by Arrangement, 72 The Drive, Newcastle upon Tyne (Newcastle upon Tyne 855668 or Stamfordham 406). Any flower arrangements, pot plants, bouquets or posies. It is possible to collect from Sue May or Lynne Black in Gosforth or Stamfordham, but they will deliver locally. They also have vases and containers for hire and are happy to visit clients to discuss colour schemes and plans for a small or large event. Prices start at £3 for a small dinner-table arrangement.

Pets

CUMBRIA

Low Lowood Kennels, Armathwaite, Carlisle (Croglin 636). Anne Latimer, who runs the kennels, will visit clients within easy reach of Carlisle and charges about £4.50 to £5.50 for an average-size dog whose coat is clipped regularly. Out-of-condition dogs are charged by the time taken; a neglected old English sheepdog's coat could take five to six hours.

LONDON

Pet Plan Ltd, 35 Horn Lane, W3 (01-993 6423). Illness and accident insurance for cats and dogs from eight weeks old for life. For an annual premium of between £20 and £29.50 per animal, three policies are offered, insuring against veterinary fees, money spent in advertising rewards for lost animals and up to £500,000 third-party claims for injury by animals to people or property.

Vehicles

WARWICKSHIRE

Ladbroke Avon, Millers Rd, Warwick (Warwick 491377). The oldest privately owned coach builders in the country, established in 1919, who will undertake conversions of saloon cars into estates and bring back traditional coachwork crafts into modern mass-produced vehicles. Their estate conversions are usually on new Jaguars, Sunbeam Lotus and Triumph Acclaims. The only second-hand car they accept is the Jaguar coupé, now out of production, which they turn into a convertible. Prices are from £1,450 to retrim a Triumph Acclaim in leather and walnut and give it a sunshine roof, carpeting and soundproofing and two-tone paint. A Jaguar saloon-to-estate costs around £7,500, but you then have 'the fastest and most exclusive load-lugger in the world'. One-offs are possible too – they have fitted Range Rovers with perches for Arab falcons and even one with a machine-gun rack. They are also the largest crash-repair centre in the country, with their own radiator shop and trimming department, and do work for private clients as well as insurance companies and car dealers. Ladbroke, incidently, has nothing to do with the betting company – the managing director comes from the village of Ladbroke, near Warwick.

Video

LONDON

Montevideo Film and Video Productions Co. Ltd, 15 Cleveland Rd, South Woodford, E18 (01-530 5083). A specialist video company of high quality. Peter Akehurst is a well-known photographer of fashion and people and he produces videotapes for social events, company promotions, fashion shows, portfolios, recording artists and commercials. The company has its own sound and light engineers; all editing and titles are done in house to ensure a personal service and high standard. A reliable company in a field crowded with cowboys.

Prices were correct at the time of printing, but are only intended as an indication and means of comparison. Do not send cheques to any company without checking first by telephone on postal charges and availability.

---

9 Getting Cleaned Out

Blinds

LONDON

Centuryan Blinds, 44 Southside, Clapham Common, SW4 (01-720 5566).
Complete renovation service for Venetian and other blinds. Cleaning, recording and providing new slats where necessary costs from £5 to £50, according to size and condition. They also supply roller blinds, louvre blinds and black-out or dim-out blinds for computer rooms.

MIDDLESEX

Contravent, 1 Eskdale Rd, Uxbridge (Uxbridge 37988), and at 274 Davidson Rd, Croydon, Surrey (01-656 8325). Maintenance and supply of all types of blinds, and cleaning of Venetian and louvre blinds. The smallest Venetian blind would cost about £7.50 for cleaning and recording.

Drycleaning and dyeing

CHESHIRE

Harry Berger, 25 Station Rd, Cheadle Hulme, Cheadle (061-485 3421).
Old-established drycleaners and dyers who operate a postal service. They clean wedding dresses, suedes, leathers, sheepskin and furs, and they alter and repair all types of fabric and skin clothing as well. They will even turn collars – the last company to offer this tailoring service. The postal dyeing service is particularly useful and extremely efficient; the order form comes with a list of fabric types describing how they dye and a chart of light-fastness ratings from one to ten for velvet curtains – the higher the number the better the resistance to fading. There are thirty dyeing shades – a better range than the average postal dyeing service – and prices, including return postage, are from £8.90 for a coat, £14.74 for a fur

fabric jacket, £6.90 for a candlewick bedspread, £3.45 per square yard for curtains. There are seventy Harry Berger agents throughout the country, but you may prefer to go to the fountainhead; the company was established in 1912 as dyers, cleaners and bespoke outfitters, so their knowledge of the properties of various textiles is of great value. Send a large stamped addressed envelope for information before sending orders.

Park Dry Cleaning Company, 30 Park Rd, Hale (061-928 8061). A family-run drycleaning business specializing in difficult cleaning jobs that other firms won't tackle. Suedes and leathers are cleaned and re-oiled, silk garments are hand-cleaned and pressed. They also clean furs, lace and beaded dresses, undertake alterations and invisible mending, and dye clothes and soft furnishings. Cleaning costs from £14 for a suede or leather coat, £17 for a fur coat, £3.60 for a man's suit, £3.80 for a silk dress. A postal service is available.

LEICESTERSHIRE

ServiceMaster Ltd, 50 Commercial Square, Freeman's Common, Leicester (Leicester 548620), and 150 local centres. A franchised cleaning service operating worldwide and cleaning ten million square feet of carpet every *day*. They clean on site and will rescue furnishings from flood damage, drying out the carpets and stretching them back into place. Local franchisees are in the Yellow Pages; or you can contact the head office, above. Charges, which vary among the licensees, depending on their area and travel expenses, are about 85p to £1 per square yard.

LONDON

Chalfont Cleaners & Dyers Ltd, 222 Baker St, NW1 (01-935 7316). Dyeing of clothes and furnishings in twenty colours, all fairly strong. Advice given on the possibility of achieving certain colours on certain fabrics (not suede and leather). Sample prices: coats from £17.30, dresses from £11.90, unlined curtains £3.40 per square metre, blankets from £11. A leaflet is available with full price list and colour chart. Full drycleaning service also. Postal service anywhere.

Cleanrite, 122 Acre Rd, Kingston-upon-Thames, Surrey (01-549 7346). Cleaning on site of carpets, upholstery, fabric wall-coverings and lampshades by their mobile plant which operates from the van by its own heat and power. Curtains are cleaned on their premises – you can take down and they will collect and deliver, or they will provide a complete take-down and rehang service which guarantees against shredding and shrinkage. One width of lined velvet curtain 6 ft long would cost about £4.80. They give a discount on quantity.

Collins Cleaners, 99 Gloucester Rd, SW7 (01-373 8069), and fifteen West End branches. High-quality cleaning of clothes, curtains, duvets, pillows, suedes and leathers (jackets from £10.50). They will remake eiderdowns and repair clothes, from replacing zips, remaking cuffs and relining skirts to major alterations to garments and repairs to sheepskin. They also offer a Permacrease service for most types of trousers, excluding jeans and cords; the creases are guaranteed for one year. Good-value hand-cleaning of silk ties (£1.50) and a new dyeing service for clothes, candlewick bedspreads, velvet curtains and other plain fabrics.

Curtain Cleaning Services Ltd. Head office: 172 Hoe St, E17 (01-521 8691 or 01-520 1556). This company will take down, clean, rehang and re-dress curtains for about £1.25 per square yard – guaranteed no shrinkage – and will undertake velvet curtain dyeing. They also make, fit and maintain curtains for homes, offices and hotels and have a carpet and upholstery cleaning service. On-site cleaning charges are from £1 per square yard.

Guillaume, 59 Davies St, W1 (01-629 2275). Old-style high-quality cleaners who have been in business for thirty-five years and say 'By tradition you can ask us to clean anything, and we do.' They specialize in fine clothes in fine fabrics and charge accordingly: men's two-piece suits £5.50, wedding dresses from £30 to £50. They dye in fifty colours and will undertake special colours on fabrics by the yard. They also reline, invisibly mend and alter.

Harding's of Kingston, 122 Acre Rd, Kingston-upon-Thames, Surrey (01-549 7346). Specialists since 1859 in cleaning theatrical costumes, theatre drapes, wedding dresses and uniforms, and also in flameproofing. An associate company of Cleanrite at the same address.

Jeeves, 9 Pont St, SW1 (01-235 1101), and branches in NW3 , W2 and W1. Hand-finished drycleaning and laundry of fine linen, antique clothes, soft toys, curtains, suede, leather and fur. Repairs include replacement of pockets and zips and lengthening and shortening hems; furs are repaired and relined. There is a depository where clothes may be stored and a packing service for holidays. Deliveries are made in central London; otherwise there is a postal service or, if you can't get to Belgravia during shopping hours, you can have a key to the night hatch and leave your clothes and instructions there.

Lewis & Wayne, 9 Streatham High Rd, SW16 (01-769 8777), and branches in SW3 and SE20. One of the very few specialist cleaners who will still clean trilby hats. They charge £2.25 and will also do fur hats from £3. They have a hand-laundry shirt service, will dryclean church and masonic regalia, beaded dresses and fur coats, and have a take-down and rehang curtain-cleaning service anywhere in Central London (about £2 per square yard).

Lilliman & Cox Ltd, 34 Bruton Place, Berkeley Square, W1 (01-629 4555).
Specialist cleaners of furs, suede and leather, uniforms, riding wear, theatrical
costumes, wedding dresses, raincoats, soft furnishings and everyday clothes. The
company, which has three royal warrants, was founded in 1944 by Sidney
Lilliman, a master tailor, with Arthur Cox, a technical expert in drycleaning, and
the high standards they set are carried on by the present directors. A two-piece suit
costs £8.50 to clean, £5 to press only, a lady's suede jacket from £14, day dress
from £9.50. Delivery in London or postal service.

**Patent Steam Carpet Cleaning Co., Furmage St, Wandsworth, SW18
(01-874 4333).** On-site carpet cleaning using shampoo, hot-water extraction
('steam') or drycleaning. Prices are from 95p per square yard. The company, which
has a royal warrant for carpet cleaning, also cleans upholstery and soft furnishings
and offers a flood damage service. It specializes in cleaning oriental carpets (prices
from £1.10 per square yard), and for these there is a collection and delivery service.

**Permaclean Marie Blanche, 154 Battersea Park Rd, SW11 (01-622 0151),
and branches.** One of the few cleaners in the country who will deal with silk and
fabric lampshades. Most cleaning is done on site – a small wall light costs about
£1, a large standard lampshade £5. The company specializes in the cleaning of
furnishings and fine fabrics, including antique materials and wedding dresses.
There are branches in Cardiff and Nottingham.

**Pilgrim Payne and Co. Ltd, Latimer Place, Latimer Rd, W10 (01-960
5656); and Coit Drapery & Carpet Cleaners (UK) Ltd, at the same
address (01-969 2424).** Cleaners with 130 years' experience – and a royal
warrant. They clean carpets and upholstery on site by extraction or shampoo, and
take down curtains, clean and rehang. Curtains can be relined to extend their life
or new sets can be made. Everything is individually estimated, but as a guide the
cleaning of unlined curtains would be from 75p per foot drop per width.

Thuro Steam, 55 Bondway, SW8 (01-582 6033). Cleaning of curtains,
carpets and upholstery. Carpets and furniture can be steam-cleaned on site or in
the factory; curtains are removed for cleaning and rehung. They will also treat with
a Scotchgard or anti-static finish and are one of the few people to dye carpets,
either in their depot or on site. Almost any colour is possible, depending on the
yarn, as they mix their own colours.

MERSEYSIDE

**North of England Carpet Cleaning Co. Ltd, 86 Aigburth Rd, Liverpool 17
(051-727 7278), and 17 Birchenall St, Moston, Manchester 10 (061-205
1086).** Cleaning and renovation of all kinds of carpets on site or in the factory. The

company will repair small wears and tears and will dry, clean and refit water-damaged carpets after flooding. They also restore oriental carpets, undertake insurance inspections and reports, and will also clean upholstered furniture and clean and dye carpets and curtains. Carpet cleaning is from about £21 for 20 square yards, three-piece suites from £31. There is also a carpet adaptation service for house moves. There is an associate company, W. E. Franklin Ltd in Sheffield.

NOTTINGHAMSHIRE

Giltbrook Dyers & Cleaners Ltd, Hampden St, Giltbrook (Nottingham 382231), and branches. Specialists in drycleaning and fabric dyeing. They have a standard range of sixteen colours, plus black, and they can also dye to specific requirements. Velvet curtains cost about £2 per square yard to dye, a lady's coat £8.80. A postal service is available, and there are fourteen branches in the Nottingham and Derby areas. They also clean and repair suede and leather.

OXFORDSHIRE

Safeclean International, Freepost, Upton, Didcot (Blewbury 850387), and local franchises. This is the headquarters of a franchised chain of cleaners specializing in hand-cleaning and using natural substances wherever possible, rather than harmful chemicals. Ebullient Desmond Cook, who runs it, was working as a contract cleaner twenty years ago when he decided he could improve on the old squirt-and-suck methods of redistributing grime around clients' carpets. 'I didn't have the accent that goes with a full-scale conservation course at the V&A, so I got it all out of Mrs Beeton,' he admits cheerfully. His treatments are based on saponaria, a natural plant which can't harm fibres, and he travels to embassies and stately homes to deal with antique tapestries, oriental rugs, tented ceilings and fabric walls. Associates trained in his methods will cope with the more usual three-piece-suite jobs. Sample prices: £40 to £60 for a ten- to twelve-cushion three-piece suite, £1.20 a square metre for fitted carpet. Fifty franchised cleaners round the country; write to the address above for your nearest.

TAYSIDE

Pullars of Perth, 35 Kinnoull St, Perth, Tayside (Perth 23456). One of the last companies who will clean gloves. Prices are about £1.90 for fabric, £2.80 for leather, any length.

House cleaning

BUCKINGHAMSHIRE

Skivvies, Unit C, Progress Rd, Sands Industrial Estate, High Wycombe (High Wycombe 442788). Complete house cleaning, ceiling to floor. They wash, scrub, resand floors, clean carpets, take down and rehang curtains. Their usual clients are owners of large houses whose staff can't or won't cope with the heavy work, but they deal with smaller premises too. They handle a lot of properties rented out while the owners are abroad, cleaning throughout when there is a change of tenant.

CHESHIRE

Bank Vale Help at Home, Bank Vale House, Bank Vale Rd, Hayfield, Stockport (New Mills 45994). A private home-help service for the elderly and disabled. Linda Heaton, who was formerly a local-authority home-help organizer, has personally interviewed all her staff and offers a reliable domestic help, cleaning, cooking and caring service by sincere, capable people. The service ranges from a single hour's cleaning or a visit to prepare a meal to an all-night sitting or a weekend stay to care for someone ill or frail. Daily domestic help is £2.50 per hour (Sunday rate £3 per hour); night sitting is £22.

LONDON

B C S Ltd, 108 Fulham Palace Rd, W6 (01-741 2153). Contract cleaners who will also spring-clean private houses throughout, washing walls, paintwork, utensils, turning out cupboards, scrubbing floors, stripping, repolishing and sealing. A valuable service if you are moving into an old house that has not been looked after. There is a minimum charge of £40.

Deluxe Services, 12 Great Western Rd, W9 (01-289 2038). A team of responsible people who will do routine cleaning chores in private houses and flats. A basic three-hour session costs £10, plus fares, and the client provides the cleaning materials. This company will also arrange carpenters, electricians, plumbers, builders, painters and decorators or whatever professionals you need to put your house in order.

NORTHUMBERLAND

Shiners, Heathcote, Main Rd, Stocksfield (Stocksfield 842276 and 843088). A small domestic agency employing twenty-five girls who will come to clean your house or office either on a regular basis or for a once-a-year spring-clean. They will also clean new houses after the builders have left and before the removal men come. They will arrange for someone to come to clear up and wash up after a dinner-party and shampoo the carpet if necessary. Monica Jewitt and Linda Lamb personally transport the girls to their work within a twenty-mile radius of the Tyne Valley, so they are closely involved with their Shiners (and will provide deputies if your regular cleaner cannot come for any reason). They charge £2.55 per person per hour (day rate), £3.10 per hour (night rate), plus 50p petrol charge beyond ten miles of Prudhoe.

Invisible mending

LONDON

British Invisible Mending Service, 32 Thayer St, W1 (01-487 4292 or 01-935 2487). Any type of hand-sewing, alterations, reweaving and reknitting. They will narrow lapels, taper legs, restyle, alter jersey fabrics, reweave buttonholes. They have been established for thirty-nine years, and although their work is not cheap – £34.50 for a simple lapel narrowing, not involving a buttonhole – it is expert.

Wholesale Invisible Mending, 30 Brewer St, W1 (01-437 8541). Invisible mending, tailoring and drycleaning, including complicated, beaded evening gowns. This is a third-generation family business started by Eric Robert's grandfather in 1910, and a high standard is maintained. Everything is done on the premises, and a specially quick service can be provided when needed. Invisible mending is possible on most fabrics other than silk: expect to pay from £8 for a very small hole.

YORKSHIRE

Neville-Sechic Ltd, Wellington Rd, Dewsbury, W Yorks (Dewsbury 464281). High-quality invisible repairs on most fabrics. The company was established in 1952 for the repair of stockings and textiles, and now concentrates on repairs to garments in wool, worsted, mohair, Terylene and other man-made fibres, knitwear and jersey. Most of its work is for the trade, but it will accept a few garments from private clients. Prices are from £5.50 for a $\frac{1}{4}$-in. to $\frac{1}{2}$-in. repair to £17.50 for a $2\frac{1}{2}$-in.; each is individually estimated.

Oriental carpets

DORSET

J. T. H. Green, Whitcombe Farm, Beaminster (Beaminster 862366).
Repairs to oriental rugs up to 11 × 5 ft. Toby Green has been fascinated by oriental rugs since he was about six years old, and now that he has retired he has more time to concentrate on them. He charges about £50 to repair the sides and ends of a hearth-size rug; holes will depend on the size and complexity of the design. He will travel anywhere, but if you want to visit him, just go to Beaminster and ask for 'the retired doctor'. Everyone within twenty miles will be able to direct you.

GLOUCESTERSHIRE

Julian Homer, Stoneleigh, Parabola Rd, Cheltenham (Cheltenham 34243). Cleaning and restoration of most oriental hand-knotted rugs. Julian Homer started collecting thirteen years ago when he was furnishing a flat and when old rugs were the cheapest form of floor covering. He now deals in many collectable items, from saddle bags and cushions to carpets, at prices from £100 to £1,000, and will tackle all aspects of his subject, including valuations.

Eric Pride, 8 Imperial Square, Cheltenham (Cheltenham 580822). Hand-made oriental rugs and kelims, cleaned and restored. Eric Pride has a wide selection of Persian and tribal rugs and hangings and is also a broker. All work is done on the premises; there is a range of 700 shades of wools and these can be blended to achieve intermediate colours. Cleaning is 50p per square foot. Restoration is charged at £6.50 per hour. Silk rugs are also accepted for restoration.

HERTFORDSHIRE

Sheelagh Lewis Ltd, 10 Stockings Lane, Little Berkhamsted, Hertford (Cuffley 875044); and The Old School House, Bury, Dulverton, Somerset (Dulverton 23715). Restoration of all hand-knotted rugs, Persian, oriental and English. Sheelagh Lewis's business began as a hobby after travelling in the Middle East, where she became fascinated by the rugs. Later, in London, she freelanced in research and cataloguing of rugs and learned all aspects of the trade, including buying and selling. Now she concentrates on restoration, and also lectures throughout the country. Apart from insurance work – restoring areas burned or chewed by occidental pets – the most usual repair is to fringes (about £25 for both ends). She can undertake the finest silk rugs and can arrange for special vegetable dyes to be made up when necessary.

LONDON

David Black Carpets, 96 Portland Rd, W11 (01-727 2566). Restoration and hand-cleaning of all kelims and flat-woven oriental rugs. David Black and his partner Clive Loveless will also value clients' own rugs for insurance.

Calaora Carpets, 214 King St, W6 (01-741 4106). Cleaning and restoration of handmade oriental carpets up to 150 years old (it is difficult to find suitable materials to restore older ones). This family business began in the mid-1830s in Turkey and was established in this country by the present owner's grandfather in the early 1900s. Since then successive generations have been among the leaders in their field of restoration, and they undertake work for the trade, the National Trust and similar organizations and private clients. They will also repair modern fitted carpets which have been damaged by scorching, burning or flood.

Coats Oriental Carpets, 4 Kensington Church Walk, off Holland St, W8 (01-937 0983). Retailers of oriental rugs who will also hand-clean, mend and reweave on site if necessary. All estimates are individual.

Nissim & Co. Ltd, 23 Charlotte Rd, E C2 (01-739 5051). Handwoven oriental rugs and machine-made copies cleaned and restored. Axminster and Wilton re-tufted on site – small burns from cigarettes or coal, for instance – on behalf of insurance companies only. All estimates are individual.

The Oriental Carpet Clinic at Portman Carpets, 7 Portman Square, W1 (01-486 3770). Hand-cleaning of valuable oriental rugs, including expert repair where necessary. The company will also give valuations.

SOMERSET

Michael and Amanda Lewis, 8 North St, Wellington (Wellington 7430). Dealers in old and new handmade oriental rugs and kelims who also clean and restore. Michael and Amanda Lewis hand-clean rugs with non-chemical solutions and use fibres of appropriate age and colour for their restoration work. They will travel all round the West Country.

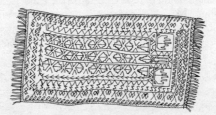

Suede, leather and fur

AVON

Westmans Cleaners (Suedecare), Devonshire Rd, Weston-super-Mare (Weston-super-Mare 28165). Specialist cleaners of sheepskin, operating a nationwide postal service. They clean and renovate sheepskin, suede, leather, pigskin and split hides, repigmenting when necessary. The repair service includes rebinding, reinforcing button fixings, replacing suede collars and cuffs and relining suede garments. They have twenty-two years' experience behind them. Cleaning charges are from £14.25 for coats. A full list of prices and services is available.

Suede Services Ltd, 2a Hoop Lane, Golders Green, NW11 (01-455 0052). Experts in the cleaning and repair of all skins – leather, suede, sheepskin, fur. Leon Simons has been a specialist for forty years and will re-oil, retint, resurface, replace panels, match and mend. He offers a postal service throughout the country, but if you have a problem with any skin garment you can send him a stamped addressed 9 × 6 in. envelope, and he will put you in touch with a local leather specialist.

SUSSEX

Suede and Leather Care, 30 Preston St, Brighton, E Sussex (Brighton 27488). Cleaning and renovation of all suedes, leathers, sheepskins and fur. They will resurface, retint, match panels, remodel, and they offer a postal cleaning service all over the country and abroad. For a three-quarter-length coat to be cleaned, redressed and siliconed to prevent marking in the rain costs from £18.50. They also make suede and leather clothes and motorcycle outfits to order (a pair of trousers is from £175), and as Martin Gould is a model aircraft enthusiast, he will also make replicas of period flying helmets and jackets.

Prices were correct at the time of printing, but are only intended as an indication and means of comparison. Do not send cheques to any company without checking first by telephone on postal charges and availability.

10] Getting Married

Cars and carriages

CHESHIRE

Heyeswood Carriages, Heyeswood Farm, Chester Rd, Hatford, nr Northwich (Sandiway 882334). For the bride who wants to arrive in style, John Barlow can provide a vintage Royal Mail Coach, a nineteenth-century open carriage and horses, a white Rolls Royce or a dark blue Bentley. Prices are around £85 for a coach or a car with a driver in full livery. There is an additional mileage charge for long distances.

Vintage Carriage Hire, Roseacre, Spout Lane, Mobberley (Mobberley 3651). Rolls Royce limousines from the twenties and thirties to hire for weddings, special events and theatre trips. A Rolls Royce for a three-hour booking midweek would cost from £55, including a chauffeur in period costume.

LONDON

Getting Married, 201 Walworth Rd, S E17 (01-701 1750). Hire a carriage-and-pair for your wedding. There is a choice between an open landau and a Victorian 'glass coach', drawn by bays or greys. They are accompanied by two livery men, and the charge would normally be between two and three hundred pounds, depending on the distance involved. Coach, horses and attendants travel to the destination by lorry, set up near the bride's house, take her to the church and to and from the reception. The company also provides fashion, photographic, catering and floral services, all done personally, not sub-contracted.

London Transport Tours and Charter Office, 55 Broadway, S W1 (01-222 5600). If you want a stylish marriage and can't afford a carriage, how about hiring a double-decker bus? You can have one for a minimum of four hours for £250. Coaches are available too; charges depend on time and mileage.

The Wedding Bureau, 214 Evelyn St, Deptford, S E8 (01-692 7038).
Vintage Rolls Royces in white, colours or two-tone from about 1916. They also
have two horse-drawn carriages, a Victoria and an open landau (both convertible
in case of rain), with matching greys, bays or black or white horses to pull them.
Vintage cars are £224.25, carriages £241.50 in and around London. They will go
as far as the south coast. At least six weeks' notice is needed for carriages in the
summer.

Wedding Services, 16 Daleham Gardens, N W3 (01-794 8244). Harry
Greenberg will not only provide vintage Rolls Royces for weddings anywhere in
the country, but will also arrange the photography and flowers and provide a
discotheque. For central London he charges an inclusive fee of £100 for the
vintage cars, £80 for Silver Shadows and Silver Clouds in white or colours.
Ceremonies further than fifteen to twenty miles will have an additional mileage
charge, and for really long distances the basic charge is waived and fees are based
on a £12 an hour and 90p per mile hire charge. Photography is around £4 per
colour print, plus £22 for a leather album. Discos £65 for four hours. A very flexible,
willing-to-tackle-anything service.

**White Lady Weddings, 1 Drewstead Rd, Streatham, S W16 (01-677
5432).** Modern and vintage Rolls in many colours, £160; Victoria and Landau
carriages and pairs, £235. The prices are for Central London; individual quotations
for longer distances. Other services, including photography, video, flowers and
cutlery, are available.

TYNE AND WEAR

**Benton Oval Garage, Benton Rd, Four Lane Ends, Newcastle upon Tyne
(Newcastle upon Tyne 661908/668909 and Wideopen 363126).** Rolls
Royces and vintage cars for hire. There are eight Rolls Royces, and hiring charges
for a wedding in the Newcastle area start at £80.50. A green-and-black 1937
vintage Rolls would be from £92 and a 1931 yellow-and-black Rolls £103.50.

WARWICKSHIRE

**Stratford Motor Museum, 1 Shakespeare St, Stratford-upon-Avon
(Stratford-upon-Avon 69413).** 'One of the most valuable Rolls Royces in the
world' is available for wedding hire during the summer months only (so that its
pristine condition will be maintained). It is a Phantom II built specially for the
Maharajah of Rajkot in 1934 and has his crest on both doors and windows.
Restored in the original saffron colour, the P II has a drop hood and eleven
forward-facing lights – some originally manipulated by servants from the running
board during night-time panther shoots. It costs £100 to hire, plus £1 per mile, plus

VAT, and is also used for publicity occasions – an extra £100 and mileage for a whole day's use. Worth going to the museum just to inquire, because the consultant, Peter Hugo, is the number-one Prince Charles look-alike.

Fashion and beauty

CHESHIRE

Happy The Bride, 319 Hale Rd, Hale Barns, Altrincham (061-980 6014). Anything and everything to do with weddings. Sarah Dunning's shop specializes in unusual and exclusive wedding dresses in silk and antique lace from Britain, America and the Continent at prices ranging from £150 to £950. She will hire out an extra large white umbrella in case it rains on the day, and can supply a hooped crinoline petticoat for £20. Real rose-petal confetti available (95p, plus 20p postage and packing). Personalized stationery for the table includes printed napkins, place cards and book matches. At no extra cost Sarah Dunning will arrange any aspect of your wedding or all of it – the cake, the flowers, the reception, the photography. Advice in the shop is free. Consultations in clients' houses are charged by the hour. Closed Mondays.

Heather Jackson, 23 St Mary's Rd, Sale (061-973 5256). A wedding-day make-up at your home. Charges are from £4.95 to £9.95 per person, depending on numbers. A rehearsal is always advised for the bride (£6). Heather Jackson also does special photographic make-up if you are having a studio portrait.

LONDON

Alison Combe, Unit 111, Clerkenwell Workshops, 31 Clerkenwell Close, E C1 (01-251 3864). A designer who specializes in exclusive handmade headdresses. Alison Combe has often worked with Bill Gibb and regularly makes collections for Harrods and other top stores here and in Houston and Paris. She undertakes special commissions for bridal head-dresses or, for less formal weddings, hair ornaments, and she designs corsages and accessories for evening wear. Prices are from £25 for hair ornaments to over £100 for an elaborate head-dress.

Liberty, Regent St, W1 (01-734 1234). Wedding veils repaired and refreshed from £20. Lace veils mounted on a family tiara from £35. Hats made to match an outfit in customer's own fabric or in a Liberty fabric from £45, plus the cost of the fabric. All in the wedding dress and millinery department.

Joan Price's Face Place, 33 Cadogan St, SW3 (01-589 9062), and 31 Connaught St, W2 (01-723 6671). Brides – and their mothers – can learn how to create a natural and lasting make-up with exactly the right colours for their complexions. Once you have had a lesson (£7.95) you can also call on the Face Place for professional help with your make-up on the day itself (£12 an hour, plus fares, Central London only), but Joan's girls will not do a bridal make-up on someone they have never seen before.

Flowers

BERKSHIRE

Anna Plowden, 30 Bridle Rd, Maidenhead (Maidenhead 27553). Pictures made from wedding bouquets, pressed and mounted on velvet in a range of frames, from walnut and gilt ovals to miniatures. Anna Plowden began to make flower pictures from bouquets in 1974 because her husband Anthony was such a keen gardener he couldn't bear her to filch his flowers for the house. He now grows rare varieties of silver foliages for her and does all the framing, which seems a happy compromise. Brides who live some distance from Maidenhead are sent a container for the bouquet to be posted. Anna will reproduce the bouquet exactly or will make up an original flower picture. Prices are from £9 for miniatures to £185 in 23-ct gold-leaf, all with non-reflective glass.

CHESHIRE

Frames and Flowers, 11 Greenbank Drive, Bollington, Macclesfield (Macclesfield 72815). Wedding bouquets pressed and mounted as pictures, or dried flower pictures created specially for wedding anniversaries. These, in tones of gold, silver or whatever is required, are from £15, including postage, for a picture in an oval frame. Pictures made from clients' wedding bouquets are from £27.50 to £350. An airtight container to keep the flowers fresh is sent in advance; orders should be placed at least three weeks before the wedding.

CORNWALL

Foye Forge, Fowey (Fowey 2248). Specialists in gold, silver and copper plating. A single bloom from the bride's bouquet can be turned into a piece of jewellery, or the stem can be extended for use as an ornament in a specimen vase. The flower, with its stem wrapped in moist cotton wool, must be packed in a strong carton and posted first-class to arrive fresh, and the service takes about four weeks. Prices are from £17.25 in gold plate for, say, a freesia, £14.95 in silver, £11.50 in copper. When Foye Forge turned from blacksmithing to plating twenty years ago, they were the first to plate leaves and acorns as jewellery. They now also plate babies' first shoes (from about £12.50) and toddlers' shoes (from £14.50).

ESSEX

Yvonne Saunders, 70 New St, Great Dunmow (Great Dunmow 3986). Wedding bouquet pictures mounted on a background of the wedding-dress fabric or on cream silk, and framed in wood, with or without gold leaf. Yvonne Saunders sends a special airtight container to the bride-to-be, so that the bouquet can be dispatched in it immediately after the wedding and so remain as fresh as possible. She makes a sketch of the original design and reassembles the flowers after pressing. Prices are from £35 to £75, including postage.

HERTFORDSHIRE

A–Z Flowers, Hertfordshire (Albury 245, Royston 838341 and Brent Pelham 239). Three Constance-Spry-trained florists who work from home and between them cover an area from London to Cambridge. Leone Ayres, Jenny Arnell and Diana Zurlinden specialize in wedding bouquets and receptions, and flower arrangements for marquees, churches, dinner tables and hospital presentation. They also make arrangements from flowers they have grown and dried themselves. Prices are from £20 for a bride's bouquet.

LONDON

Caroline Evans, Unit C, 49 Atalanta St, S W6 (01-381 5494). Flower arrangements for all occasions. As a change from conventional arrangements, flower 'trees' make delightful wedding decorations and are one of the specialities here. A large bay-shaped 'tree' 5 ft high with a spread of three or four feet costs about £60 – it looks enchanting composed of daisies and ribbons, or you can have whatever flowers you like to match your theme. Caroline Evans likes to visit the venue with the bride to discuss colours. Bouquets are from £21, pedestal arrangements from £50. She also does wedding arrangements and bouquets entirely in silk – these will be about 75 per cent more than fresh flowers – and arrangements in dried flowers for winter displays.

SUSSEX

Pippa & Co., Trout Hall, Virginia Cottage, Scaynes Hill, Haywards Heath, W Sussex (Scaynes Hill 225). Wedding bouquets pressed and mounted on a piece of your wedding-dress fabric if you wish – and framed. Airtight containers are sent before the wedding, and the finished picture can be supplied unframed from £12, or in a selection of wood or gilt frames from £16, plus postage.

Photography and video

CHESHIRE

Patrick McGlade, Precious Moments Video, 15 Oakwood Court, Bow Lane, Bowdon (061-941 3190). Weddings video-recorded from the moment the bride leaves home, during the church service, and at the reception until the honeymoon departure. The client gets the entire original tape of up to three hours. Patrick McGlade can also supply a shorter version with music, edited to any length. Prices are from £200, and a demonstration tape is available. He also provides the same service for sporting occasions, anniversary dinners, barmitzvahs and amateur operatics.

HERTFORDSHIRE

The British Institute of Professional Photography, Amwell End, Ware (Ware 4011). For those seeking a portrait or wedding photographer, the BIPP has lists of their members throughout the country, and although the Institute does not recommend individuals you can be sure that members all reach reasonable standards. There are three membership qualifications: Licentiates (LBIPP) have to submit ten examples of their current work and are assessed for competence by a judging panel; Associates (ABIPP) have their work judged by an annual meeting of distinguished Fellows of the Institute, who require a high degree of ability, presentation and content; and Fellows (FBIPP) have to demonstrate distinguished ability.

Receptions

Note

See also the sections on *Party catering* in Chapter 5 (pp. 153–8) and *Hire services* in Chapter 8 (pp. 218–21).

DORSET

Western Marquees, Stables Farm, Bradford Peverell, Dorchester (Martinstown 312). Hexagonal blue-and-white marquees for wedding receptions and other functions. These special marquees have no centre pole and no guy ropes, and their hexagonal shape makes them suitable for large modules, like a honeycomb. Two sizes, the smaller with 10-ft-long sides, the larger 20-ft. Charges are subject to a site survey. They also provide tables, chairs, lighting, heating and whatever else is necessary.

HEREFORD AND WORCESTER

W. H. Burgoyne & Sons, Lyonshall, nr Kington (Lyonshall 283). All types of marquees for private parties, weddings, agricultural shows. A fourth-generation family business who will also supply all the fittings – dance floor, lighting, heating – and will travel anywhere.

LONDON

Searcy Tansley, 136 Brompton Rd, SW3 (01-584 3344). A Georgian-style house for hire for wedding receptions, dinners or parties. The house, at 30 Pavilion Road, SW3 (between Harrods and Sloane Street), has been carefully renovated to maintain the atmosphere of a private house, yet incorporating improvements to make large-scale catering easy and efficient. There is a library and a ballroom which will accommodate 400 people for a buffet (catered of course by Searcy's). Prices are £200 hiring fee, plus catering from £4.50 per head for cocktail parties to £15 per head for buffets and meals, based on 100 guests.

Chandos House is also sometimes available on loan from the Royal Society of Medicine, care of Searcy's, who have twenty venues for hire.

TYNE AND WEAR

Max Murray, Cater Hire, Walbottle Rd, Lemington, Newcastle upon Tyne (Newcastle upon Tyne 674098, 24-hour answering service). Everything you can think of in the catering line, from champagne buckets, white damask tablecloths and fine china with gold rims, to fish knives, heart-shaped cake tins and kettles big enough to boil twelve pints of water. No order is too small for Max Murray, and he can manage to cater for 2,000 people. Everything can be delivered to the door (delivery charge minimum £4) or collected from his warehouse. There is also a comprehensive range of disposable plates, napkins, wedding-cake boxes, straws and confetti. Hiring charges are from 3p. Sample prices: punchbowls with eight glasses £2, flambé lamp £5, wedding-cake stand £1, fish kettle £2.

11] Getting Posted

Chocolates

LONDON

Army & Navy, 105 Victoria St, SW1 (01-834 1234), and Barkers of Kensington, 63 Kensington High St, W8 (01-937 5432). Handmade cream truffles in ten flavours – milk chocolate, vanilla, caramel, coffee, rum, Grand Marnier, whisky, cognac, Gaelic and cherry. Made by a young, Swiss-trained confectioner in Tunbridge Wells and delivered fresh each week. Presentation boxes £3.96 lb., £8.50 2 lb., or loose at 99p per quarter, plus postage. Will keep for four weeks. Also available in Army & Navy at Camberley, Guildford, Kingston and Bromley.

Prestat Ltd, 40 South Molton St, W1 (01-629 4838). *The* people for truffles. They are all handmade to the recipes that have made Prestat famous for more than eighty years. An assortment including rum and brandy flavours can be sent for £8.85 per lb. box, including postage, anywhere in the UK. A variety of other delicious chocolates too, but the truffles are the connoisseur's choice.

MIDDLESEX

Village Fayre, 389 Uxbridge Rd, Hatch End (01-421 0363). Handmade confectionery from recipes invented by Angela Jay and Yvonne Field, who went straight to the top when they began six years ago by winning an order from Fortnum & Mason. They do mixtures of plain, milk and white chocolates filled with orange, mint and cassis truffle at £5 per lb. and liqueur chocolates at £7 per lb. Send a stamped addressed envelope for details of postal charges and other confections.

Flowers

Interflora: any branch. As a replacement for the late-lamented telegram, this well-known flower delivery service organizes a message service called an Interfloragram. For about £6 you can send a single flower and a message of up to twenty-two words (address free) to anywhere in Britain – same-day delivery if ordered before noon.

CHANNEL ISLANDS

Flying Flowers, PO Box 373, Jersey (Jersey 71788). One dozen carnations for £5.50, sent anywhere at the drop of a credit card. You can have them in white, pink, red, yellow, peach or mixed, and should give five working days' notice if you need them for an anniversary.

CORNWALL

Cornish Bulb Company, Little Greystones, Passage Hill, Mylor, Falmouth (Penryn 72720). Your substitute memory for birthdays and anniversaries. Martin Drake, who started in 1971 by sending out three bunches of daffodils from a packing shed, now undertakes to send roses, anemones, carnations or a choice of thirty-six bulbs to people whose birthdays you can't afford to forget. You send the names, addresses and dates; they do the rest. Prices from £5 for anemones and daffodils in season; roses ten for £8; carnations fifteen for £7.50.

LONDON

Flowerland Ltd, Box No. 377, The Flower Market, New Covent Garden, SW8 (01-622 6488). Fresh flowers direct from New Covent Garden, delivered anywhere in the UK within twenty-four hours. There are twelve bouquets, from a single red rose and fern at £3 or ten red roses at £10, to a mixed bouquet at £20, all including a message card.

MIDDLESEX

John Grooms Craft Centre, Edgware Way, Edgware (01-959 2418). Handmade artificial flowers. There are twenty varieties, all made by craft workers of the John Grooms Association for the Disabled. A complete price list is available. Other gifts in cane, basketwork, wood and mosaic too.

SUSSEX

Chesswood Postal Flowers, Chesswood Nurseries, Thakeham, Pulborough, W Sussex (West Chiltington 2340). A variety of freshly cut flowers sent with a message anywhere on the UK mainland. There are roses in a choice of colours at £8.50 for ten, £15 for twenty (red ones £10 and £17.50), orange and yellow lilies £9, spray carnations £6.50, seasonal assortments £7, these all for ten; freesias £7 for twenty. All flowers are sent by first-class post, or can be expressed for an extra fee to guarantee next-day delivery.

Food

HAMPSHIRE

Goldesborough Quail Farm, Clements Farm, Wheatley, Bordon (Bordon 23174). Poultry farmers who will send quail by post within 150 miles. The cost is £5.20 for six and they should arrive the next day, Post Office willing. They don't like orders from further afield – and certainly not from Scotland at Christmas – because of the possibility of postal delays.

LEICESTERSHIRE

Dickinson & Morris Ltd, 10 Nottingham St, Melton Mowbray (Melton Mowbray 62341). The first Melton Mowbray pork pies are said to have been baked in this seventeenth-century building. The shop now belongs to Dickinson & Morris Ltd, who also make Melton hunt cake – a 'secret recipe' rich wedding-cake-type mixture first made 120 years ago. This they can send all over the world. U K charges are £9.60 for the large size, £6.90 for the smaller. (Check current postal charges before ordering.)

LONDON

The Drury Tea and Coffee Company, 3 New Row, W C2 (01-836 1960); also at 37 Drury Lane, W C2 (01-836 2607), 1 Mepham St, S E1 (01-928 2551); and branches in Bath and Bristol. Originally tea specialists when they opened in Drury Lane in 1936 – long before coffee caught up as a popular drink. Now there are twenty-five types of coffee beans as well as a wide variety of teas and all the equipment for making both. Mail order is available through the New Row address. They particularly recommend their Bahamas blend coffee.

Higgins, 42 South Molton St, W1 (01-629 3913). Still, as far as they know, the sole shop in the country to specialize only in coffee. When Harold Rees Higgins opened in 1945, coffee was still a minority drink and everyone predicted his downfall; but nearly forty years later the shop is still going strong under the direction of his son Tony and daughter Audrey, who are fascinated by the whole subject of coffee. They will tell you the tale of the arrival of coffee in Europe in 1615, and the opening of the first coffee-house in England (in Oxford in 1650) and in Vienna – via the Turkish army in 1683. Thanks to a Polish officer called Kolschitzky, who swam the Danube several times with messages for the Austrian and Polish troops, the Turks were routed, leaving behind bags and bags of coffee beans. The canny Pole, having lived among the Turks for years, was the only one who knew what to do with the beans, and he claimed them as part of his reward – his first step to opening Vienna's first coffee house and making himself a fortune. Higgins are making their fortune by offering forty-one different and distinctive flavours from £2.20 to about £4 per lb., and will send any weights over $\frac{1}{2}$ lb. by mail. Orders of 5 lbs. and over are sent post-free.

Paxton & Whitfield, 93 Jermyn St, SW1 (01-930 9892); The Paxton & Whitfield Cheese Club (01-928 5262). Cheese by mail order? What will it be like by the time it arrives? The answer is 'Perfect', for Paxton & Whitfield have a cheese club and send a monthly selection specially chosen to arrive in its prime. Having been in the business for nearly 200 years, they know what they are about, and the selection includes English and Continental cheeses, each piece weighing about 12 oz. You are not committed to a regular order (£7.50 per month) – there are twelve selections a year and you can wait as long as you like before ordering again.

LOTHIAN

McSween of Edinburgh, 130 Bruntsfield Place, Edinburgh 10 (031-229 1216). One of my few excursions over the border, but then where else would you expect to go, should you feel so inclined, for a haggis fit for a laird? This company has specialized in making traditional, natural-skinned haggis for more than thirty years, and I was told by a genuine Scottish connoisseur of this boiled bladder that it is worth every penny of its 98p per lb., plus postage. Weights available range from a 1-lb. size to a ceremonial size at 6–8 lbs., serving 15–45 portions.

NORFOLK

The Mustard Shop, 3 Bridewell Alley, Norwich (Norwich 27889). English, French and flavoured mustards. The shop is owned by Colman's and was opened to commemorate their 150th anniversary in 1973. Many attractive pots and packs: a list is available, and products can be mail-ordered.

NORTHUMBERLAND

L. Robson & Sons, Fish Curer, Craster, Alnwick (Alnwick 76223). Kippers smoked in the traditional way, using oak sawdust, are a Northumbrian delicacy available by post. Craster kippers can be sent between June and September in a specially designed box – three or four kippers, weighing about 1 lb., cost about £2.20 – or you could order smoked salmon at any time of year. Robson's guarantee to replace their fish if it does not arrive in perfect condition.

Wine and other gifts

DERBYSHIRE

Pearl Derby, 96 Derby Rd, Chellaston, Derby (Derby 701100). The most exciting gift you are ever likely to get in a can – an oyster guaranteed to contain a pearl. Each one, cultured in Ago Bay off the Japanese coast, comes packed in a special preservative; rinse it off, open the oyster and your pearl could be round or baroque, white, pink, golden or, the most valuable, black. They vary from 5 mm to 10 mm in diameter, and if you send yours back to Pearl Derby, Yvonne Swann and Jo Chittenden will drill it and fit it to wear on a chain, or they can match it from their stock of loose pearls if you want a pair for earrings. The cost of each can is £8.50; silver or gold settings are from £9 to £63.

LONDON

Songbird Ltd, 60 Goldney Rd, W9 (01-286 8090). Singing telegrams specially composed to enchant or embarrass. You can choose to have them performed by, among others, Tarzans and Don Juans, schoolgirls, nurses or somewhat under-dressed ladies in suspenders. Birthday telegrams are £25, others specially composed from details submitted by the sender £35. Also Songbird Balloon Bouquets – bunches of balloons delivered from £15, or a balloon-in-a-box £7.50 by post or £11 delivered.

Unirose, 6 Rabbit Row, W8 (01-727 3922). Champagne, roses, chocolates and a selection of gifts both nice (pink, striped or white satin-bordered mirrors to stand by the bed – with a message written in smudgeproof lipstick if you wish) and naughty (black stockings and suspender belt). Other ideas include caviar, cigars, smoked salmon, pâté de foie gras, jewellery and one or two Design-Council-approved toys – handy if your memory is not as long as your budget. Prices from £5 to £115.

SURREY

Alexander Dunn & Co. Ltd, 42 Walton Rd, East Molesey (01-941 3030). Smoked salmon and whisky, port, stilton and biscuits, whisky or champagne with three pâtés – these are examples of a variety of gifts available by mail order anywhere on the U K mainland. A brochure and price list are available.

Prices were correct at the time of printing, but are only intended as an indication and means of comparison. Do not send cheques to any company without checking first by telephone on postal charges and availability.

12] **Getting Around**

Group craft workshops and craft courses

Note

Unless group workshops specifically say they welcome visitors it is best to make inquiries first by telephone. Some light industrial premises are not able, for reasons of safety and security, to cope with casual window shoppers.

AVON

Clevedon Craft Centre, Moor Lane, Clevedon, Bristol (Clevedon 872867). Craft workshops in a group of converted stables where visitors are welcome to watch a variety of work in progress. At the last count there was a potter, a knitter, a silversmith, a tiler and a leatherworker among others – check if you are seeking a particular craft. There is a tea room and museum (not open Mondays).

CHESHIRE

Red Rose Guild of Designer Craftsmen. Secretary: Shan Bristow, 4 Victoria Rd, Wilmslow (Wilmslow 520193). Set up in 1921 to hold annual exhibitions in Manchester showing craftwork of high quality, this Guild was well ahead of its time. It has always had a North-West bias but shows work from all parts of the country. The 120 members are admitted by selection committee, and crafts include weaving, furniture-making, glass, mirrors, pottery, silver, jewellery and embroidery. The Guild acts as an information bureau, supplying names of people available for commissions. The annual exhibition is held in the autumn.

CORNWALL

Anne Hulbert Creative Ventures, Tremayne, St Martin-in-Meneage, Helston (Manaccan 555). Four-day residential craft courses, twice monthly.

Anne Hulbert teaches patchwork, beadwork, quilting, appliqué, beginners' fabric painting and machine embroidery, designing cushions and blinds. Accommodation and full board is included in course fees of about £85 per person.

The Mid-Cornwall Craft Centre and Galleries, Biscovey, Par (Par 2131). An attractive crafts centre in a nineteenth-century school house offering glass engraving, needlework, toys, cabinet-making, ceramics, jewellery, paintings and prints. Craft courses available. The gallery is on the A390, three miles east of St Austell.

HEREFORD AND WORCESTER

Gaffers Gallery, Brewers Passage, Commercial St, Hereford. A co-operative craft gallery and coffee-shop with studio glass-blowing workshop attached. Apart from glass you will find designer-made furniture, ironwork and jewellery always on show, plus a range of work by other local artists and craftsmen shown in regularly changing exhibitions.

The Jinney Ring Craft Centre, Hanbury, Worcs (Hanbury 272). A group of craftsmen established in a series of beautifully converted farm buildings. You will find a wood-turner, weaver, potter, dolls'-house maker, glass blower, and stained-glass maker. Refreshments are available and you can make your own cyder on an old press. Closed Mondays and Tuesdays.

LONDON

The Clerkenwell Workshops, 31 Clerkenwell Close, E C1 (01-251 4821). London's longest-established light industrial and craft workshops. There are 140 businesses representing fifty trades and services, including dental technicians, musical-instrument makers, antique restorers, fashion designers and printers. The traditional Clerkenwell trades of silver and goldsmithing, jewellery making, and watch repair and restoration are represented, and you will also find sandwich making and harpsichord manufacture listed. Inquiries about specific crafts should be sent to the address above, where they will be dealt with or passed on to individual workshops.

Coldharbour Works, 245a Coldharbour Lane, S W9 (01-274 7700). A converted granary housing thirty-five craft workshops. Among the specialists you will find furniture restorers, electronic and audio experts, knife and tool sharpeners, jewellers, potters and makers of security grilles and gates, upholsterers and toymakers.

Kingsgate Workshops, Kingsgate Rd, N W6 (01-328 7878). A group of workshops and studios in a converted ex-factory. The services you will find there include cabinet-making and furniture makers and restorers, pine and kitchen specialists, potters, silk screeners, textile weavers, upholsterers and dress designers.

Portobello Green Craft Workshop Arcade, next to Westway Market, corner of Portobello Rd and Cambridge Gardens, W10. Twenty-five workshops including fabrics, leather goods, knitwear, jewellery, picture framing, antique restoration, bicycle repairs and spares, beads and pine furniture.

Regeneration Ltd, Finsbury Business Centre, 40 Bowling Green Lane, Clerkenwell, EC1 (01-278 9261); also at Acton, Stratford, Hackney, Camberwell, Wandsworth, Portsmouth, Hove, Southampton and Deptford. A countrywide series of converted warehouses, factories and other premises, all converted into small workshops. In mid-1983 there were 500 small businesses flourishing with Regeneration's help, and by March 1984 they intend to have more than one thousand.

MANCHESTER

North West Craftsmen. Chairman: Brenda Morrison, The Cottage, 1 Hawthorn Avenue, Monton, Eccles, Manchester (061-789 5591). An enterprising young crafts group who hold a Christmas Craft Shop at the Royal Northern College of Music in Manchester. Music-lovers get out their cheque books in the intervals and do their Christmas shopping. Smaller exhibitions are held throughout the region in the summer. Work includes embroideries, jewellery, silver, pottery, patchwork. Prices from about £1 to £200.

SUSSEX

The Earnley Concourse, nr Chichester, W Sussex (Bracklesham Bay 670392 or 670326). An adult education centre which runs residential courses from two to seven days; subjects include techniques of china restoration, portrait painting, care and restoration of antique furniture, soft-toy making, mounting and framing pictures, upholstery and jewellery-making.

Useful addresses

British Woodworking Federation, 82 New Cavendish St, London W1 (01-580 5588). An association of more than 700 firms specializing in working with wood – doors, wood windows, joinery, kitchen cabinets or timber-framed housing components. Members guarantee to use modern preservatives to rotproof wood windows. The Federation will put inquirers in touch with local members.

The Building Centre, 26 Store St, London WC1 (01-637 1022). Advice on the most suitable materials and fittings for your redecoration or rebuilding scheme. For a fee of around £20 you get an hour's consultation with one of a group of designers, who will give impartial advice on design problems, including rough plans or layouts where appropriate. Appointments are necessary.

CoSIRA (Council for Small Industries in Rural Areas), 141 Castle St, Salisbury, Wiltshire (Salisbury 6255). Business and technical advice, training and finance offered to small manufacturing and service businesses located in villages or rural towns up to 10,000 inhabitants.

The Crafts Council Conservation Section, 12 Waterloo Place, London SW1 (01-930 4811). As well as its index of approved individual craftsmen, with slides of their work, the Council organizes the National Register of Conservation Craft Skills in the Building Industry. This is run with the co-operation of county planning departments, which keep registers of local craftsmen who have carried out successful restoration work. If a local planning department cannot help, the Council will suggest someone from a nearby borough.

Directory of Consultants and Contractors, The Arboricultural Association, Ampfield House, Ampfield, nr Romsey, Hampshire (Braisford 68717). A list of tree surgeons and specialists approved by the association for the quality of their work. All covered by insurance.

Drycleaning Information Bureau, Lancaster Gate House, 319 Pinner Rd, Harrow, Middlesex (01-863 8658). The DIB has lists of all members of the Association of British Launderers and Cleaners on its word-processor and can put you in touch with specialist cleaners. They prefer written inquiries, with a stamped addressed envelope.

English Tourist Board, 4 Grosvenor Gardens, London SW1 (01-730 3400). Activity and hobby holidays. The Board produces an annual guide to activity holidays which includes an arts and crafts section – rug-weaving, spinning, dyeing, pottery, printing, needlework, cookery, beauty care among them. Details of duration and cost of holidays are given. The price is £1.25 from bookshops.

The Kitchen Specialists Association, 31 Bois Lane, Chesham Bois, Amersham, Buckinghamshire (Amersham 22287). An association of shops specializing in kitchen design, supply and installation. There is a consumer-protection scheme so that, if for any reason (kitchen fitters have been known to go out of business in the middle of a contract) your member-contractor does not complete the kitchen you have ordered, the Association guarantees to have it installed to the original specification. This is subject to a maximum deposit of 20 per cent of the total contract. Addresses of local members are available from the Association.

Research & Development Department, Shetland Islands Council, 93 Olaf St, Lerwick, Shetland (Lerwick 3535). A list of designers and manufacturers of Shetland and Fair Isle knitwear, with a note on whether the garments are hand-knitted, hand-framed or machine-knitted.

Tourist Information Office, City Hall, Bradford, W Yorks (Bradford 729577). A booklet (about 40p) is available from the Tourist Office and from the Central Library listing shops where low-priced clothes and cloth are available straight from the Bradford mills. They are usually end-of-lines, so there is no guarantee that you will find the style and colour you want, but men's worsted suits are under £100, all-wool skirt lengths are from £1.50, and velvet curtains can be half price, so it could be worth calling in on one of these fairly scattered shops if you are in the area.

Index

After-dinner speakers, 162
Antiques removals, 223
Antiquities, 187
Appliqué, 56–7, 57–8, 60
Archery, 210
Architectural restoration, 30, 119–20, 124, 126, 145
Arms and military, 187
Art and craft materials:
  artists' materials, 179, 208
  bamboo, 199
  candle-making, 181
  felt, 181
  jewellery-making, 183, 184, 185
  kid, gold and silver, 181
  leather, suede 184
  marquetry, 181
  raffia, 199
  rattan, 179
  rug-making, 181, 184
  rush: English, 179; synthetic, 102
  seagrass, 199
  sheepskins, 184
  sheet copper and pewter, 185
  shellac, 179
  soft-toy kits, 186
  spinning and weaving, 186
  timber, 179
Artists:
  house portraits, 176, 177; ceramic, 177–8; embroidered, 176
  landscapes, 175, 177

  miniatures, 45, 176
  oils, 175, 176, 177
  pastels, 176
  pets, 176, 178
  portraits, 23, 176–7
  sculpture, 178
  watercolours, 23, 175, 176, 177
Awnings:
  for hire, 121
  made to order, 121
  repaired, 116

Baby shoes, gold plated, 240
Babysitting, 224
Ballet wear, 161
Balloons:
  balloon-in-a-box, 159, 247
  balloon gas cylinders, 159
  printed to order, 159, 161
Banister ropes, 139–40
Barbecues, 206
Barman, cocktail party, 160
Barometers, 191
  repaired, 91
Basketwork, 65, 244
  repaired, 65
  supplies for, 179
Bathroom fittings:
  Victorian, 119, 121
  wood, 122
Baths:
  jacuzzi conversions, 122

Baths *cont.*
  made to order, 121
  re-enamelled, 121
Batik dyeing, 28
Beauty:
  cosmetics, 216
  hair, 216
  products, herbal, 204, 215, 217
  remedial make-up, 215
  scents, limited editions, 174, 215, 216–17
  skin-care products, 217
  skin blemishes, treatment, 216
  wedding make-up, 238, 239
Bedding:
  bedlinen and covers, 20, 21, 56, 57, 58, 59
  canopies and drapes, 19, 20, 21, 22
  futons, 205, 206
Bedheads, 21, 29, 32
  mirror mosaic, 61
  tapestry, 183
Bedlinen: *see* Bedding
Beds:
  four-posters, 19, 20, 21, 22
  made to order, 19, 21–2, 30, 33, 35–6, 101
  sofa beds, 32, 33, 207
  tubular, 21
Bedsteads, brass, 20
Benches, 33
Bicycle repairs, 251
Billiard tables, made and restored, 97
Blinds:
  cleaned, 226
  made to order, 56, 57, 58, 59, 127, 199
  re-corded, 226
Bookbinding etc., 83, 85, 86, 88
  account books, 85
  albums, 84, 85
  conservation, 83, 85
  family bibles, 84
  game books, 83
  manuscripts and theses, 84

  private-press printing, 25
  racing scrap books, 83, 88
  restoration, 83–6, 88
  visitors' books, 84, 85
Bookcases, 29
Bookplates, 173, 188
Booksellers:
  antiquarian, 188, 189
  children's, 201
  computing and electronics, 200
  country lore, 201
  out of print, 188
  private-press, 188
  spiritual and mystical, 200–201
  zen and acupuncture, 207
Bootscrapers, 135, 136
Bowls, wood, 30
Brass, 134
  curtain rails, 135
  door fittings, 135, 138
  grilles, 135
Bronze, 134
Brushes, rebristled, 106
Building advice, 252
Bureaux, 31
Butlers, 162
Buttons, 180, 181, 189
  antique, 180, 181, 189

Cabaret artistes, 162
Cabinet-making, 28–31, 32, 33, 35–6, 37
  supplies for, 179
Cabinets, 19
Cakes, fancy shapes, 154, 155, 156, 157
Cake tins, for hire, 161
Calligraphy, 23, 24
Cane panels, 31, 126
Carpet bags, 233
Carpets and rugs, 205
  cleaning of, 227, 228, 229–30
  conservation, 116, 117
  dyeing, 229–30

made to commission, 39, 54–6, 57, 79, 186
oriental, 197–8, 222, 233, 234; restoration, 222, 230, 233–4; valuations, 198, 222, 233, 234
Cars:
coach builder, 225
conversions, 225
crash repair, 225
vintage, for hire, 236, 237–8
wedding, 236–8
Cartoons, 189
Catering: see Party catering; Weddings
Ceramics, 38
Chairs, 29, 30, 31, 33, 34, 35–6, 37
Champagne by post, 247–8
Chests, 19, 32, 33
Child escorts, 213, 224
Children's parties:
catering, 155, 157–8
entertainers, 147–50
Chimney pots, 125
Chimneys, smoking, to cure, 124, 125
China:
Art Deco, 191
commemorative, 191–2
discontinued lines, 172
matching odd pieces, 214
restoration, 86, 87, 88–9, 89–90, 98, 104; studio pottery, 89; classes, 89
Chintz, 21, 38–9
Christening robes repaired, 116
Christening shawls, 71
Church bell ropes, repaired, 117
Church furniture, 31, 32
Church embroidery, 28, 41
Church inscriptions, 23
Church metalwork, 110
Church vestments, 28
repaired, 116
Cigars, 248
Cleaning:
blinds, 226

carpets, 227, 228, 229–30; oriental, 230
fabric walls, 230
houses, 231–2
lampshades, 229
on site, 227, 228, 229
soft furnishings, 227, 228, 229
tented ceilings, 230
upholstery, 227, 229, 230
wall-coverings, 227
See also Drycleaning
Clocks:
antique, 190–91
made to commission, 25–6, 26–7, 44, 52
repaired, 88–9, 90–91, 92, 93–4, 96, 190–91
spare parts, 92
Clothes:
Accessories
bags, 55, 69; evening bags, 67, 108
fingerless gloves, 73
scarves, 67, 71, 73, 79
shawls, 67, 71
shooting stockings, 73
socks, 73
umbrellas, 80
Menswear
clerical shirts, 82
discounted, 253
dressing robes, 82
knitwear: see under Clothes (Women's) below
large sizes, 81
motorcycle leathers, 235
pyjamas, long legs, 82
silk blazers and raincoats, 82
shirts: made to measure, 81, 82; ready to wear, 81–2
Shoes
ballet, 77
clogs, 76
handpainted, 77
large sizes: women's, 76, 78; men's, 78

Shoes *cont.*
　　made to measure, 76–7, 78
　　mail-order, 78
　　narrow fittings, 76
　　odd feet, 75, 76
　　orthopaedic, 78
　　sandals, 78
　　small sizes, 78
　　Women's
　　antique, 70
　　appliquéd, 69
　　corsetry, 75; maternity and
　　　　mastectomy, 74, 75
　　fur, 70–71; hire, 70
　　handpainted, 67
　　knitwear; made to order (women's,
　　　　men's, children's), 57, 71, 72, 73,
　　　　74; ready to wear, 73, 74;
　　　　Shetland, 253
　　large sizes, 68, 69, 81
　　leather, 80, 235
　　lingerie, made to order, 69, 74–5
　　quilted, 67
　　second-hand, 68
　　silk, 67, 69
　　smocks, 69
　　swimwear: made to order, 75;
　　　　mastectomy, 75
　　tall sizes, 68
　　waistcoats, 69, 80
Clowns, 147, 148, 149–50
Coats of arms:
　　decorative, 23, 24, 30
　　heraldic, 214–15
Cocktails, 160
Coffee tables, gemstone-topped, 25
Comforters, 20
Commemorative addresses, 23
Commemorative plaques, 23
Commemoratives, 191–2
Conservatory extensions, 122, 123
Continental quilt conversions, 20, 21
Copperware, 206
Corner cupboards, 29
Corsetry: *see* Clothes

Cosmetics, 216
Cot covers, 57
Courses, 42, 43, 252
　　china mending, 89
　　embroidery, 183
　　herbs, 204
　　needlepoint, 183, 186
　　pottery, 174
　　spinning and weaving, 186
Court cupboards, 19
Craft galleries and shops, 192–4,
　　　　204–5, 207, 250
Craft workshops groups, 249, 250–51
Crafts Council, 252
Crafts supplies: *see* Art and craft
　　　　materials
Cribs, 29
Crochet, 20
Croquet mallets reshafted, 115
Curtains, 20, 56, 57, 58, 60
　　flameproofing, 228
　　taking down and rehanging, 228,
　　　　229
Cushions, 20, 28, 54–5, 56–7, 57–8,
　　　　59, 60, 116, 233
　　interiors, polybeads and foam, 40
　　kits, 182
Cutlery:
　　replating, 105
　　sales and repair, 105
Cutwork embroidery, 27–8

Dental technicians, 115, 250
Desks, 29, 32, 33, 34, 35, 37
　　releathered, 94, 96, 98, 99, 107
Disability aids:
　　repairs, 93
　　to order, 93
Discos:
　　adult, 160, 237
　　junior, 149
Display cabinets, 29
Divans, extra wide or long, 22
Dolls, 62–4
　　antique, 195

houses: *see below*
kits, 210
prams, 195
rag, 112
repairs, 63, 86, 87, 111–12
wax, 64, 111, 112
wooden, 62
Dolls' houses, 194–5, 250
furniture, 194–5
restored, 111
Domestic help, 222, 224
Doors, period, 119–20
Double-decker bus, 236
Dressers, 30, 33
Dressing mirrors, 30
Dressmaking:
materials, 41, 180, 181
services, pleating, 180
Drinks cabinets, 29, 33
Drycleaning:
beaded dresses, 227, 228, 232
church regalia, 228
clothing, 228, 229, 232
curtains, 227, 228, 229, 230
daywear, 226, 227
duvets, 228
evening wear, 226, 227
fur, 226–7, 228, 229, 235
gloves, 230
information service, 252
lace, 227
leather and suede, 226, 227, 228, 230, 235
pillows, 228
riding wear, 229
sheepskin, 226, 235
soft furnishings, 226–7, 229
soft toys, 228
theatrical costumes, 228, 229
ties, 228
trilby hats, 228
uniforms, 228, 229
wedding dresses, 226, 228, 229
Duvets, 21

covers, 20, 57
repaired, 62
Dyeing:
blankets, 227
candlewick, 227, 228
carpets, 229–30
clothing, 226–7, 228, 230
curtains, 227, 228, 230
fabric, 227, 228, 230
fur fabric, 226–7
soft furnishings, 226–7

Eiderdown quilts:
recovered, 20, 228
to order, 21
Embroidery, 27–8, 47, 176, 251
conservation, 116, 117
supplies, 181–4, 186
Emergency rescue, 24 hrs, 223
Enamel, repairs, 89
Engraving, 26
glass, 89
silver, 89

Fabrics: *see* Dressmaking; Furnishing fabrics; Textiles
Fake grass, 130
Family trees, illustrated, 23, 24
Fancy-dress:
hire, 151–3
make-up, 151, 153
Fans:
conserved, 116
framed, 52
Fashion counselling, 217
Fashion plates, 189
Feathers conserved, 116
Fences, 129, 130, 131
Fêtes and carnivals:
decorations to buy, 159
equipment to hire, 159
Filing cabinets, 34
Fire:
bellows: made, 28; repaired, 28
canopies, 109, 110, 125, 133, 134

Fire *cont.*
  dog grates, 123, 125
  gas, coal effect, 124
  screens, 125; gemstone, 25;
      papier-mâché, 35
  stoves, 123, 124, 133
Fireplaces and surrounds:
  modern, 123, 142
  period, 120, 123, 124, 125, 136
  reproduction, 123, 124, 125
  restoration and fitting, 124, 136
Flood and fire rescue, 224, 227, 229,
      230, 234
Flowers:
  arrangements, 224, 240; dried, 240
  artificial, 244
  by mail, 244–5, 247
  pot plants, 224
  telegrams, 243–4
  trees, 240
Food:
  caviar, 248
  cheese, 246, 248
  chocolates, 201, 202, 243, 247
  coffee, 245–6
  confectionery, 201–2
  Cumberland rum butter, 202
  delicatessen, 156
  fudge, 202
  haggis, 246
  Kendal mint cake, 202
  kippers, 246
  Melton hunt cake, 245
  mustard, 246
  pasta, 203
  pâté, 248
  picnics, 202–3
  quail, 245
  smoked salmon, 248
  tea, 203, 245
  toffee, 202
  trout, 202
  truffles, 201, 202, 243
  wholefood, 203
  wine, 203

Foreign specialities:
  Chinese and Japanese, 207
  Indonesian, 206
  Spanish, 206
  Russian, 208
Foundation stones, 23
Freezer foods, 155, 156, 157, 158, 224
Furnishing fabrics, 38–9, 40, 41
  designed to order, 40, 55
  handpainted, 39
  quilted, 40–41
Furnishing trimmings, 39
Furniture:
  bedroom, 33
  bookcases, 120, 127, 146
  cane, 31, 32
  designed to commission, 28–9,
      29–32, 50, 93, 96, 101, 126, 127,
      251
  fifties and Deco, 195–6
  fitted, 126, 127, 128, 145
  laminated, 32
  nursery, 29, 32, 33
  painted, 50, 51, 126–7
  pine, 33, 126
  reproduction, 29, 34, 36
  restoration: *see below*
  rocking chairs, 30
Furniture restoration, 29, 34, 66, 91,
      92, 93–4, 94–5, 96, 97, 98–9, 100,
      102, 250–51
  boulle, 94, 95, 96, 98
  gilding and resilvering, 94, 95, 96,
      98, 99
  ivory, mother-of-pearl, 94, 98
  lacquer, 94, 95, 98, 99
  leather inlay, 94, 96, 98, 99, 100
  leather upholstery, 99
  marquetry, 94, 95, 96, 107
  ormolu, 96
  pine stripping, 94, 95, 145
  polishing, French and wax, 94, 95,
      98, 99, 100, 102
  upholstery, 94, 95–6, 97, 98, 99,
      104

Games: *see* Sports equipment; Toys and games
Garden:
  fake lawn, 130
  fencing, 129, 130, 131
  gates, 130
  maintenance, 129
  paths, 131
  planning, 129
  pots, 130–31
  stonework, 129–30
  troughs, 129
Genealogical research, 214–15
Geriatric chairs, 19
Gifts by post, 247–8
Glass:
  blue glass linings, 87, 88, 105
  engraving: *see below*
  repair, 86, 87–8, 89, 104
  scent bottles, 208
  stoppers, 87
  studio glass, 192
  tantalus, 89
  to commission, 37–8
Glass, engraving:
  crests, 163, 164, 165, 166
  initials and anniversary designs, 89, 163, 164, 165, 166–7, 168, 172
  landscapes and houses, 163, 164, 165–6, 167, 168
  portraits, 164, 166, 167
  wildlife, 163, 164, 165, 166, 167–8
Guns, 187, 211, 212

Hair, 216
Hampers, 153
Handbag and luggage repairs, 108, 109, 117, 118
Hassocks, 19
Headstones, 23
Heraldic:
  carving, 30, 31
  illumination, 23, 24
Herbs:
  fresh, 204

products, 204, 215, 217
Hire:
  camping equipment, 220
  car transporters, 221
  catering equipment, 242
  dance floors, 242
  Highland wear, 220
  heart cake tins, 242
  horse boxes and trailers, 221
  house maintenance, 218, 220–21
  lighting, 219, 242
  lounge suits, 220
  machinery, 218
  musical instruments, 218
  photographic equipment, 220
  pictures, 219–20
  plants, 220
  reception venues, 242
  skiwear, 220
  stuffed animals, 219
  tableware, 221, 242
  tents and marquees, 219, 242
  theatrical effects, 219
  wedding wear, 220
  yachts, 219
Hobby horses, 58
Home helps, 231
Horse-drawn carriages, restored, 118
House maintenance, 231
House names, 23
House-sitting, 221, 222
House-swaps, 222

Ice cubes, 156
Incense, 206
Interior design, 21, 27, 32, 33, 39, 60, 205, 213
  props, 208
Invisible mending and repairs, 115, 226, 227, 232
  collars turned, 226
  cuffs remade, 228
  leather and suede, 230
  relining, 228
  sheepskin, 228

Invisible mending and repairs *cont.*
zips replaced, 228

Jazz, 197
Jewellery:
Islamic, Greek and Roman, 116
repairs: beads restrung, 104; pearls restrung, 106
reproduction, 42
to commission, 41–2, 43, 44–5, 46–7, 105, 166, 176, 247, 250, 251
Jigsaws and puzzles, 62, 64–5, 209
Joinery, 127, 145, 146, 251

Kangaroo, 223
Kimonos, 59, 207
Kitchen:
equipment, 206, 207
furniture, 33–4, 252–3
units, made to measure, 126, 127–8, 145, 250–51
Kitchen Specialists Association, 252
Kites, 210
Kneelers, 19
Knitting, 185–6
Knitwear: *see* Clothes (Women's)
Knives:
hunting and sports knives, 106
rebladed, 105
rehandled, 105
sharpened, 105, 223, 250
Knobs, handpainted, 50–51

Lace, 20
antique, 181, 198–9
bobbins, 30, 65
repairs, 98, 116, 117, 183
Lampbases:
antique, 38, 48, 50
converted from vases etc., 47, 48, 110
handpainted, 38, 48, 50
wood, 47

Lampshades:
from customers' fabric, 58
handpainted, 38, 50
re-covering, 47, 48
to commission, 47–8
Lavatory seats, wood, 121, 122
Leaded lights, 141
restoration, 141
Leather, upholstery restored, 107, 108, 109
Leathergoods:
bags, 78, 79, 80
belts, 78, 79, 80
briefcases, 78, 79, 80
instrument cases, 78, 79, 109
saddles, 79; repaired, 78–9
to commission, 78, 79–80, 251
Left-handed, 205
Light fittings:
chandeliers, 110, 118, 132
gas, 132
modern, 208
period, 132
repairs, 48, 132
reproduction, 132, 134, 139
spare parts, 132
Limited editions, 196
Locks:
made to order, 133
period, 133
Locksmiths, 222, 223
Looms, 186
Loose covers, 56

Machinery, repair, 109
Magazines, for collectors, 189
Make-up, remedial, 215
See also Beauty
Maps, 190
Marble, cut to size, 142
Marquetry, 52
Mattresses, 21–2
caravan, 19
pads, 20
Memorials, headstones, 23

Metal repairs, 109, 110
  brass and copper, 110
Metalwork and forged iron to
    commission:
  balustrades and railings, 109, 134–5,
    135–6, 137, 138
  fire furniture, 133, 134–5, 136, 137,
    138
  garden furniture, 136, 137
  gates, 109, 133, 135, 136, 137, 138
  ironmongery, architectural, 138
  iron sculpture, 134
  repairs and restoration, 96, 97, 109,
    110, 134, 135, 136, 138
  shoeing, 136, 138
Military memorabilia, 187
Mineral specimens, 42, 199
Miniatures, 45
Miniature weaving, 28
Mirror mosaics, 61
Mirrors, 127, 207
  cane, 32
  framing, 52, 53
  resilvering, 114
  restored, 114
Model kits, 209
Model trains:
  for sale, 209
  restored, 112
Moses baskets:
  to order, 65
  repaired, 65
Mother-of-pearl, 46–7
Motorcycle repair, 119
Mountaineering, 211
Murals, 51
Museum replicas, 42, 193
Musical boxes, repaired, 88, 93
Musical instruments:
  cellos, 49
  double bass, 49
  for hire, 218
  guitars, 48, 50
  reproduction medieval, 48
  violas, 49–50

  violins, 49–50, 250

Nannies, 213, 222
Needlecraft supplies:
  beads, 181, 183, 184
  embroidery, 181–4, 186
  knitting, 185–6
  metal threads, 184
  samplers, 182
  tapestries and yarns, 182, 183, 184,
    186
Newspapers:
  birthday editions, 188–9
  for collectors, 188–9
Nursery clocks, 25

Objets d'art, restoration:
  bronzes, 106
  ivory, 96, 106, 107
  marble, 104, 106
  mother-of-pearl, 104, 107
  papier-mâché, 104
  sculpture, 96, 106
  terracotta, 96
  tortoiseshell, 104, 107
Orchestras, 162
Orchids, 204
Oysters, 247

Paintwork:
  dragging, sponging, ragging, 50, 51
  marbling, 50, 51, 58
  stencilling, 50, 51
  stippling, 50, 58
Panelled interiors:
  made to measure, 19, 120, 146
  period, 119
Pans:
  rehandled, 109
  repaired, 110, 206
  retinned, 109, 206, 223
Paper:
  conservation, 84
  handmade, 22–3, 24
  marbled, 24–5, 188

Paper *cont.*
  posters, prints, watercolours, 84, 85
  restoration, 83
  wrapping, 161, 207–8
Paper knives, 25
Paperweights:
  ready-made, 165
  to commission, 165, 166, 167, 176
Papier-mâché, repair, 87, 98
Party catering:
  barbecues, 157
  business luncheons, 153, 154, 155,
    157, 158
  children's, 155, 157–8
  dinner parties, 153, 154, 155, 156,
    157, 158
  food for freezers, 155, 156, 157, 158
  hampers, picnics, 153, 155–6, 157,
    158
  receptions, 153, 154, 155, 156, 157,
    158
  See also Weddings
Party equipment:
  invitations, 177
  lighting, 159
  presents, 159, 160, 161
  tableware and decorations, 152, 160,
    161
Patchwork, 59–60, 251
Patio doors, 141
Pearls: *see* Jewellery
Personalized gifts:
  bedlinen, 168, 169, 173
  bookends, 170
  bookplates, 173
  china and glass, 171, 172
  clocks, 170
  cushions, 170
  embroidery, 173
  enamel boxes, 170
  flagons, 174
  furniture, 168, 169
  hotwaterbottle covers, 173
  house plaques, 175
  jigsaws, 64–5, 171

  knitwear, 168, 169
  labels (clothing), 175
  leathergoods, 79, 171, 172
  mugs, 168, 175
  name pictures, 33, 168, 170
  pens, pencils, 171, 172
  pets, 172
  picture frames, 172
  picture table mats, 172–3
  pottery, 169, 173, 174, 175
  scent, 174
  silver, 45, 169–70
  stationery, 175–6
  sunglasses, 172
  tiles, 176
  umbrellas, 172
  wine: bottles, 172; labels, 172, 174
  wood, 169–70
Pets:
  dog clipping, 224
  insurance, 224–5
  presents for, 172
Pewter:
  antique, 196
  restoration, 110
  sale and repair, 106
Photographs:
  for decoration, 190
  old, copied, 112–13
  restored, 84, 112–13
Pianolas, restored, 113
Picture framing, 52–4, 101, 113, 251
  DIY, 53
  materials, 52–3
Pictures:
  cleaning, 54, 113–14, 115
  etchings, 52
  miniatures, 113
  oriental prints, 207
  restoration: *see below*
  watercolours, 52
Pictures, repair and restoration:
  drawings, 114
  oils, 53, 54, 113–14, 114–15
  prints, 114

tempera, 114, 115
  wall paintings and panels, 114, 115
  watercolours, 53, 54, 98, 113, 114
Pigeons, 211
Pillowcases, 20
  antique, 198–9
Pillows:
  square continental, 199
  to order, 21
Pinchbeck platters, 134
Pine stripping, 119
Plaster mouldings, 123, 138–9
Port by post, 248
Postcards, for collectors, 118
Pottery and stoneware, 169, 173, 174,
  251
Presentation scrolls, 23, 24
Programmes, for collectors, 189
Props, TV and display, 208
Pub signs, 30
Puppet shows, 147–8, 148–9, 150
  for handicapped children, 149
  Punch and Judy, 148, 150
Puzzles: see Jigsaws

Quilting, to order, 40–41, 47
Quilts, 20, 21, 57, 59, 60
  antique, 20
  cot, 56, 57, 59

Racquets, restrung, 115
Rattan, 179
  plastic, 179
Records, 197, 206
Rocking horses:
  repaired, 61, 111
  to commission, 61, 62–3, 64
Rope, 139–40
Rose-petal confetti, 238
Rush:
  English and Dutch, 179, 181
  seagrass, 181
  synthetic, 102

Saddlers, 79, 109
Samplers, conservation and repair, 116
Sauna equipment, 122
Scents, handmade, 174, 215, 217
Screens, 32, 35, 61, 126–7
Security gates and grilles, 250
Sewing: see Needlecraft supplies
Sewing machines, sales and repair, 110
Sharpening:
  chisels, 105
  hair clippers, 105
  knives, 105, 223
  pinking shears, 105
  saws, 105
  scissors, 105, 223
Shellac, 179
Shells, 199
Shelves and storage, 31, 32
Shoe repair, 108
Shoes: see Clothes
Shop signs, 136
Silks, 39, 41, 180, 181
Silver:
  antique, 196
  engraving, 89
  plated leaves, 240
  rehandled (teapots), 105
  repaired, 89, 97, 106–7
  replated, 105
Silver and goldsmiths, 41, 42, 43–4,
  44–5, 45–6, 133, 176, 250, 251
  church silver, 43, 45–6
  cutlery, 45
  platters, 134
  reproduction, 46
Singing telegrams, 247
Ski clothing, repairs, 211
Skin-care, 215–17
  treatments, 216
Skin rugs, repaired, 107–8
Sleeping bags, converted, 20, 21
Small business advice, 252
Smocking, 28
Sofas, sofa beds, 32, 33, 207
Soft furnishings, 56, 57, 60

Soft toys, repairs, 111–12
Spare parts:
  art metal, 110
  machinery, 109
Speakers, 162
Spectacle repairs, 115
Spinning, 23
  wheels, 34, 186
Spiral staircases, 135, 136
Spit engines, repaired, 134
Sports equipment, 210–12
  repairs, 115
Stained glass:
  hanging decorations, 168
  period, 125, 144
  repair, 61, 119, 140, 141
  to commission, 60, 61, 140–41
Stationery, 24, 25, 161, 208
  personally illustrated, 175–6, 177
Stonework:
  artificial castings, 130
  cast, to order, 129–30
  Cotswold, 130
  for fire surrounds, 142
Stuffed birds, recased, 107–8
Stump work, conserved, 116
Suites, three-piece, 19
Survival kit, 210
Swimwear: *see* Clothes

Tablelinen, 20
Table mats, 172, 173
Tables:
  bedside, 32
  coffee, 25, 29, 32, 33, 36, 118
  conference, 35
  dining, 29, 30, 31, 32, 33–4, 35–6,
    37
  gateleg, 33
  mirrored, 61
  sofa, 32
  tilt-top, 33
Tapestries:
  conservation, 116

  made up and mounted, 108, 181–2,
    183, 184
  repair, 116
  restoration, 97, 183
  to commission, 27, 28, 182, 183, 184
  tramé, 183
Tented ceilings, 58, 230
Tents and canvas, repairs, 109, 116
Terracotta:
  flagons, 174
  garden pots, 130, 131
  Spanish, 206
  wedding platters, 174
Textiles:
  conservation, 115–16, 117
  repairs, 115, 116
  Turkish and Asian, 116
Thatch, 142
Thimbles, 199
Tiles, 40, 143, 144
  handpainted, 50, 143, 144, 145
  mosaics, 144
  murals, 143, 144
  period, 144
Timber supplies, 179
Toastmasters, 162
Toolmaking, 109
Toys and games, 61–2, 64, 209
  jigsaws and puzzles, 62, 64–5, 209
  mechanical toys, repaired, 93, 111,
    112
  See also Dolls; Rocking horses
Trays, 35, 172
Tree surgeons, 131, 252

Umbrellas, 80
  repaired, 117–18
  wedding, to hire, 238
Upholstery, 34, 250, 251
  from customers' fabrics, 58

Valentines, 23
Valuations, 94, 221, 223
Victorian sheet music, 189

Victorian workboxes, reproduction, 29
Video photography, 225, 236, 237, 241
Video units, 29
Vintage motorcycles, repair, 119

Wall-coverings, fabric, 38, 39
Wall-hangings and panels, 27, 55, 56, 182, 183
    repaired, 116
Wallpapers, 38, 40, 41
    printed to order, 39, 40
Wall plaques, carved, 30
Watch:
    repairs, 92, 93, 250
    spare parts, 92
Weather vanes, 110, 134, 137
Weaving, 23, 57
    supplies, 186
Weddings:
    bouquets pressed and framed, 239, 240, 241
    cakes, 153–4, 154–5, 156, 157, 238
    carriage and pair, 236, 237
    cars, 236, 237, 238
    catering, 153, 154, 155, 157–8, 236
    dresses, 236, 238
    double-decker bus, 236

flowers, 224, 236, 237, 238, 240;
    gold-plated, 240
    make-up, 238, 239
    marquees, 219, 242
    photography, video, 225, 236, 237, 238, 241
    rose-petal confetti, 238
    stationery and paperware, 238, 242
    tableware and equipment for hire, 221, 237, 242
    umbrellas for hire, 238
    veils, repaired, 239
    venues, 242
Welding, 109
Welsh dressers, 29
Whisky by post, 248
Wigs, 152
Wind dials, 134
Windmill, 135
Window frames, 141, 145, 146, 251
Windsor chairs, 29
Wine:
    antiques, 200
    by post, 247–8
Wood:
    carving, 146
    stripping, 145
    timber supplies, 179
    turning, 30, 65–6, 91, 119, 146, 244

More about Penguins, Pelicans and Puffins

For further information about books available from Penguins please write to Dept E P, Penguin Books Ltd, Harmondsworth, Middlesex U B7 0D A.

In the U.S.A.: For a complete list of books available from Penguins in the United States write to Dept D G, Penguin Books, 299 Murray Hill Parkway, East Rutherford, New Jersey 07073.

In Canada: For a complete list of books available from Penguins in Canada write to Penguin Books Canada Ltd, 2801 John Street, Markham, Ontario L3R 1B4.

In Australia: For a complete list of books available from Penguins in Australia write to the Marketing Department, Penguin Books Australia Ltd, P.O. Box 257, Ringwood, Victoria 31 34.

In New Zealand: For a complete list of books available from Penguins in New Zealand write to the Marketing Department, Penguin Books (N.Z.) Ltd, P.O. Box 4019, Auckland 10.

In India: For a complete list of books available from Penguins in India write to Penguin Overseas Ltd, 706 Eros Apartments, 56 Nehru Place, New Delhi 110019.

THE PENGUIN LONDON MAPGUIDE

The Penguin London Mapguide contains everything you need to know to enjoy yourself and get the best out of London. It includes

* Art Galleries and Museums
* Markets
* Underground Stations
* Places of interest

* Theatres and Cinemas
* Parks
* Bus Routes
* Tourist Information Centres

and

Detailed plans of the National Gallery, Regent's Park Zoo and the Tower of London.

ROSES FOR ENGLISH GARDENS

Gertrude Jekyll and Edward Mawley

Gertrude Jekyll brings her garden sense to the best-loved flower of all. In collaboration with Edward Mawley, a practical rose gardener, she shows the nearly limitless possibilities for planting between walls, on pergolas, along wood posts, on verandas, and on trees, never instructing so much as inspiring. To instil practical principles of successful gardening and the experience of her gardening eye to the enthusiastic gardener is her aim.

Edward Mawley provides details for plantings, pruning and propagating different varieties of roses along with defence against disease and ways to exhibit roses for shows.

GERALDENE HOLT'S CAKE STALL

Honey Crunch Tea-Bread, Praline Cream Gâteau, Harvest Cake, Iced Gingerbread, Chocolate Cup Cakes, Easter Biscuits

These are only a selection of the delicious wares that Geraldene Holt sold from her enormously successful cake stall at Tiverton Pannier Market. (Now there are a string of similar cake stalls all over the country.) Collected into this book, her recipes will tempt even the most hard-hearted into action, and her advice on equipment, techniques and useful short cuts to success will ensure that hungry families everywhere are treated to amazing tea-time delights.

JOSCELINE DIMBLEBY'S BOOK OF PUDDINGS, DESSERTS AND SAVOURIES

Puddings to make the family gasp, desserts to amaze a formal gathering, savouries to round off a perfect meal . . .

Here Josceline Dimbleby has gathered together a selection of pies, tarts, gâteaux, mousses, cheesecakes, ice-creams and savouries which will inspire even the most jaded cook. Practical, easy and often inspired by the flavours of the Orient, they can be relied on to add a new dimension to your cooking.